Brevity and the Short Form in Serial Television

Screen Serialities

Series editors: Claire Perkins and Constantine Verevis

Series advisory board: Kim Akass, Glen Creeber, Shane Denson, Jennifer Forrest, Jonathan Gray, Julie Grossman, Daniel Herbert, Carolyn Jess-Cooke, Frank Kelleter, Amanda Ann Klein, Kathleen Loock, Jason Mittell, Sean O'Sullivan, Barton Palmer, Alisa Perren, Dana Polan, Iain Robert Smith, Shannon Wells-Lassagne, Linda Williams

Screen Serialities provides a forum for introducing, analysing and theorising a broad spectrum of serial screen formats – including franchises, series, serials, sequels and remakes.

Over and above individual texts that happen to be serialised, the book series takes a guiding focus on seriality as an aesthetic and industrial principle that has shaped the narrative logic, socio-cultural function and economic identity of screen texts across more than a century of cinema, television and 'new' media.

Titles in this series include:

Film Reboots
Edited by Daniel Herbert and Constantine Verevis

Reanimated: The Contemporary American Horror Remake
By Laura Mee

Gender and Seriality: Practices and Politics of Contemporary US Television
By Maria Sulimma

European Film Remakes
Edited by Eduard Cuelenaere, Gertjan Willems and Stijn Joye

Superhero Blockbusters: Seriality and Politics
By Felix Brinker

Hollywood Remakes of Iconic British Films: Class, Gender and Stardom
By Agnieszka Rasmus

East Asian Film Remakes
Edited by David Scott Diffrient and Kenneth Chan

Brevity and the Short Form in Serial Television
Edited by Shannon Wells-Lassagne, Sylvaine Bataille and Florence Cabaret

Brevity and the Short Form in Serial Television

Edited by Shannon Wells-Lassagne,
Sylvaine Bataille and Florence Cabaret

EDINBURGH
University Press

Edinburgh University Press is one of the leading university presses in the UK. We publish academic books and journals in our selected subject areas across the humanities and social sciences, combining cutting-edge scholarship with high editorial and production values to produce academic works of lasting importance. For more information visit our website: edinburghuniversitypress.com

© editorial matter and organisation Shannon Wells-Lassagne, Sylvaine Bataille and Florence Cabaret 2024
© the chapters their several authors 2024

Grateful acknowledgement is made to the sources listed in the List of Illustrations for permission to reproduce material previously published elsewhere. Every effort has been made to trace the copyright holders, but if any have been inadvertently overlooked, the publisher will be pleased to make the necessary arrangements at the first opportunity.

Edinburgh University Press Ltd
13 Infirmary Street
Edinburgh EH1 1LT

Typeset in 11/13 Ehrhardt MT by
IDSUK (DataConnection) Ltd, and
printed and bound in Great Britain

A CIP record for this book is available from the British Library

ISBN 978 1 4744 8204 2 (hardback)
ISBN 978 1 4744 8206 6 (webready PDF)
ISBN 978 1 4744 8207 3 (epub)

The right of Shannon Wells-Lassagne, Sylvaine Bataille and Florence Cabaret to be identified as the editors of this work has been asserted in accordance with the Copyright, Designs and Patents Act 1988, and the Copyright and Related Rights Regulations 2003 (SI No. 2498).

Contents

List of Figures vii
Acknowledgements ix
Notes on Contributors x

    Introduction 1
    Shannon Wells-Lassagne, Sylvaine Bataille and Florence Cabaret

Part 1 Confirming – and Deconstructing – Television Traditions of Brevity

1 *Alfred Hitchcock Presents*: Subverting Anthology TV Series 17
    Julien Achemchame

2 *The Jewel in the Crown*: A Miniseries between Short and Long 32
    Florence Cabaret

3 Short Middle Ages: Comic Dramatisation of Rhythm in French Shortcom *Kaamelott* 59
    Justine Breton

4 Short but Serious? Slimming Down the Episode in 'Prestige' Drama *Homecoming* 74
    Sylvaine Bataille

5 *Twin Peaks*, 25 Years Later: Whatever Happens Happens Now, and Nothing Else Matters 92
    Benjamin Campion

Part 2 New Media and New Forms: Web-series, Streaming Platforms and the Short Form

6 Orders of Magnitude: Fractality and Granularity in Contemporary Television Series 107
Florent Favard

7 'Minute by Minute': Short Form Seriality and Social Viewing and Waiting in *SKAM* 121
Sara Tanderup Linkis

8 Narrative Efficiency and the Constraints of the Short Form in *Les Engagés* 134
Stéphane Sawas

9 *Crisis on Earth-X* or the Status of the Crossover Event 145
Claire Cornillon

Part 3 Blurring Boundaries: Production, Paratexts and Reception of the Short Form

10 Loops, Bottles and Clips: Structuring Brevity in American Television 159
Shannon Wells-Lassagne

11 Ovulate and Repeat: Temporal Uncertainties and the Serialising Effect of Narratives of 'Women's Time' in the Sitcom *Friends* 174
Jessica Thrasher Chenot

12 'Spoilers Ahead!': Short-circuiting Complex Series in Explainer Online Videos 189
Sébastien Lefait

13 Writing *En thérapie*: A Conversation with Vincent Poymiro 206
Sylvaine Bataille, Florence Cabaret and Shannon Wells-Lassagne with Vincent Poymiro

Index 224

Figures

1.1	Hitchcock's shadow joining his caricatural self-portrait: self-directed irony.	21
2.1	Watching from afar (E13).	36
2.2	Watching at close hand (E13).	36
2.3	The culmination of the fire motif (excipit of E14).	43
2.4–2.5	Entangled but stifled narrative 'branching out' (E13).	47
3.1	'But we're just here to complain' ('Mais nous, on venait juste se plaindre') – Perceval and Karadoc as medieval precursors to modern-day workers' rights protesters ('Les Exploités').	63
4.1	The barrel distortion of the shot makes the wall of boxes even more imposing and is a visual nod to the title of the episode.	83
4.2	Heidi (Julia Roberts) in her office at the Homecoming centre, inside the frame formed by the vertical curtains and the horizontal windowsill (E01).	84
4.3	Carrasco (Shea Whigham) in the stairs leading to the archive: the geometrical overhead shot uses architectural elements to embed rectangular and square frames within its reduced square boundaries and may evoke the absurdity of M.C. Escher's stairs through its flattening effect (E03).	85
4.4	A shot of Heidi's car gradually replaces the matching overhead shot of Heidi shopping, creating continuity between the two shots separated by a black horizontal line (E10).	86

FIGURES

4.5	All in one: Heidi's road trip as a way for her to start putting together the pieces of her splintered identity (E10).	87
5.1	A mushroom cloud in White Sands, New Mexico, on 16 July 1945 (S03E08).	94
5.2–5.3	Early signs of the forthcoming deflagration: a painting of a mushroom cloud and a portrait of Franz Kafka (S03E03).	96
5.4	Sonny Jim Jones tries to play baseball with his catatonic dad, Dougie (S03E12).	99
5.5	Gordon Cole has a great time with an exquisite French lady dressed in red (S03E12).	99
5.6	Albert Rosenfield appears alone on-screen, in front of Gordon Cole and his French conquest sharing intimacy (S03E12).	100
7.1	'Even and Isak – minute by minute' (S03E10).	121
7.2	Clip from Saturday 10.15, (S03E10).	122
7.3	SMS chats on screen (S04E07).	125
8.1	Nadjet (Nanou Harry) lays a sticker 'rue Olympe de Gouges' at the end of E05.	138
8.2	Hicham (Mehdi Meskar) and Murielle (Claudine Charreyre) discover the homophobic tags at the start of E09.	139
8.3	Thibaut (Eric Pucheu) receives a message from Hicham before sleep at the end of E04.	141
10.1	Troy and Abed's portrait (background centre): repetition with (limited) variation.	166
13.1	Philippe Dayan (Frédéric Pierrot) meeting his supervisor Esther (Carole Bouquet) at the end of each week (S01E05).	214
13.2	Dayan listening to an initially reluctant Adel Chibane (Reda Kateb) (S01E02).	216
13.3	Dayan trespassing the rules with Ariane (Mélanie Thierry), visiting her at her place (S01E35).	220

Acknowledgements

This book is one of the many collective projects that have been carried out by GUEST (Groupe Universitaire d'Études sur les Séries Télévisées), a national network of French academics working on television serial fiction, to which most of the contributors to this volume belong. GUEST was founded in 2013 in Normandy and selected for funding by the Région Haute-Normandie for six years. We are deeply grateful for this financial support, which benefited *Brevity and the Short Form in Serial Television* from its inception to the later stages of its making. We are also greatly indebted to the Région Bourgogne-Franche Comté for its generous financial contribution through the regionally-funded research program ADAPT. We extend our sincerest thanks to the research centre TIL, at the University of Burgundy, which was another important source of financial help for this project.

During the editing process we were lucky to have Juliet Powys on board and we warmly thank her for her eagle-eyed readings of the chapters and her invaluable help in the translation of Vincent Poymiro's interview. Special thanks also go to Lucy Garnier, whose professionalism, flexibility and efficiency we greatly appreciated.

We want to thank our main interlocutor at EUP, Sam Johnson, for his availability and patience. Many thanks also to Richard Strachan, Gillian Leslie and Kelly O'Brien for their attention to our project. Finally this book could not have been completed without Screen Serialities series editors Con Verevis and Claire Perkins' precious advice; they have our gratitude.

Notes on Contributors

Julien Achemchame is a Senior Lecturer in Film Studies at the Université Paul-Valéry in Montpellier, France, and a member of the research group RIRRA21. He is the author of two books on the American filmmaker David Lynch, *Lost Highway: Errance dans le labyrinthe de la modernité cinématographique* and *Entre l'œil et la réalité: le lieu du cinéma*. Mulholland Drive *de David Lynch* (2010). His current research focuses mainly on the circulation of filmic forms in cinema history, especially through the example of reflexive films and, in particular, Hollywood metafilms, and on the analysis of the forms of seriality found in contemporary television series. He has published several articles in the online journals *TV/Series* (on *The Wire*, *The Shield* and *Dexter*; and on *Dollhouse*) and *Mise au Point* (on *Breaking Bad* and *Better Call Saul*).

Sylvaine Bataille is a Senior Lecturer in Literature and Film Studies in the English department at the University of Rouen Normandie, France and co-head of the research group ERIAC. Her research interests cover the questions of appropriation, adaptation, translation and reference, with a focus on Shakespearean screen adaptations and drama television series. She has been head and co-head of the GUEST consortium, a regionally funded research program on television serial fiction (between 2013 and 2019). She has co-edited three issues of the online journal *TV/Series* (with Sarah Hatchuel, *TV Series World-Wide: Changes and Exchanges*, 2012; with Florence Cabaret, *TV Series and Intermediality*, 2013 and *Cultural, Social and Ideological Representations in TV Series*, 2013), and has published several papers on television series, such as *Rome* ('Haunted by Shakespeare: HBO's *Rome*', in *Television Shakespeare*, 2008); *Sons of Anarchy* ('"Hamlet on Harleys": *Sons of Anarchy*'s appropriation of *Hamlet*', in *Shakespeare On Screen:* Hamlet, 2011); *Battlestar Galactica*

('*Battlestar Galactica* et l'héritage gréco-latin', in *L'Antiquité dans l'imaginaire contemporain*, 2014); *Boss, Empire* ('Between Political Drama and Soap Opera: Appropriations of *King Lear* in US Television Series *Boss* and *Empire*', written with Anaïs Pauchet, in *Shakespeare on Screen:* King Lear, 2019); or *Fargo* ('*Fargo* (FX, 2014–) and Cinema: "Just like in the movie?"', in *Exploring Seriality on Screen*, 2020).

Justine Breton is a Senior Lecturer in French Literature at the University of Reims, France, a member of the CRIMEL research team, and webmaster for the French association 'Modernités médiévales', which focuses on the study of medievalism. Following her work on the Arthurian legend and its movie adaptations, and her interest in the works and posterity of British author T. H. White, she studies audio-visual medievalism and fantasy, particularly in movies and TV series, from *Monty Python and the Holy Grail* to *Game of Thrones*. She is especially interested in the comical use of the Middle Ages and its implications, about which she wrote several papers. She co-edited Kaamelott, *un livre d'histoire* (2018) and published books on contemporary medievalism, including *Une Histoire de feu et de sang. Le Moyen Âge de* Game of Thrones (2020), written with historian Florian Besson and focusing on the way the HBO series depicted a dark, biased and stereotypical image of the European Middle Ages; *Monty Python: Sacré Graal!* (2021), which presents how the historical and cultural background of the movie serves its comedy; and *Un Moyen Âge en clair-obscur. Le médiévalisme dans les séries télévisées* (2023), which analyses the diachronic representation of the Middle Ages in TV series, from 1949 to 2022.

Florence Cabaret is a Senior Lecturer in Indian Literatures in English at the University of Rouen Normandie, France, and a member of the interdisciplinary research group ERIAC. After a PhD about Salman Rushdie's novels, she has worked on novelists from the Indian diaspora (Amitav Ghosh, Rohinton Mistry, Anita Desai, Jhumpa Lahiri, Mira Syal), as well as on films and TV series directed by Indian diasporic artists in the English-speaking world (Deepa Mehta, Mira Nair, Gurinder Chada) and Indian characters in British and American TV series (*The Jewel in the Crown*, *E.R.*, *Skins*, *Upstairs, Downstairs*, *Goodness Gracious Me*, *The Mindy Project*). She co-edited several collective works such as *Mauvaises Langues!* (2013) with Nathalie Vienne-Guerrin, *Retranslating Children's Literature* (2014) with Virginie Douglas, and several issues of the online journal *TV/Series* with Sylvaine Bataille and with Claire Cornillon. She is also the French translator of the novels of Hanif Kureishi and of Chloé Hooper.

Benjamin Campion teaches Film and Audiovisual Studies at the Université Paul-Valéry in Montpellier, France and is a member of the research group

RIRRA21. He has a PhD in Cinema and Audiovisual studies and has published two books on the American premium cable network HBO: one on the network's history and programming strategies (*Le Concept HBO. Élever la série télévisée au rang d'art*, 2018), the other on its borderline representations in terms of language, nudity and sex (*HBO et le porno. Raconter des histoires par le sexe*, 2022). His work is driven by a desire to transcend disciplines and to establish a dialogue between arts and media, looking at the serialisation of cinema as well as its narrative and formal expansion to television and the Internet. He also works on borderline representations, censorial modalities, and the history and practice of film criticism.

Claire Cornillon is a Senior Lecturer in Comparative Literature at the University of Nîmes, France and a member of the research group RIRRA21. She is co-chair of the Masters' program in Humanities and Creative Industries at the University of Nîmes. Her main field of research is narration and fiction, specifically in TV series. She published *Sérialité et Transmédialité. Infinis des fictions contemporaines* in 2018. She has co-edited an issue of the online journal *Series. International Journal of TV Serial Narratives* on The CW, with Shannon Wells-Lassagne and Mélanie Bourdaa (2018) and an issue of online journal *TV/Series* on US network series, with Sarah Hatchuel and Dennis Tredy (2022). Other recent publications include 'Le statut de l'ellipse dans quelques séries semi-feuilletonnantes formulaires', *Sens public*, 2021; 'The Ethics of Serial Narrative Structures', written with Sarah Hatchuel, *Series. International Journal of TV Serial Narratives*, 2020.

Florent Favard, Senior Lecturer in Theory and Practice of Cinema, Audiovisual Media and Transmedia at IECA (Institut Européen de Cinéma et d'Audiovisuel, Université de Lorraine, Nancy, France) and member of the Crem research group, focuses on the narrative complexity of contemporary science fiction television series and transmedia franchises. He has published two books on television series narratives (*Écrire une Série TV*, 2019; *Le Récit dans les séries de science-fiction*, 2018). He is a regular contributor to online journal *TV/Series* ('Where the physical world meets the digital world: representations of power structures and cyberspace in television series set in New York', co-written with Julie Ambal, 2020; '"The maze wasn't made for you": Artificial consciousness and reflexive narration in *Westworld* (HBO, 2016–)', 2018) and co-edited an issue of the journal on seriality in contemporary television series in 2019.

Sébastien Lefait is a Professor at Aix-Marseille University, France and a member of the research team LERMA. His research focuses on the way in which the arts of representation interact with human societies. His work therefore examines the areas of interference between a socio-cultural issue and its textual or audio-visual renditions, showing the existence of bilateral influences. In particular, he studies surveillance societies and their impact on fiction; the overlapping areas between American literature and contemporary visual culture; racial tensions and the challenges of their representation; post-September 11 paranoia and the corresponding media vehicles; the influence of military fiction on armed conflicts, et cetera. In his works, he concentrates on the ways in which artworks and cultural productions, beyond merely reflecting a state of reality, can act as vehicles of change. His publications include *La Question raciale dans les séries américaines* (co-written with Olivier Esteves, 2014) and *Surveillance on Screen. Monitoring Contemporary Films and TV Programs* (2013). He has also co-edited *The Faces and Stakes of Brand Insertion*, with Sandrine Villers (2022) and *Modern Representations of Sub-Saharan Africa*, with Lori Maguire and Susan Ball (2020).

Stéphane Sawas is a Professor at the INALCO (Institut National des Langues et Civilisations Orientales) in Paris. He is the Director of the CERLOM (Centre d'Étude et de Recherche sur les Littératures et les Oralités du Monde) and also teaches at the ENS (École Normale Supérieure). His research interests include Modern Greek Literature, Mediterranean Cinema and Music, History and Aesthetics of TV Series. He was awarded the Gold Medal of the Hellenic Society of Translators of Literature in 2013.

Sara Tanderup Linkis holds a PhD in Comparative Literature. She is a Senior Lecturer in Digital Cultures and Publishing Studies at Lund University, Sweden. Her research focuses on serialisation and serial narratives, transmedia storytelling, audiobooks and born-audio storytelling, publishing and digital book culture, and she has published extensively on these topics in acclaimed international journals such as *Narrative*, *SoundEffects*, *Image & Narrative*, *Orbis Litterarum*, *Children's Literature Association Quarterly*, *Memoires du Livre/Studies in Book Culture* and *Passage*. She is the author of two monographs, *Serialization in Literature across Media and Markets* (2021) and *Memory, Intermediality and Literature* (2019).

Jessica Thrasher Chenot is a Senior Lecturer in Civilisation of the English-speaking world in the department of Applied Foreign Languages at the University of Rouen Normandie, France. She is currently co-chair of the department and teaches courses on the history and the culture, including the popular culture, of the United States for students at the Bachelor's and Master's level. Her doctoral dissertation focused on the multiplicity of representations of mothers and motherhood in the blockbuster sitcom *Friends*, including the generic, narrative and ideological implications of these representations. She has published several articles on this topic, and her contribution to this collection finds its roots in this doctoral research. Other publications have turned their focus to issues of paternity in twentieth-century United States sitcoms and she continues to pursue this line of inquiry in her research, reflecting on the intersections of popular culture, parenthood, genre and gender. Recent publications include: 'Watching Mothers: Seeking New Normativities for Motherhood in the Sitcom *Friends* (NBC, 1994–2004)' (*Genre en Séries*, 2017) and 'Bursting at the (Generic) Seams: Pregnancy Narratives in the Twentieth-Century American Situation Comedy' (*RFEA*, 2020).

Shannon Wells-Lassagne is a Professor of Film and Television Adaptation in the English Department at the University of Burgundy/Université de Bourgogne (Dijon, France). She has written a monograph, *Television and Serial Adaptation* (2017), and co-edited volumes: *Screening Text* (2013), *Adapting Endings* (2019), *Adapting Margaret Atwood:* The Handmaid's Tale and Beyond (2021) and *Illustration and Adaptation: New Cartographies* (forthcoming), among others, as well as special issues or dossiers in *Screen*, *The Journal of Screenwriting*, *Interfaces*, *TV/Series* and *Series*. Her work has appeared in *Critical Studies in Television*, *Screen*, *The Journal of Adaptation in Film and Performance*, *The Journal of Popular Film and Television* and *Irish Studies Review*, among others.

Introduction

Shannon Wells-Lassagne, Sylvaine Bataille and Florence Cabaret

From John Ellis on, television studies have long considered segmentation to be central to the very nature of the medium (Ellis 1982); as Caren Deming reminds us,

> In stark contrast to the classical Hollywood narrative (often characterized as seamless), the televisual text is always about seams, or segment markers, which don't interrupt the programs so much as help to constitute them. (. . .) More often than disguising divisions, then, the televisual flow manifests a preoccupation with division at the expense of continuity. (Deming 2005, 129)

Though the nature of 'flow' might suggest an uninterrupted movement of audiovisual messages directly to the viewer, in fact from its inception, television was defined by its limitations, be it in its original limited broadcast schedule at certain hours of the day, its strict scheduling timeframes to facilitate commercial interruptions (and make its cookie-cutter uniformity easier to insert into local programming from one broadcast network to another), or its 'seasonal' appearance (which was not just the number of episodes to appear in that year, but a period of months between September and May when only the new fictions would be broadcast, the summer months being relegated to reruns). As Jason Mittell shows, the privileged form was the episode, largely unfettered by the idea of continuity, for primarily economic purposes:

> Economic strategies privileged the episodic form – in large part, serialized content posed problems for the production industry's cash cow, syndication. Reruns distributed by syndicators could be aired in any

order, making complex continuing storylines an obstacle to the lucrative aftermarket. Additionally, network research departments believed that even the biggest hit series could be guaranteed a consistent carryover audience of no more than 1/3 from week-to-week, meaning that the majority of viewers would not be sufficiently aware of a series's backstory to follow continuing storylines. (Mittell 2009)

The repeated delimitation of televisual storytelling, then, necessarily foregrounded the notion of brevity, where episodes were conceived for brief periods of sustained attention, and where even this attention was short-lived, and not meant to carry on from one week to the next – hence explaining the presence of rebroadcast episodes. One could argue that technology facilitated this emphasis on brevity, for example through the popularisation of the remote control and its corollary, the ability to 'channel surf', allowing the viewer to more easily view television by fragments, changing the channel between acts of a series to avoid advertisements and catch another show in the meantime.

If more recent television studies have focused overwhelmingly on the ever-increasing number of fictions that have foregrounded seriality and long-form narratives, investigating claims like that of *Game of Thrones* (HBO, 2011–19) showrunners David Benioff and D.B. Weiss that they were making a 73-hour film rather than television[1] – what Newman and Levine refer to as 'cinematisation', television's 'ubiquitous legitimating strategy' (Newman and Levine 2012, location 204) – ultimately television studies have always recognised that seriality goes hand-in-hand with segmentation, what Sean O'Sullivan refers to as being 'broken on purpose' (O'Sullivan 2010). Indeed, even with the advent of the '*auteur* television' heralded by HBO and *The Sopranos* (1999–2007), this new narrative continuity was accompanied by a renewed emphasis on brevity:

> Central features of the way in which texts became bingeable were the focus on writing and narrative complexity, the shortening of seasons to 12 or 13 episodes, the high investment in cast and the creation of 'cinematic' aesthetics. The 18-month hiatus between seasons that was once given to the writers of *The Sopranos* (...) to develop stories for the next season would remain a rarity, but the story highlights the importance that was assigned to creative processes and how much HBO aimed to market itself as purveyor of this kind of creativity. (Jenner 2021, 9)

Though the ongoing storyline of a landmark serial fiction like *The Sopranos* may have initially seemed to foreground duration and the length of the story of Tony Soprano and his clan, this was carefully balanced by generalising a tendency towards brevity, both in the number of episodes that would hereafter constitute a season, and in the ultimate duration of that season (shown weekly without the interruption of reruns,[2] and then with an extended hiatus between seasons that makes each seem even shorter). As Anthony Smith concludes in *Storytelling Industries*, it is in fact brevity that makes seriality feasible:

> A season's relative shortness and continuous frequency of transmission (or simultaneous release of episodes) raises the chances of viewers 'keeping up with' intricate season-length storylines, as the format lessens the demand placed on viewers to keep track of what has occurred previously in the narrative. (Smith, 2018, 93, quoted in Kozak and Zeller-Jacques 2021, 210)

As such, the authors of this volume do not seek to deconstruct or contradict the work of our many esteemed colleagues in the field of television studies, or to harken back to an older form of television (and television studies); rather, we hope that this volume on brevity in television offers a complement to their work on seriality, an acknowledgement of the inherent tension in all television storytelling between brevity and duration, between the part and the whole. Matthew Poland's witty phrasing could summarise our intentions:

> Serials are full of holes – those gaps that yawn across individual instalments – but they are also full of *wholes*, i.e. constituent parts that also demand to be read as self-contained entities in their own right. Consequently, serials are both always ending and never ending; they are both broken and unfinished. As such, they challenge our inherited notions about aesthetic unity, continually raising questions as to the boundaries that constitute an aesthetic whole. (Poland 2014, 77)

Indeed, this volume makes clear that far from being a 'throwback', focusing on the ambiguous nature of brevity in television allows us to shed new light on the ever-evolving landscape of storytelling for the small screen. Indeed, recent work on our tendency towards binge-watching confirms that despite the new technologies first of box sets, and then of streaming media, in the end viewers come back to the notion of the episode:

> The episode, not the hour, is the unit of the 'binge-watch'. [. . .] Episode boundaries provide an opportunity for users to decide whether or not to keep watching. The quantitative analysis [. . .] shows that the more episode boundaries are provided, the more users abandon a season. This suggests that despite the strength of features like auto-play which reduce friction and keep viewers in the 'insulated flow,' episode boundaries are

still a more pronounced cue to trigger user habits than their internal sense of the passage of time. (Pierce-Grove 2021, 98)

This emphasis on the episode is equally apparent in popular and journalistic discourse, in never-ending lists of 'best episodes' for different series each year – or indeed in our own academic practices, as the difficulty of imposing long serial narratives necessarily encourages university lecturers to privilege specific episodes as representative of an overly large whole (at least within the framework of a semester-long course).[3] Even while breaking the mould in terms of narrative complexity, we're told, *The Sopranos*' David Chase was more interested in 'discrete little movies' than soap opera (O'Sullivan 2013, 66). In fact, resistance to soap opera is characteristic of the long-form series that have been acclaimed both by critics and the audience since the beginning of the twenty-first century. Newman and Levine have shown that drama identified as 'quality' like *The Sopranos*, although heavily serialised, strives to distinguish itself from the lesser valued genre of soap opera, notably by 'containing' its serialised seriality. Introducing a dose of episodic storytelling is indeed one of the ways in which it is achieved: 'prime time dramas distinguish themselves from soaps by becoming more like the episodic dramas against which they also seek separation. Yet they escape the denigrated status of an episodic procedural by articulating such instances to movies' (Newman and Levine 2012, location 2171), as Chase's vision of *The Sopranos* as a series of 'discrete little movies' makes clear, thus making the episode structure a key feature of 'quality' televisual storytelling.

Another way of imposing limitations on seriality is simply to make sure that the series ends. This is another strong distinction tool that differentiates dramas seeking cultural prestige from soap opera, a long format that typically tells never-ending stories. The 'quality' dramas of the last two decades share this desire for narrative closure with the 'miniseries', which started in the 1970s and was characterised by the limited duration of a finite number of episodes (Newman and Levine 2012, location 2081). The recent trend of 'limited series', the term which has lately been preferred over 'miniseries', is an illustration of the continued value associated with relative brevity at the scale of the whole narrative of a series. While the term 'limited' or 'event' series certainly has an aura of prestige in the era of Peak TV (see McNutt 2014), distinguishing the show from the more common several season-long series, it can also guarantee[4] that the series will provide a satisfying sense of conclusion, a narrative trait that plays a role in the viewers' selection of whether or not they will stream a show, according to a survey showing that 'whether or not the show has concluded has a significant impact on whether people sample it' (MacCary 2023).

Brevity has also played an important role in the relations between broadcast or cable television and online television. Web-series were originally characterised by extremely short formats, both for technical reasons and, as Aymar Jean Christian points out in his book on independent web television, due to 'perceptions of audience attention' (Christian 2018, 33). Indeed, the devices on which online videos were watched (laptops, mobile phones, iPads) were initially thought to potentially prevent long attention spans: in the words of J.P. Kelly,

> Within such close proximity to the numerous other competing windows of a computer screen, viewers might be tempted to shift their attention elsewhere: to quickly check their email, to update their social networking status, or to interact with any of the various other files that sit just one click away. (Kelly 2017, 79)

Webisodes of broadcast or cable series were an early example of traditional television's use of the Internet in relation to the airing of complex serialised dramas like *Lost* (ABC, 2004–10), *Heroes* (NBC, 2006–10), *The Walking Dead* (AMC, 2010–22) or *Battlestar Galactica* (Sci Fi, 2004–9). In many ways, these very short online episodes filled the 'holes' of the serials, for instance helping fans wait for the return of their favourite show during the summer break, maintaining interest in the series before the airing of a new season, or even attracting new viewers to the show (Glater 2006, Hale 2008, *TVWeek* 2007). Even as broadcast television and cable television increased their presence on the Internet, and as Netflix and other streaming platforms launched their own long-form series, embracing the possibilities allowed by technological improvements which now made streaming long videos a comfortable and pleasurable experience, online television's tradition of extreme brevity has continued with independently produced web-series.

More recently, the popularity and visibility of some of these online series has become obvious in the mainstream success of their stars, like Issa Rae's *Awkward Black Girl* (2011–13), which gave way to *Insecure* (HBO, 2016–21), or Quinta Brunson's *Girl Who Has Never Been on a Nice Date* (2014), which led to the popular and critical darling *Abbott Elementary* (ABC, 2021–present)[5] – though the relatively longer forms of their more conventionally accessible shows suggest that extreme brevity may not necessarily be becoming the norm, but instead a new option among others for television fictions.

Likewise, technological innovations have introduced another paradox into our perception of brevity: while episodes, acts or seasons might be brief, physical and streaming media suggest that unlike the origins of television, broadcast live and not necessarily recorded for posterity, fictions of today are more permanent than ever (though the versions available may not always be official).[6] Indeed, we hope that this volume will contribute to making these short forms, however brief, a long-lasting part of our understanding of television narratives.

CONFIRMING — AND DECONSTRUCTING — TELEVISION TRADITIONS OF BREVITY

The first part of our analysis explores the ways that television has structured itself around traditions of brevity, and how these traditions have been upheld or deconstructed in later fictions. Even in our earliest example, Julien Achemchame shows how Hitchcock was already using the television anthology format of *Alfred Hitchcock Presents* (CBS, 1955–60, 1962–4; NBC 1960–2, 1964–5) as a subversion of earlier dramatic anthology formats, both longer and live, even while his own work as occasional director but systematic producer and script advisor made him a proto-showrunner as we know them today. Television allowed Hitchcock both the freedom to more amply examine the genres and themes that interested him – and the ability to poke fun at sponsors, viewers, the code of morals that predominated at the time, and indeed at himself. Achemchame's careful delineation of episodic structure, with the story itself providing two acts and a twist, and Hitchcock's introduction and conclusion bookending the narrative, foregrounds the way that brevity is an integral part of the creator's desired effect. By making his own persona and his characteristic irony the foremost unifying elements of the series, by limiting the viewer's experience with each episode's characters, Hitchcock allows us to watch for narrative mechanisms rather than empathy or catharsis – and perhaps, frees the viewer to briefly empathise with the criminals, as Achemchame suggests: 'not only are we made to understand the murderer's motivations but our empathy might even lead us to wish they will elude the police.'

While Julien Achemchame focuses on the brevity of the episode of television (particularly in relation to its forerunner, the dramatic anthology), Florence Cabaret focuses on a case study of a short form whose brevity is global: the miniseries, or 'classic serial'. Because of its structural emphasis on closure, but its longer episodes and focused narrative, Cabaret highlights its inherently hybrid status, between television tradition and filmic ambition. In *The Jewel in the Crown*'s (ITV, 1984) depiction of strictly maintained boundaries between countries, and hierarchies between peoples, Cabaret also detects an implicit and ironic commentary on the very nature of television traditions in Britain, and ITV's attempts to puncture them.

Indeed, Cabaret insists on the miniseries' refusal to conform to either linear progression or traditional serial storytelling, notably in its paradoxical use of incipits and excipits that largely eschew the cliffhanger, preferring instead abstract or symbolic images of fire and landscape that are evocative of previous scenes rather than foreshadowing of elements to come, or the repeated use of still images (photographs, paintings, news images) or flashbacks. As such, Cabaret shows, 'the miniseries *pro*gresses by *re*gressing', but also interrupts the forward momentum of the narrative with 'potential spin-offs' or alternate histories, a mise-en-abyme of *The Jewel in the Crown*'s own vision of history.

The attention paid to narrative structure is similarly highlighted in Justine Breton's analysis of French shortcom *Kaamelott* (M6, 2005–9). The shortcom – a fusion of English terms 'short' and 'sitcom' – has become a staple of French broadcast television in the last few decades, offering very brief sketches (clocking in at 10 minutes or less) situated between the evening news and the primetime slot. In her examination of *Kaamelott*, a comic retelling of Arthurian legend, Breton focuses on the series' adoption of traditions old and new (both from vaudeville and classic theatre as well as from preceding shortcoms) that are then honed in this new context. She insists that the transformation of the tragic myth into a comic series largely relates to time, notably in its incorporation of a static diegesis typical of the sitcom in its first three seasons, where each episode 'resets' after the crisis of its preceding instalment, and reinforces that lack of narrative impetus through fixed shots of similarly static actors, limiting production costs while reinforcing the importance of dialogue and language in the series. Like Cabaret, Breton's analysis suggests that this narrative stagnation forces the viewer to focus on the individual episode, an assertion compounded by the series' own diegetic discussion of Aristotelian principles.

Breton's examination of *Kaamelott*'s debt to the theatre is another example of the generic hybridity that Jason Mittell has rightly identified as being endemic to television (Mittell 2004), and will be a recurrent issue in this collection, from Hitchcock's use of his filmic persona on *Alfred Hitchcock Presents* to *The Jewel in the Crown* tapping into techniques previously reserved for film, while foregrounding its inclusion of newsreel, photography and painting. The final two authors of this section, Sylvaine Bataille and Benjamin Campion, highlight these intermedial borrowings as a means to better establish their series' status as innovative television, broadening the horizons of the media. Bataille studies Sam Esmail's *Homecoming* (Prime Video, 2018–20), a fiction that foregrounds markers of prestige television (notably in its numerous homages to film *auteurs* like Hitchcock, DePalma or Antonioni), while simultaneously insisting on a notably brief duration for its episodes (a half-hour format traditionally reserved for comedy). This tension between adherence to the televisual traditions of 'quality television' on the one hand and the refusal to relegate the short form solely to comedy could be diminished by its presence on the streaming platform Prime Video, Bataille writes, but instead the fiction doubles down on the notion of smallness, of the individual episode, through an emphasis on the incipit and excipit of each (with title cards that offer only the episode number, and extended end credits with lingering *temps morts*), thus slowing down the consumption of streaming's traditional binge watch. As such, this series, devoted to the notion of 'lost time', echoes its themes structurally, offering a reduction of the visual narrative that is both temporal and spatial (borders of the frame, image ratio, shot scale and camera angle), and perhaps suggesting a parallel with streaming video's decreasing size of screens, as people now watch on computers or tablets rather than televisions.

Though Benjamin Campion's work on *Twin Peaks: The Return* (Showtime, 2017) offers yet another association with film, given the *auteur* status afforded to series creator and director David Lynch, Campion seeks to establish the way Lynch ultimately eschews this link with the medium that made him famous in an effort to foreground not just the individual episode, but indeed the individual scene, in a contemporary TV landscape that tends to favour the notion of television as simply a more lengthy form of film. In so doing, Campion echoes Constantine Verevis's reading of *Fire Walk with Me* (1992) as a 'ruinous sequel', given that like Verevis, he sees *The Return* as a means to 'rend further holes in [*Twin Peaks*'s] narrative fabric' (Verevis, 69). Thus Lynch makes a series that is uniquely televisual, all while overturning a certain number of clichés specific to small screen storytelling, in order to offer a new understanding of television as art beyond its status as commercial entertainment:

> what is striking when studying *Twin Peaks*' third season is the extent to which the series' move to premium cable evidently freed it from the constraints of narrative 'efficiency' and the unnatural cliffhangers intended to make viewers more or less consciously want to tune in again the following week. TV series are not just a matter of postponed delight and 'oh-now-all-is-clear' resolution; they also – and above all – engage perception and comprehension of images full of life, spontaneity and, in Lynchian cases, mystery. Perhaps it is time to consider TV series as a contemporary art form instead of systematically underlining their legacy – serial literature, radio dramas, daytime soap operas –, as has become customary for many scholars over the past decade, in television and elsewhere.

NEW MEDIA AND NEW FORMS: WEB-SERIES, STREAMING PLATFORMS AND THE SHORT FORM

Florent Favard opens this section devoted to the impact of new media on television and brevity by pinpointing the fundamental elements of television narrative, and how these different levels of narrative are impacted by the evolving nature of production and distribution in television. Favard uses celebrated texts by Jason Mittell and Michael Z. Newman to re-examine the building blocks of the series, from the scene or 'beat', to the act, the episode, the arc, the season, a multi-season 'movement', and finally the series, before going on to discuss how these different blocks have taken on changed importance as their mode of dissemination changes (how the act shrinks as broadcast networks insist on more commercial breaks, or the erasure of all intermediate forms other than the season in the era of Netflix's 'next episode' push towards binge-watching).

Several of our authors ironically associate brevity with slowness (Bataille, Campion); Sarah Tanderup Linkis's chapter title, 'Minute by Minute,' associates Norwegian series *Skam* (NRK1, 2015–17) not only with the passing of time, where each minute counts in this real-time transmedial series, but also with its production company of the same name, who famously popularised the notion of 'slow television' on NRK. This fascinating balance between broadcast traditions and transmedial possibilities is characteristic of this second part of our collection. *Skam*'s use of real-time differs radically from the first television series to focus on that storytelling strategy, Fox's *24* (2001–10, 2014). Instead of constantly emphasising the idea that time was running out, that the end was nigh (with the end of the series' 24-hour duration being directly paralleled with a catastrophe), *Skam* focuses on the importance of each moment to be savoured (or endured). Likewise, by integrating social media into its storytelling in a way that was previously unheard of, *Skam* was particularly successful in blurring the boundaries between paratext and text: while previous (and subsequent) series rely on social media primarily as a marketing tool, through tweeting creatives or publication of behind-the-scenes featurettes, *Skam* made what was generally peripheral to the narrative central to its storytelling. In so doing, Tanderup Linkis writes, *Skam*'s novel storytelling actually harkens back to the communal experience of storytelling, be it Victorian *feuilletons* or broadcast favourites.

The coexistence of broadcast and streaming television apparent in Favard's chapter, like *Skam*'s reliance on both traditional public broadcast and novel uses of social media, is a recurrent tension in this section, as each of our authors acknowledges how new media remains if not dependent, then at least indebted to the broadcast traditions that preceded it. Thus Stéphane Sawas's work on the web-series *Les Engagés* shows another European public broadcaster, France Télévision, which, like *Skam*'s NRK, took advantage of new media to offer both a novel form for drama and groundbreaking content (as France's first LGBTQIA series) on its streaming platform Studio 4, in an effort to attract an audience that had escaped them in a more traditional format. Sawas's careful analysis of the series short form focuses notably on its ellipses (partially due to the production context of abridging screenplays initially intended for 30-minute episodes to the 10-minute web-series format). Ellipses condense the narrative, speeding up the pace of plotlines, but also paradoxically motivating the viewer to slow down, to rewatch and redouble their investment on/in the series.

Finally, our last chapter in this section, Claire Cornillon's examination of the DCverse's crossover event 'Crisis on Planet X' offers a savvy analysis of how broadcast networks might respond to the popularity of new media. While *Skam* and *Les Engagés* offer examples of how broadcast seeks to incorporate new media either in its fictions or on its new platforms (also known as the 'if you can't beat 'em, join 'em' strategy), the CW, whose network was at one point home to no less than eight superhero series, chose instead to create a crossover event for the four of its series broadcast at the time in opposition to the notion of binge-watching, and instead dependent on the televisual notion of flow. By scheduling each of the individual series in a two-night viewing event, the CW broke each fiction out of its binge-watching mould, instead offering 'appointment television' that Cornillon posits constitutes an ersatz miniseries within the framework of the DCverse, a coherent and discrete whole within each ongoing narrative. However, she argues, this reliance on older traditions (of flow, of the crossover) does not necessarily forgo the possibilities of new media; on the contrary, the crossover is 'geared towards fan interaction and fan service' and 'strengthen[s] links inside the fan community', making the CW's insistence on their stars' presence on social media part of a new media strategy to push online audiences towards broadcast screens – at least for the duration of this 'special episode' miniseries.

BLURRING BOUNDARIES: PRODUCTION, PARATEXTS AND RECEPTION OF THE SHORT FORM

The final section of our collection deals with the blurring boundaries of reception, production and paratext in television. One of the small screen's defining qualities, after all, was its ability (and indeed need) to adjust its diegesis to the changing context of production, be it in the availability of actors over the course of multiple years, or the available budget (or indeed renewal of contracts) for an ongoing fiction. Thus our first two authors focus on the relationship between production constraints and their diegetic impact on narrative time in television. Shannon Wells-Lassagne joins Claire Cornillon in her analysis of 'special episodes,' using the series *Community* (NBC, 2009–14; Yahoo, 2015) as a case study. She suggests that the micro and macro scales of analysis can overlap, investigating three high-concept special episodes (the bottle episode, the time loop and the clip show), which she suggests focus on the episode, the sequence (or act), and the clip (or beat), respectively. These episodes may have been conceived as cost-cutting measures, a means to balance the budget for a season, but in so doing, these forms highlight the structuring nature of brevity in television storytelling – in its proximity to the viewer in a real-time narrative, in its repeated segmentation balancing familiarity and novelty, or in its changing relationship to memory.

Jessica Thrasher offers a similar study of production influencing television narrative: her introduction notes that the diegetic choice to draw out *Friends* (NBC, 1994–2004) characters Chandler and Monica's efforts to conceive was ultimately imposed by behind-the-scenes concerns (in other words, production negotiations for a tenth season of the show). *Friends* is one of the more traditional sitcoms/short forms discussed in this volume, but its production context, though extraordinary in its success (very much at odds with the 'on the bubble' productions that predominate the TV landscape), underlines the way that even in a short form that is largely episodic, there is an increasing focus on long-term/ongoing narratives, and the uncertainty of conceiving a child in the fiction ultimately echoes the uncertainty of conceiving a coherent narrative and resolution for long-running fiction.

While Thrasher and Wells-Lassagne focus on how production impacts diegetic time in television series, our final author highlights the blurred boundaries between paratext and reception. Indeed, in the era of physical media and streaming video, reception, too, has been impacted by modes of viewing: Florence Cabaret notes that the retrospective viewing of *The Jewel in the Crown* through DVDs influences our perception of its genre, foregrounding its similarities with the soap opera after the fact, while Justine Breton remarks on the way the tightly structured sketches of *Kaamelott* are made even more apparent in the decision to first have three 3-minute sketches broadcast together, and later to heighten this impression of both brevity and ubiquity by offering hours of reruns of the series. Bataille's discussion of streaming series *Homecoming* likewise highlights how the fiction ultimately fights against the impression of never-ending (and unstructured) narrative in streaming's binge-watching model through its emphasis on the episode. Lastly, Sébastien Lefait takes on the issue of dramatic television's often epic length through the use of paratext. The 'explainer videos' made by popular culture journalists are both paratext (using images and information made available through press kits and interviews) and reception (featuring fan theories making sense of lengthy narratives), using short videos (and indeed precise examples) to point out themes, important details and other paratexts for audiences involved in forensic fandom. As such, the brevity of these online videos offers a solution to the impossible absorption of these increasingly lengthy and complex television narratives, to the 'contradiction between the (potentially limitless) proliferation of TV show narratives and the (equally endless) dissolution of their meanings, which in turn give[s] rise to orienting, riddle-solving videos'.

Finally, as a conclusion and epigraph to this study of brevity, the editors of this volume interviewed screenwriter Vincent Poymiro, a celebrated author whose work featured in Cannes's famous film festival and at the Césars, France's equivalent of the Academy Awards. He is the author of the French adaptation of *BeTipul* (HOT3, 2005–8, adapted in the US as *In Treatment*

[HBO, 2008–21]), entitled *En thérapie* (Arte, 2021–2), and in this wide-ranging interview, while focused particularly (and logically) on the production side of television fiction, he shares his thoughts on the state of French, British and American television and its evolution. *En thérapie*, as another example of a short form made accessible through a public broadcaster's plans for its streaming platform, confirms much of the work of Sawas and Tanderup Linkis, while his thoughts on television's rivalry and intermingling with other art forms like theatre and film echoes remarks made by Breton, Campion, Bataille or Achemchame. This peek outside of the ivory tower of academic discourse is valuable in and of itself, of course, but the resonance it offers with the considerations of our authors suggests not only that screenwriters take the study of their work as seriously as academics do, but also that their awareness of this constantly evolving television landscape opens up future avenues of exploration both for artists and the academics who study their art.

NOTES

1. 'We've had this sense from the first time we pitched the show to HBO that we wanted basically to tell a 70-hour movie. Actually it's going to turn out to be 73 hours, but still it's stayed relatively the same in terms of a beginning, a middle and now we're coming to the end.' (Miller 2018)
2. See also O'Sullivan 2010, 67–8.
3. Our thanks to Julie Grossman for this comment.
4. The definition of 'limited series' varies according to the context (between broadcast and cable television for instance): see McNutt 2014. Moreover, recent series initially labeled as 'limited', such as *Big Little Lies* or *The White Lotus*, were followed by a second season.
5. See also Nguyen 2019.
6. See also Grainge 2011.

WORKS CITED

24, created by Joel Surnow and Robert Cochran, Fox, 2001–10, 2014.
Abbott Elementary, created by Quinta Brunson, ABC, 2021–present.
Alfred Hitchcock Presents, created by Alfred Hitchcock, CBS, 1955–60, 1962–4; NBC 1960–2, 1964–5.
Awkward Black Girl, created by Issa Rae, YouTube, 2011–13.
Battlestar Galactica, created by Ronald D. Moore, Sci Fi, 2004–9.
BeTipul, created by Hagai Levi, Ori Sivan and Nir Bergman, HOT3, 2005–8.
Big Little Lies, created by David E. Kelley, HBO, 2017–19.
Christian, Aymar Jean, *Open TV: Innovation Beyond Hollywood and the Rise of Web Television* (New York: New York University Press, 2018).
Community, created by Dan Harmon, NBC, 2009–14; Yahoo, 2015.

Deming, Caren, 'Locating the Televisual in Golden Age Television', in *A Companion to Television*, eds Janet Wasko and Eileen R. Meehan (Wiley-Blackwell, 2005), 126–41.
Ellis, John, *Visible Fictions: Cinema, Television, Video* (New York: Routledge & Kegan Paul, 1982).
En thérapie, created by Éric Toledano and Olivier Nakache, Arte, 2021–2.
Les Engagés, created by Sullivan Le Postec, Studio 4, 2017–21.
Friends, created by David Crane and Marta Kauffman, NBC, 1994–2004.
Game of Thrones, created by David Benioff and D.B. Weiss, HBO, 2011–19.
Glater, Jonathan D., 'Sci Fi Creates "Webisodes" to Lure Viewers to TV', *The New York Times*, 5 September 2006. Available online: https://www.nytimes.com/2006/09/05/arts/television/sci-fi-creates-webisodes-to-lure-viewers-to-tv.html (Accessed February 2023).
The Girl Who Has Never Been on a Nice Date, created by Quinta Brunson, YouTube, 2014.
Grainge, Paul (ed.), *Ephemeral Media: Transitory Screen Culture from Television to YouTube* (London: British Film Institute, 2011).
Hale, Mike, 'NBC Bridges Series Gaps with Online Minidramas', *The New York Times*, 28 December 2008. Available online: https://www.nytimes.com/2008/12/29/arts/television/29webi.html (Accessed February 2023).
Heroes, created by Tim Kring, NBC, 2006–10.
Homecoming, created by Eli Horowitz and Micah Bloomberg, Prime Video, 2018–20.
In Treatment, created by Rodrigo Garcia, HBO, 2008–21.
Insecure, created by Issa Rae and Larry Wilmore, HBO, 2016–21.
Jenner, Mareike, 'Introduction', in *Binge-Watching and Contemporary Television Studies*, ed. Mareike Jenner (Edinburgh: Edinburgh University Press, 2021), 1–22.
Jewel in the Crown, created by Christopher Morahan, Jim O'Brien, Ken Taylor and Irene Shubik, ITV, 1984.
Kaamelott, created by Alexandre Astier, M6, 2005–9.
Kelly, J.P., *Time, Technology and Narrative Form in Contemporary Television Drama: Pause, Rewind, Record* (Cham: Palgrave Macmillan, 2017).
Kozak, Lynn and Martin Zeller-Jacques, 'Digressions and Recaps: The Bingeable Narrative', in *Binge-Watching and Contemporary Television Studies*, ed. Mareike Jenner (Edinburgh: Edinburgh University Press, 2021), pp. 207–23.
Lost, created by Jeffrey Lieber, J.J. Abrams and Damon Lindelof, ABC, 2004–10.
MacCary, Julia, 'Frequent TV Series Cancellations Altering Viewer Behavior, Survey Shows', *Variety*, 16 March 2023. Available online: https://variety.com/2023/tv/news/frequent-tv-series-cancellations-affect-viewership-1235553780/ (Accessed March 2023).
McNutt, Myles, 'Limited Series Are a Product of Brand Management, Not Innovation', Carsey-Wolf Center's Media Industries Project, UC Santa Barbara, CLI Short Articles Archive, 2014. Available online: https://www.carseywolf.ucsb.edu/research/industry/cli/#1519677514758-87a80cd0-7d68 (Accessed February 2023).
Miller, Donna Marie, 'A 73 Hour Movie: David Benioff and D.B. Weiss on *Game of Thrones*', *Creative Screenwriting*, 1 March 2018. Available online: https://www.creativescreenwriting.com/game-of-thrones/ (Accessed February 2023).

Mittell, Jason, *Genre and Television: From Cop Shows to Cartoons in American Culture* (New York and London: Routledge, 2004).

Mittell, Jason, 'Previously On: Prime Time Serials and the Mechanics of Memory', *Just TV*, 3 July 2009. Available online: https://justtv.wordpress.com/2009/07/03/previously-on-prime-time-serials-and-the-mechanics-of-memory/ (Accessed September 2022).

Newman, Michael Z. and Elana Levine, *Legitimating Television: Media Convergence and Cultural Status* (New York: Routledge, 2012, Kindle edition).

Nguyen, Terry, '"I'm Here Because of the Internet": How Web Series Made New TV Stars', *Vice*, 2 January 2019. Available online: https://www.vice.com/en/article/qvq9qb/inclusion-television-shows-web-series (Accessed April 2023).

O'Sullivan, Sean, 'Broken on Purpose: Poetry, Serial Television, and the Season', *Storyworlds: A Journal of Narrative Studies* 2 (January 2010): 59–77. Available online: https://www.jstor.org/stable/10.5250/storyworlds.2.1.59 (Accessed April 2023).

O'Sullivan, Sean, '*The Sopranos*: Episodic Storytelling', in *How to Watch Television*, eds Ethan Thompson and Jason Mittell (New York: New York University Press, 2013), 65–73.

Pierce-Grove, Ri, 'What Defines a Binge? Elapsed Time versus Episodes', in *Binge-Watching and Contemporary Television Studies*, ed. Mareike Jenner (Edinburgh: Edinburgh University Press, 2021), 98–111.

Poland, Matthew, 'Full of Wholes: Narrative Configuration, Completion, and the Televisual Episode / Season / Series', *GRAAT On-Line*, no. 15 (April 2014): 76–92. Available online: http://www.graat.fr/4poland.pdf (Accessed September 2022).

Smith, Anthony, *Storytelling Industries: Narrative Production in the 21st Century* (Cham: Palgrave Macmillan, 2018).

Skam, created by Julie Andem, NRK1, 2015–17.

The Sopranos, created by David Chase, HBO, 1999–2007.

TVWeek, 'NBC Finds Webisode Workaround', *TVWeek*, 26 March 2007. Available online: https://www.tvweek.com/in-depth/2007/03/nbc-finds-webisode-workaround/ (Accessed February 2023).

Twin Peaks: The Return, created by David Lynch and Mark Frost, Showtime, 2017.

The Walking Dead, created by Frank Darabont, AMC, 2010–22.

The White Lotus, created by Mike White, HBO, 2021–present.

Verevis, Constantine, 'The W/hole David Lynch: *Twin Peaks: Fire Walk with Me*', in *Networked David Lynch: Critical Perspectives on Cinematic Transmediality*, eds Marcel Hartwig, Andreas Rauscher and Peter Niedermüller (Edinburgh: Edinburgh University Press, 2023), 61–77.

Part 1

Confirming – and Deconstructing – Television Traditions of Brevity

CHAPTER 1

Alfred Hitchcock Presents: Subverting Anthology TV Series

Julien Achemchame

INTRODUCTION: THE CONTEXT OF TV DRAMA ANTHOLOGY AND THE ARRIVAL OF HITCHCOCK ON TELEVISION

In 1955, television was still a young medium and industry, though it was already becoming a powerful presence in North American homes. The initial competition with cinema, started in the early 50s, was being resolved as Hollywood studios finally agreed to sell their old film catalogues and started to produce television series in place of B-pictures. From that point on, the rivalry between the two media became a sort of commercial complementarity (Balio 1990). It was that same year, 1955, that one of Hollywood's most important directors, Alfred Hitchcock, bridged the two media by producing his own television show: the anthology suspense series *Alfred Hitchcock Presents* (CBS, 1955–60; NBC, 1960–2). The anthology format, where each episode tells its own story with different characters and plots, and which thus combines brevity and discontinuity, was in and of itself nothing new: it had been quite popular since the beginning of the 50s. *Studio One* (CBS, 1948–58), *Danger* (CBS, 1950–5) and *Television Playhouse* (NBC, 1948–57), for instance, were very popular and critically acclaimed anthology dramas from that period.[1] Adapting mainly short stories and plays from famous and popular authors, those anthologies were shot live from the New York studios of the main networks and were introduced by an invisible host whose voice mainly served as the sponsor of the show. But in 1955, those fictional primetime anthology dramas were steadily being replaced by programs filmed and recorded in Hollywood, marking the 'end of the golden age of the great dramatic anthologies' (Delavaud 2013, 69[2]). Cinema's model seemed to have won this battle over that of television.

Mittell reminds us that 'technological, industrial, and reception shifts [. . . were] functioning not as straightforward causes of these formal innovations but certainly as essential factors to allow particular creative strategies to flourish' (Mittell 2015, 6). The major shifts occurring in US television in the mid-1950s might explain Hitchcock's interest in both the medium and the format. They may also partially account for the reflexive and ironic dimension of Hitchcock's anthology series, particularly visible in the presentation and conclusion of the episodes in which 'Hitchcock tells us [. . .] about television as an institution and a device' (Delavaud 2013, 69). Anthology drama was coming to an end, and Hitchcock, in a way, was mocking it in order to renew it, thereby confirming Robert Stam's contention that '[w]hen artistic forms become historically inappropriate, parody lays them to rest. Parody highlights art's historicity, its contingency and transcience (sic)' (Stam 1985, 135). But perhaps there is something about the anthology format that makes it especially rife for parody, something having to do with the way it served, according to William Boddy, to assert 'mutually reinforcing dichotomies: anthology format/serial format, live/canned, New York Theater/Hollywood cinema, realism/spectacle, character/plot and independence/subservience of the "playwright"/screenwriter' (Boddy in Horwitz 2013, 41).

Hitchcock's involvement in television was a real novelty because of his status as Hollywood Star director. We could say that he used his popular public image to ironically change the rules of anthology dramas. Introducing and concluding every episode, talking directly to the viewers, Hitchcock started a new era for the anthology format, which led, for instance, to Rod Serling's presentations in his famous science-fiction anthology series *The Twilight Zone* (CBS, 1959–64) (Potts 2005, 46). But Hitchcock had already played the role of a presenter – or rather editor – in the 1940s when he published a series of crime anthologies, some of which would provide the material for certain episodes of *Alfred Hitchcock Presents* (Delavaud 2013, 91). Delavaud explains that the purpose of the TV anthology series was 'to satisfy his deep taste for short fiction, mainly for "suspense and mystery stories" such as those that, in the 1940s, and on his own initiative, he had gathered in a volume and published under his name for Dell Publishing' (70). Moreover, Hitchcock had long been interested in multiple media; in addition to popular literature and cinema, he also used radio, taking part in a 30-minute-long radio adaptation of *The Lodger* for CBS in July 1940. His interest in the increasingly popular medium of television is manifest in his 1954 film *Rear Window*, a work that interrogates the reception of moving pictures in general; Rauger goes so far as to describe L.B. Jefferies as the 'first zapper in the history of the cinema' (Rauger 2014, 50), and considers Hitchcock's later œuvre to be informed by television. Hitchcock saw in the medium an opportunity to reconfigure his own style in the special format of short episodic anthology series.

I will first highlight how the reflexive devices (Stam 1985) used in this anthological program create the characteristics of the show's formula. I argue that this reconfiguration of Hitchcock's style and narration by means of the short episodic form allows experimentation with personal themes, classical genres (crime story, suspense, dark comedy, Gothic) and narrative form (the particular uses of suspense and surprise). Then, by analysing the links between the introductory and conclusive presentation of host Alfred Hitchcock, special cases of brevity inside the short form, and the stories from a selection of weekly episodes directed by the Master of Suspense himself (*Revenge* – S01E01, *Breakdown* – S01E07, *The Case of Mr. Pelham* – S01E10, *Wet Saturday* – S02E01, *One More Mile to Go* – S02E28, *The Perfect Crime* – S03E03, *Lamb to the Slaughter* – S03E28, *Arthur* – S05E01, *Mrs. Bixby and The Colonel's Coat* – S06E01, *Bang! You're Dead* – S07E02), I will show how the anthology, because of its particular short form, creates a mode of permanent irony. Subverting the rules of morality, Hitchcock, using his image as a star director, directs the irony against the institutional advertising sponsor of the program, against the audience, and against the characters of the weekly stories: ordinary people belonging to the upper middle class who commit terrible crimes that often go unpunished, though Hitchcock's ironic concluding remarks sometimes verbally bring a form of moral punishment to the criminal, as a postscript to the story. The brief and discontinuous form imposed by the TV anthology format is thus endowed with a unity based on a playful and complex relation with the viewer.

THE SHOW'S FORMULA: THE REFLEXIVE DEVICES

In addition to the industrial context that allows for the emergence of reflexivity, we note that the formula of *Alfred Hitchcock Presents* is apparently simple: each half-hour episode corresponds to 'a construction in two acts' (Delavaud 2013, 71) and ends 'with a gag or an unexpected turn of events' (Rauger 2014, 23). When a 2-hour film is typically structured in three to four acts and features several median climaxes, US network television imposes two 10-minute acts with a climax, because of multiple commercial breaks. The second act then culminates with a final twist, marked with Hitchcockian irony, that is like an 'emotional punch' (Mittell 2015, 169) for the viewer. Every episode is interrupted by three 1-minute-long commercial breaks: the first occurs after Hitchcock's introduction, the second in the middle of the episode, and the last one before the host's concluding words. The Hitchcock sequences are highly reflexive, inasmuch as they point to their 'own mask and invite the public to examine [the series'] design and texture' (Stam 1985, 1). More precisely, Hitchcock's presentations and conclusions, using different settings and props rarely related directly to the story of the week, operate like paratexts and metatexts (Genette 1982) that frame each episode with ironic and subtle comments on the narratives (Potts 2005, 102), and establish both a distance with television as a medium and an industry, and a complicity between the commentator and the audience. Hitchcock thus resorts to irony and macabre humour in order to leave his mark on the show, both in terms of style and of tone. Nevertheless, the director builds his introductions 'on a tradition of sarcastic, playful horror and suspense hosting, dating back to Wyllis Cooper's *Tights Out!*, which started as a radio program in 1933, continued by Arch Oboler, and perfected by William Castle' (Mock 2015, 70). This is particularly true of the season openers that he directed (*Wet Saturday* – S02E01, *Poison* – S04E01, *Arthur* – S05E01, *Mrs. Bixby and The Colonel's Coat* – S06E01).

'[T]he chief function of a television pilot,' Jason Mittell writes,

> is to teach us how to watch the series and, in doing so, to make us want to keep watching [. . .]. Pilots must orient viewers to the intrinsic norms that the series will employ, presenting its narrative strategies so we can attune ourselves to its storytelling style. (Mittell 2015, 56)

This is clearly the case for 'Revenge' (S01E01). In the prologue, Hitchcock explains the show's formula by offering a sort of tutorial to explicitly educate the viewers about his role and the series' overall tone. The opening credits are particularly important too. The caricatural self-portrait of Alfred Hitchcock appears, followed by the title of the series, with the name of the illustrious film-maker; his shadow in profile is then inserted into the self-portrait just before he steps forward to address the audience directly (Figure 1.1). The presentation then begins.[3]

After politely introducing himself, Hitchcock refers to the 'odd' title of the show bearing his name. The comical accumulation of references to Hitchcock's persona is reinforced through its association with the dark yet trivial soundtrack he chose for the show, featuring Charles Gounod's *Funeral March of a Marionette* (1872) (Potts 2005, 66). Hitchcock guarantees the series' (Hitchcockian) quality, all the while indulging in self-parody. The pilot also features the first occurrence of 'oddly enough', a phrase that will play a central role in his presentations. Hitchcock thus establishes that the series' tone is predominantly ironic. He teaches the audience to understand quite the opposite of what he says and not to trust his words (Potts 2005, 91), and he goes so far as to mock the viewer's misunderstanding of the story and possible illiteracy! His attitude to his sponsor is obsequious, and he praises the latter's foresight in being able to air his commercial because of the simulated delay of the actors, who are not ready to perform (though everything is pre-recorded). The irony is thus directed at television as a medium and as an institution (Potts 2005, 92).

Figure 1.1 Hitchcock's shadow joining his caricatural self-portrait: self-directed irony.

It points to the paradigmatic shift from live broadcasting to Hollywood modes of production; it also seeks to question the relationship established with the television audience, with direct address and allegedly live broadcast simulating two-way communication (Potts 2005, 93).

Returning at the end of the episode, Hitchcock concludes:

> Well, they were a pathetic couple. We had intended to call that one 'Death of a Salesman'. But there were protests from certain quarters. Naturally, Elsa's husband was caught, indicted, tried, convicted, sentenced and paid his debt to society for taking the law into his own hands. You see, crime does not pay. Not even on television. You must have a sponsor. Here is ours. After which I'll return. [Commercial break] That was beautifully put. In fact, after hearing that, there's nothing more I wish to add. So goodnight, until next week.

The conclusion does not explain the story, which is crystal clear – a husband whose wife had allegedly been raped kills a salesman she claims to have recognised but, in the end, she accuses another man of being her rapist, thus making her husband the murderer of the innocent salesman. Hitchcock indicates what happens next and evokes the fate of the husband, who was punished for this unnecessary act of revenge. Black humour is present with the reference to Arthur Miller's famous 1949 play *Death of a Salesman*. By referring to a work of fiction and to the innocent victim of the episode, the salesman, Hitchcock invites the audience to think of the story from a different point of view than that of the episode's protagonists. In effect, irony thus renews the story, which is, in a sense, retrospectively rewritten by the final twist. The twist invites us to watch the episode a second time and reinterpret it in the light of this knowledge. The story's potential is thus exploited far beyond the restrictions of the short episodic form.

The moral of the story, as uttered by Hitchcock ('Crime does not pay'), is called upon in an ironic way, as well as the comic accumulation of verbs ('caught, indicted, tried, convicted, sentenced and paid his debt to society') showing what happens next to the murderous husband: we are thus made to understand the exact opposite since the crime, in the series, is the main advertising argument that attracts both the audience (those mesmerised by sordid news) and the commercial sponsor.[4] Hitchcock seems to be criticising the sponsors, the audience and television (as an institution) for their taste for the tragic and the grotesque. Finally, after the last commercial break, Hitchcock praises the quality of the sponsor's advertising message and concludes – by not concluding: 'That was beautifully put. In fact, after hearing that, there's nothing more I wish to add.' This clearly suggests that the main purpose of Hitchcock's presentations is not moral but commercial. However, by making himself the main author of the show, Hitchcock monopolises the discourse, as he always has the first and last words in every episode. Reflexivity and irony construct the formula of the anthology series and, in order to extend the possibilities of the short form, enable Hitchcock to play the central part.

AUTHORSHIP: THE MASTER OF SUSPENSE'S SHOW

Even though the characters and stories change each week, the similarities between them – and arguably the basic formula of ordinary people confronted with, and sometimes even committing, crime – constructs a special 'storyworld', a Hitchcockverse of sorts anchored in Hitchcock's larger body of work (Perry and Sederholm 2013, 94). Anthology dramas tend to privilege stories that are determined by specific genres (crime, macabre humour, Gothic) and that resort to narrative devices (the twist ending). This particular universe is partly based on the audience's familiarity with the Master of Suspense, a name coined by a publicist to promote Hitchcock's arrival in Hollywood in the late 1930s (Rauger 2014, 17). Despite its discontinuous form, *Alfred Hitchcock Presents*, as its title indicates, has a certain continuity: namely its host. This status is, according to

Thomas Leitch, the 'true power behind the screen' and what makes Hitchcock the author of the show in the eyes of the viewers (Leitch 1999, 69). Like the Crypt-Keeper of the famous EC comic series *Tales from the Crypt* from the 50s (Rauger 2014, 22–23), Hitchcock functions as the teller of the weekly story (Delavaud 2013, 73). Like Lucille Ball (*I Love Lucy*, CBS, 1951–7), Gertrude Berg (*The Goldbergs*, NBC, 1949–56) and Jack Webb (*Dragnet*, NBC, 1951–9), he is the show's producer and star. His name and multiple self-images associated with the show construct Hitchcock's authorship and persona. 'Hitchcock served up his own body [. . .] formed into a discursive package, as an open-ended project elaborated on by commentators, himself included, for decades, and most prominently in the television show' (Olsson 2015, 37). This 'open-ended project' finds a special way to flourish with the short episodic form of anthology TV series.

Even though Hitchcock directed only seventeen of the 268 episodes of the series, he directed all the prologues and epilogues (Potts 2005, 62). He produced (through Shamley Productions) every episode and even supervised the writing. He defined the general style of the series, which was modelled on his most recent film *The Trouble with Harry* (1955), a mixture of a crime story and a macabre comedy. As Glenn D. Novak notes, this film 'perfectly represents the Hitchcock brand of comedy' (Novak 1986, 12). Norman Lloyd, one of the two executive producers with ex-secretary Joan Harrison, and a long time Hitchcock collaborator, claims: 'The point of view of the program was entirely his own' (Weaver 163, cited in Delavaud 71). Harrison and Lloyd selected the stories that would serve as material for the episodes and had them validated by Hitchcock. As producer, Hitchcock supervised the shooting and editing of each episode. He viewed the first edits proposed by the directors and sometimes suggested improvements. Thus, Hitchcock functioned very much like a contemporary series showrunner, creating a hybrid authorship based on management (Mittell 2015, 88); he had the final say on the many decisions involved in the making of the show but also delegated some of the creative choices to a group of producers, writers and technicians. Hitchcock's position as producer was also a matter of 'authorial branding', providing, as Mittell would have it, 'an anchor for understanding programming, delimiting potential appeals, tone, style and genre' (Mittell 2015, 97). Like most contemporary showrunners, the Hollywood director also chose the screenplays he liked the most, including many season openers, as episodes he personally would direct (Erish 2009, Potts 2005, 28). *Alfred Hitchcock Presents*, we could argue, is a duel of 'brands' between Hitchcock as a star director and the advertising sponsor of the TV series that is the target of his constant mockery; this duel contributes to the show's entertainment value. Nevertheless, Hitchcock's prominent position in the show extends the short episodic form and allows the viewer to experience a vast Hitchcockverse: 'Hitchcock's on-screen appearance stretched the

Hitchcockian creative presence and voice beyond the prologue to encompass, infiltrate, and colour all aspects of the show, perhaps even shifting the distinction between paratext and text proper' (Olsson 2015, 143). The show's formula transcends its own shortness. At the same time, the short episodic format allows Hitchcock to experiment with genres.

THE SHORT FORM OF ANTHOLOGY SERIES AND EXPERIMENTATION WITH GENRES (CRIME STORY AND SUSPENSE, MACABRE HUMOUR, GOTHIC)

As mentioned above, the two principal genres from *The Trouble with Harry* contribute to the overall style of *Alfred Hitchcock Presents*. This approach to film genres is characteristic of the director's *modus operandi*. The short form and the anthology format, I will argue, enable the director to experiment with the formal and narrative possibilities of specific genres on a weekly basis.

The presentation of episode S06E01, *Mrs. Bixby and The Colonel's Coat*, reminds viewers of the series' main themes:

> Good evening, ladies and gentlemen, and welcome to a new season of 'Alfred Hitchcock Presents'. As has been our custom, we shall present homey stories of an unusual nature. We shall continue to give the little man, or woman, his due. When crime is occasionally dealt with, it will be crime as practiced by ordinary people, like the fellow next door.

Yet, if the stated intent is to focus on crimes committed by ordinary people, some episodes do not feature a crime, including ten out of the seventeen directed by Hitchcock (*Breakdown, The Case of Mr. Pelham, Mr. Blanchard's Secret, A Dip in the Pool, Poison, The Crystal Trench, Mrs. Bixby and The Colonel's Coat, The Horse Player, Bang! You're Dead*). The series' central theme is actually the 'irony of Fate' (Rauger 2014, 24), concerning essentially 'ordinary' people: in this case, white women and men from the middle- or upper middle-class.

'Just when Americans had begun to adjust to the presence of radio in their living rooms, television arrived as the new lure and the new threat' recalls Erin Lee Mock (Mock 2015, 74), while Rauger argues that, for Hitchcock, 'Television, a familiar and totalitarian presence, is inseparable from the idea of daily life' (Rauger 2014, 148). Domestic homes, as in sitcoms, the other type of short episodic shows, are the main settings of most episodes (Hersey 2014). Television is supposed to be a sort of mirror for viewers, showing them a version of their own living room. However, in *Alfred Hitchcock Presents*, the supposedly safe domestic places become dangerous locations where all sorts of crimes happen (Mock 2015, 72). The characters are ordinary, caught in their mundane 'and sadly matrimonial intimacy' (Rauger 2014, 69). The '*scène de ménage*' features prominently at the centre of the series, and the couple is depicted as a site of violence. Sometimes a husband kills his wife (*Back For Christmas*, *One More Mile to Go*, *Arthur* and *Wet Saturday*), but the wife can kill her husband, too. *Lamb to the Slaughter* presents an ironic inversion of the situation by making the pregnant housewife the murderess of her policeman husband with an object whose very domesticity makes it comic: a big leg of lamb (Hersey 2014). Marriage is one of the many institutions the series pokes fun at; the short discontinuous form of the anthology allows it to be assaulted on a regular basis. Hitchcock presents *One More Mile to Go* (S02E28) thus: 'Tonight's legend tells of modern life and how to solve a problem: wife.' In *The Perfect Crime* (S03E03), he explains: 'A perfect crime is like a perfect marriage – their being perfect depends on your not being caught.' The host voices ideas that will be promoted by the killers, thus enhancing the series' dark humour. In *Arthur* (S05E01), the eponymous killer, who is charming but evil, and reminiscent in this respect of Uncle Charly, the widow killer in *Shadow of a Doubt* (1943), says: 'They marry and spend the rest of their lives wondering why they are so miserable.' Monstrosity is very often lurking beneath the polished appearance of bourgeois normality in characters like Herbert Carpenter (John Williams) in *Back For Christmas* (S01E23) or Charles Courtney (Vincent Price) in *The Perfect Crime*. The anthology format thereby contributes to the idea of the universality of evil within human beings.

The anthology's short episodic format enables Hitchcock to occasionally vary the setting with each story. *Wet Saturday*, for instance, uses macabre comedy to show us a British family trying to cover up the murder of the daughter's lover, a tone foregrounded by the geographical shift, to accentuate the violence of the story and to show Hitchcock's self-deprecation and dark irony, as he is himself a British citizen exiled in the United States.

The anthology offers compelling experiments in the Gothic genre as well. As Mellier notes, this genre uses 'terror and supernatural forms' (Mellier 2000, 19). In *Banquo's Chair* (S04E29), a retired detective plans to create the ghost of a woman murdered two years ago in order to obtain the murderer's confession. The final twist of the story, which is set in 1903 in 'foggy' London, reveals that the ghost was 'real', because we learn that the actress who had to play the role was late and was not responsible for the spectre. The Gothic genre is allowed by the short form and the anthology format, since not only can it reconfigure itself from one episode to the other, but it is ultimately in keeping with the general tone (macabre irony), genre (criminal story) and structure (final narrative twist) of the series overall.

According to Mellier, the Gothic lays on a constant narrative structure of 'persecution', 'which shows the confrontation of a victim with a threatening otherness' (Mellier 2000, 19). The figure of the (evil?) double, a recurrent

Hitchcockian theme – for instance in *The Lodger* (1927), *The Wrong Man* (1956) or *Vertigo* (1958) – also appears in the series with a strong supernatural connotation. In *The Case of Mr. Pelham* (S01E10), Albert Pelham (Tom Ewell) is telling a psychiatrist how he is confronted with a double trying to steal his life from him. In the end, one of the two lookalike characters ends up in a psychiatric ward – but we cannot be certain which one. Once again, this particular theme from traditional Gothic tropes offers an opportunity for Hitchcock to experiment both with genre and narrative structure (in two short acts). The final twist in this episode proposes two different interpretations, opposing rationality and the supernatural. Paradoxically, this recurrent structure reveals the constant use of suspense and surprise.

NARRATION: FROM THE LONG SUSPENSE TO THE SHORT SURPRISE

In 1956, Hitchcock defined television aesthetics in rather disparaging terms: 'Television is, in a way, a simplified cinema. [. . .] in fact, television is photographic theatre, nothing more' (quoted in Rauger 2014, 56). From this perspective, the dramatic potential would be more central than the aesthetic style. The television medium, the anthology format and the short forms of the episodes emphasise the narrative and dramatic formula: a two-part narrative structure with an ironic final twist. This twist is grounded in the idea that the world can be seen in (at least) two ways depending on the point of view that is emphasised. This openness ultimately makes the short fictional world more complex than meets the eye. For instance, in *The Crystal Trench* (S05E02), a story that resembles a condensed version of *Vertigo*, a woman waits for forty years to see the face of her deceased husband imprisoned in a block of ice after a fall into a glacier. When the long-awaited moment arrives, she discovers that her husband had a medallion with the picture of another woman in his hand. In conclusion, she wasted forty years waiting for a man who was in love with another woman! The short form of this particular episode allows for experiments on story time in order to emphasise the final surprise of the twist; in effect, the final revelation is constructed on a forty-year ellipsis, with the husband's death taking place in December 1907 and the recovery of his frozen body in July 1947.

Hitchcock theorises the difference between suspense and surprise, which he famously illustrated in his conversations with François Truffaut. Suspense resides in the uncertainty regarding the future of actions and characters, and in the emotional implication of the viewers, through dramatic irony (the characters are unaware of major plot elements which the viewer already knows). Surprise, on the other hand, is provoked by a plot twist that neither the characters nor viewers can see coming. We can assume that the short form of the anthology format cannot fully use the effects of suspense because the characters, for instance, disappear at the end of each episode. In fact, Hitchcock uses both suspense and surprise, but prioritises the surprising final twist because of the short format. The narrative formula of *Alfred Hitchcock Presents* is thus built on an anticipation of the disruption of a plot through the irony of fate. Thanks to the irony revealed in the final narrative twist, the show can play on two registers: anticipation and surprise. The oscillation between the two allows for playful interaction with the viewer. Hitchcockian suspense is thus designed to (ironically) involve the viewer in the dramatic construction of the work. Many times, the viewers find themselves on the dark side of the 'monstrosity' (*Revenge*, *Breakdown*, *Wet Saturday*, *One More Mile to Go*, *The Perfect Crime*, *Lamb to the Slaughter*, *Arthur*); not only are we made to understand the murderer's motivations but our empathy might even lead us to wish they will elude the police (*Back For Christmas*, *The Perfect Crime*, *Lamb to the Slaughter*, *Arthur*).

Hitchcock uses suspense and surprise in the episodes and adds comments before and after the stories in order to make them more complex and to play ironically with the viewer. For Hitchcock, television allows for an increased possibility of tragic, dark, cruel endings because the viewer is at home, safe. In his conclusions, he often tells us the rest of the story (that the short program does not have the time to show the viewer) and an extra moral, both reassuring and ironic, which is playful and complex. The major dramatic role of surprise is to push forward the irony of fate, which strikes the murderers even after the episodes come to an end. Those conclusions, which expand the short narratives, reveal both themselves and the main theme to be very artificial.

THE ART OF CONCLUSION

In a way, the epilogues of *Alfred Hitchcock Presents* parody the moralistic conclusions of crime series like *Dragnet*, which pass judgement on real-life criminals (each episode of *Dragnet* is actually based on a true story) in order to respect the 1951 Television Code and safeguard social propriety. We could also argue, as Erin Lee Mock does, that: 'The bookends of the host's introduction and conclusion stand as boundaries between the scary story and the world at home' (Mock 2015, 70). Nevertheless, in order to inject the series' ironic tone, 'Hitchcock and Allardice [who co-authored the presentations] had to use their imagination to invent an outcome that respected the prescriptions of the common ethic' (Rauger 2014, 36). For instance, Hitchcock concludes the episode *Wet Saturday* thus:

> I presume that story was intended to illustrate that blood is thicker than water. I always find it heartwarming to see a family standing shoulder

to shoulder in the face of adversity. Unfortunately, the authorities were not thrilled by this sight, and were seen tossing about such phrases as, 'Obstructing justice,' 'Accessory after the fact,' 'Murder in the first degree.' Very nasty. The Princeys received substantial sentences. You see, unfortunately, Captain Smollet didn't play the game. When the police arrived, he insisted on his innocence, thus confusing poor Millicent to such an extent that she re-enacted the crime with her father as the victim.

Episode S03E03, *The Perfect Crime*, has a similar conclusion:

I regret to inform you that Courtney did not retain his last trophy very long. He was caught. A charwoman knocked over the precious vase, breaking it into pieces, a few of them identifiable as, ah, bits of Mr. Gregory. You see, the gold fillings of his teeth had resisted the heat of the kiln, but all the good doctors and all the good police couldn't put Mr. Gregory together again.

Hitchcock's comments are always ironic and make a mockery of whatever morality might be deduced from the tale; this is enhanced by the fact that the criminals of *Alfred Hitchcock Presents*, like real ones, are not always apprehended in the end. Hitchcock's mockery of the episode's cautionary value is a mockery of television conventions. As such, it reflexively highlights the artificiality of these conclusions. Some of Hitchcock's justifications turn out to be quite implausible. For instance, in the conclusion of *Arthur*, Hitchcock reveals: 'There was a very sad end to our story. Because of the excellent bone, meat and blood meal Mr. Williams kept supplying them, his chickens grew to enormous size. Then it happened. One day as he shouldered his way to the hungry flock.' Hitchcock is imagining giant carnivorous chickens that kill the murderer who remained unpunished at the end of the episode. The irony of fate, through the facetious image of enormous avenging chickens, transforms the genre of the story (from crime to horror and even supernatural mixed with macabre humour) in a playful and complex reflection on the possibilities of the short episodic form of anthology (Potts 2005, 89). These obligatory prologues/epilogues, whose economic and moral functions are imposed by the sponsors and the Television Code, work to subvert industry and format conventions. Thus irony allows Hitchcock to 'moralis[e] the story while mocking morality' (Delavaud 2013, 76).

For Hitchcock, 'television, like cinema, is a playful apparatus [. . .]' (Delavaud 2013, 69). This game with the audience is partly established through irony. In effect, irony is based on the tacit collusion between a speaker and a receiver: the latter must understand the exact opposite of what it seems to be at first sight. For Gilles Delavaud, the epilogues 'aim first of all, not so much to clarify the denouement as to comment on it, to interpret it, to make its significance explicit' (75); Hitchcock's ironic introductions invite 'the complicit viewer to adopt, for the duration of the broadcast, this distanced and ironic gaze that the epilogue will further emphasize' (Delavaud 2013, 75). It is through Hitchcock's ironic presentations and conclusions that viewers are made to comprehend the unity of the show's formula.

CONCLUSION: HITCHCOCK'S PLAY WITH THE SHORT FORM ON TV

In 1955, Alfred Hitchcock saw in the television medium an opportunity to reconfigure his own cinematographic style in the special format of the short episodic anthology series. Through reflexivity and irony, the Master of Suspense, as a star Hollywood director with a personal fictional universe, constructed the show's formula in order to extend the possibilities of the short form and to experiment with classical genres (crime story, suspense, macabre humour, Gothic) and narrative form. Using both suspense and surprise, the dramatic structure of the short episodes, constructed in two acts, emphasises the key role of the final twist. This is closely linked to the main tone of the show: irony. By means of the introductory and conclusive presentations of the host, Alfred Hitchcock, the anthology also creates a mode of permanent irony. On a moral level this irony makes it possible to question and subvert the fictional universe and the serial media device. In his introductions and conclusions, Hitchcock, while using self-parody, also mocks the show's advertising sponsor, the serial television media device and the way the public apprehends it all. Through the brief ironic form, he offers a commentary on the moral rules that govern the fictional universes of the episodes, where the crimes are committed by upper middle-class protagonists. They are generally punished – when they do get punished – in unexpected and twisted ways described in the conclusive paratexts of the episodes. Hitchcock's conclusions, by breaking the fictional narrative limits of the short episodes, thus reveal ironically the artificiality of the morality imposed on the television medium. The irony that Hitchcock uses constantly and that is visible through the recurrent irony of fate in the stories allows the brief and discontinuous form imposed by the TV anthology format to find a unity based on a playful and complex relationship with the viewer.[5]

NOTES

1. See Hawes 2002 and Baughman 2007.
2. My translation for this and all quotes from French sources.

3. 'Good evening. I'm Alfred Hitchcock. And tonight I'm presenting the first in a series of stories of suspense and mystery called, oddly enough, *Alfred Hitchcock Presents*. I shall not act in these stories but will only make appearances. Something in the nature of an accessory before and after the fact. To give the title to those of you who can't read and to tidy up afterwards for those who don't understand the endings. Tonight's playlet is really a sweet little story. It is called *Revenge*. It would follow . . . Oh, dear, I see the actors won't be ready for another sixty seconds. However, thanks to our sponsor's remarkable foresight, we have a message that would fit in here nicely.'
4. In *The Case of Mr. Pelham* (S01E10), Hitchcock mocks the fact that there will be no crime in the episode, causing the viewer's disappointment: 'Good evening. Due to circumstances beyond our control, tragedy will not strike tonight. I'm dreadfully sorry, perhaps some other time.'
5. I would like to thank David Roche for helping me through the writing of this chapter.

WORKS CITED:

Alfred Hitchcock Presents, created by Alfred Hitchcock, CBS, 1955–60; NBC, 1960–2.
Balio, Tino (ed.), *Hollywood in the Age of Television* (London: Unwin Hyman, 1990).
Baughman, James L., *Same Time, Same Station: Creating American Television, 1948–1961* (Baltimore: Johns Hopkins University Press, 2007).
Danger, created by Yul Brynner, Sidney Lumet et al., CBS, 1950–5.
Death of a Salesman, written by Arthur Miller, 1949.
Delavaud, Gilles, 'La télévision selon Alfred Hitchcock. Une esthétique de l'émergence', in *CiNéMAS. Fictions télévisuelles: approches esthétiques*, eds Germain Lacasse and Yves Picard, 23, no. 2–3 (Spring 2013): 69–95.
Dragnet, created by Jack Webb, NBC, 1951–9.
Erish, Andrew A., 'Reclaiming *Alfred Hitchcock Presents*', *Quarterly Review of Film and Video* 26, no. 5 (2009): 385–92, DOI: 10.1080/10509200802165218
Funeral March of a Marionette, composed by Charles Gounod, 1872.
Genette, Gérard, *Palimpsestes. La Littérature au second degré* (Paris: Seuil, 1982).
Hawes, William, *Filmed Television Drama: 1952–1958* (New York: McFarland and Company, 2002).
Hersey, Curt, 'The Televisual Hitchcockian Object and Domestic Space in *Alfred Hitchcock Presents*', *Quarterly Review of Film and Video* 31, no. 8 (2014): 723–33, DOI: 10.1080/10509208.2012.718982
Horwitz, Jonah, 'Visual Style in the "Golden Age" Anthology Drama: The Case of CBS', in *CiNéMAS. Fictions télévisuelles: approches esthétiques*, eds Germain Lacasse and Yves Picard, 23, no. 2–3 (Spring 2013): 39–68.
I Love Lucy, created by Lucille Ball and Jess Oppenheimer, CBS, 1951–7.
Leitch, Thomas M., 'The Outer Circle: Hitchcock on Television', in *Alfred Hitchcock: Centenary Essays*, eds Richard Allen and Sam Ishii-Gonzales (London: BFI, 1999), 59–71.

Mellier, Denis, *La Littérature fantastique* (Paris: Seuil, 2000).
Mittell, Jason, *Complex TV: The Poetics of Contemporary Television Storytelling* (New York: New York University Press, 2015).
Mock, Erin Lee, 'Where No One can Hear You Scream: Hitchcock Brings Horror into the Home . . . Where It Belongs', *Journal of Interdisciplinary Humanities* (Special Issue on Alfred Hitchcock) 32, no.1 (Spring 2015).
Novak, Glenn D., 'Humor in the Films of Alfred Hitchcock', International Conference on Wit and Humor in Literature and the Visual Arts, Atlanta, Georgia, November 1986. Available online: http://files.eric.ed.gov/fulltext/ED282269.pdf (Accessed February 2024).
Olsson, Jan, *Hitchcock à la Carte* (Durham: Duke University Press, 2015).
Perry, Dennis R. and Carl H. Sederholm, 'Adapting Poe, Adapting Hitchcock: Robert Bloch in the Shadow of Hitchcock's Television Empire', *Clues* 31, no. 1 (2013): 91–101.
Potts, Neill, *The Television Work of Alfred Hitchcock* (PhD dissertation, Warwick University, 2005). Available online: https://wrap.warwick.ac.uk/2457/1/WRAP_THESIS_Potts_2005.pdf (accessed February 2024).
Stam, Robert, *Reflexivity in Film and Literature: From Don Quixote to Jean-Luc Godard* (Ann Arbor: University of Michigan Research Press, 1985).
Rauger, Jean-François, *L'Œil domestique: Alfred Hitchcock et la télévision* (Pertuis: Rouge Profond, 2014).
Rear Window, directed by Alfred Hitchcock, Paramount Pictures, 1954.
Studio One, created by Fletcher Markle, CBS, 1948–58.
Tales from the Crypt, created by William Gaines and Al Feldstein, EC Comics, 1950–5.
Television Playhouse, created by Fred Coe, NBC, 1948–57.
The Goldbergs, created by Gertrude Berg, NBC, 1949–56.
The Lodger, adapted by Alfred Hitchcock, CBS, July 1940.
The Trouble with Harry, directed by Alfred Hitchcock, Paramount Pictures, 1955.
The Twilight Zone, created by Rod Serling, CBS, 1959–64.
The Wrong Man, directed by Alfred Hitchcock, Warner Bros, 1956.
Vertigo, directed by Alfred Hitchcock, Paramount Pictures, 1958.

CHAPTER 2

The Jewel in the Crown: A Miniseries between Short and Long

Florence Cabaret

After a relative fall from favour in the 1990s and 2000s, it appears the miniseries has been regaining momentum since the 2010s, though it is frequently referred to under a 'new' label, i.e. the 'limited series', a term dug up from the 1970s before being replaced by 'miniseries' in the 1980s.[1] An examination of the various names used to describe a TV show that is too episodic to be described as a TV film and yet too short to be defined as a 'proper' TV series may help us grasp from the start the fundamental hybridity of the miniseries as a genre caught between short and long. 'Miniseries' itself came after the original British use of 'serials', which was meant to distinguish the limited format of the serial when compared to the much longer format of 'series' – or, to be still more precise: 'The term "serial" (as opposed to series) denotes a multi-episode television drama in which a single narrative is dramatized (or a single novel adapted) across a finite number of episodes' (Monk 2011, 8). Contrary to the series, which is based on a sequence of seasons comprising between 12 to 24 episodes, the miniseries could be described as a 'one-season series', a contradiction in terms since, from the start, the scenario of the miniseries is bound to circumscribe a set story with a beginning, a middle and an ending told over a restricted number of episodes, provided there are at least two episodes. That is also why the miniseries could be described as a 'multiple-episode television film', pointing to its narrative proximity with the self-contained structure of most cinematographic works and the idea that its story is not conceived to be continued beyond the number of episodes initially planned by its creators. This number may vary quite considerably though, whether you think of *It* (ABC, 1990), which is generally described as a 'two-part drama', or more recently of *When They See Us* (Netflix, 2019), which is made up of four episodes, and quite famously of *Roots* (ABC, 1977), whose eight 'parts' ranged from 90-minute-long episodes to 45-minute-long episodes, which were then condensed to six episodes in the video version – and then remade into a new four-part miniseries in 2016 (History Channel). This last example also points to another time variation that concerns the duration of an episode in a miniseries: contrary to the majority of series, whose episodes last around 40 to 45 minutes, the miniseries tend to opt for a longer running time which doubles that of a classical television series and comes closer to the duration of a cinema or television film of 90 minutes. That is why the miniseries could be described as an essentially hybrid genre, caught as it is between brevity and length, which it combines along patterns specific to each work.

With its fourteen episodes of 90 minutes each, *The Jewel in the Crown* (Granada ITV, 1984) is an apt case in point as far as in-betweenness and play with duration and shortness are concerned. This is all the more true given that its status as one of the most famous British miniseries of the 1980s has been more widely discussed in relation to aesthetic categories, which tended to overshadow the formalistic question of duration. After its ITV broadcasting in 1984 in the UK and its PBS rebroadcasting at the end of 1984 in the US, *The Jewel in the Crown* was heavily criticised for its ostensible affiliation with the 'Raj revival' trend and its associated tendency towards 'nostalgia screen fiction'; it was accused of being a visual manifestation of the Thatcher years and their conservative yearning for the heydays of the British Empire. In the wake of the publication of Said's *Orientalism, or Western Perceptions of the Orient* (1978), British Asian novelists started to gain more and more popularity and prominence in the UK; among them were Salman Rushdie and Hanif Kureishi, who vehemently contested the marginalisation of Indian voices and narratives in Eurocentric filmic or televisual adaptations such as *A Passage to India* (David Lean, 1984), *The Far Pavilions* (HBO, 1984) and *The Jewel in the Crown*, especially at a time when Indian people had become British citizens and next-door-neighbours instead of anonymous and exotic crowds used as 'set dressing' for white lead characters in their more or less glorious colonial enterprise in the Indian subcontinent.[2] More generally speaking, 'heritage films' (epitomised by the Raj revival shows) became the target of critiques reproaching them with extolling Victorian aristocratic values in museum-like pictorial settings, which regularly downplayed the tentative criticism embodied by this or that character:

> The theatricality of the Raj, and the epic sweep of the camera over an equally epic landscape and social class is utterly seductive, destroying all sense of critical distance and restoring the pomp of Englishness felt to be lacking in the present. (Higson 1993, 124)

Interestingly enough, both heritage films and miniseries came under similar criticisms: at the end of the 1970s, television productions also started to benefit from greater financial and technological means, so that the narrative and visual quality of their fictional shows were definitely improved. In a context of growing competition between public and private funding,[3] television channels competed to showcase the possibilities for spectators to enjoy quality shows on the small screen as much as on the big screen, in the UK as much as in the US, and on Granada ITV as much as on the BBC.[4] The first British independent and commercial television channel intent on challenging the monopoly of the BBC when it was created in 1955, Granada ITV adopted the same values of entertaining and educating[5] and gradually managed to gain a global reputation thanks to miniseries such as *Brideshead Revisited* (1981) and *The Jewel in the Crown*, which it had also produced. The inordinate length of these two miniseries[6] highlights the idea of international competition involving not only the format and aesthetics of these works, but also varying broadcasting techniques as well as implicit ideological issues to rival with similar contemporary shows. *The Jewel in the Crown* was extolled as the acme of British prestige drama,[7] connecting it not only with the tradition of period and costume drama, but also with the tradition of television adaptations that brought Shakespearian plays and canonical British novels of the nineteenth century to the small screen.

This miniseries was thus described as the embodiment of a variety of small and big screen traditions, conflated at that precise moment of television history: for those reasons, *The Jewel in the Crown* appears to regularly blur several format codes and boundaries as they are being combined and reshaped under their reciprocal influences – a phenomenon which could be regarded as ironical meta-commentary on the colonial world depicted in the narrative. Even though the miniseries focuses on the very last years of the British presence in India (1942–7), the sense of tight boundaries between ethnic groups and social classes being maintained against potential intruders or 'colonisers gone soft' stands at the heart of a story which uses the well-known demise of the British Empire in India to stage the tragic outcome of the encounter between an array of characters – mainly the westernised Indian Hari Kumar (Art Malik), the newly-arrived British Daphne Manners (Susan Woolridge), and the Chief Superintendent Ronald Merrick (Tim Piggot-Smith), who, as a 'mere public school boy', feels despised by more aristocratic British people and threatened by elite young Indian men whom young British women may find more attractive. Anchored in the portrayal of these characters, the way the miniseries deals with the sequencing and staging of its own time and duration could be regarded as a mise en abyme of issues pertaining to time passing, past times remembered and time accounted for by the protagonists of the story. Indeed, the various approaches to brevity and holding onto time – at a moment when characters feel the ending of the long British Empire is at hand – are intrinsically interwoven in the miniseries format of the show.

Therefore, in this chapter, I will first consider the paradoxical temptation of length in a serial that appears to be caught between the appeal of the smooth unwinding of a historical film and the narrative structure of the soap opera, thus undermining the pattern of a short fiction organised around a circumscribed progressive plot to constantly trespass these boundaries in order to follow an ensemble cast as well as multilayered stories and timelines of varying scales. Paradoxically, *The Jewel in the Crown* is also riddled with fragments, whether it be in the form of regular insertions of news clips, immobile images (paintings, photos, freeze screens) or flashbacks which, at the other end of the spectrum of duration, tend to counter expectations of the miniseries' compact narrative and instead foreground an impression of dispersal and diffraction into micro-episodes within each episode and within the whole serial. From shooting to editing choices, the miniseries then appears to offer a reflection on time, its perception and the lessons we may draw from the fictional reconsideration of a historical period at a moment in history and in the history of television that necessarily influences that perception.

THE CHOICE OF LENGTH: BETWEEN FILM, SOAP OPERA AND PROTRACTED FAREWELL

Between the miniseries and films

ITV Granada's decision to launch the adaptation of Paul Scott's *Raj Quartet* (1966–75) into a miniseries was the outcome of the recent commercial success of the 1979 film adaptation of another novel by Paul Scott, *Staying On*, which is frequently described as a form of sequel to his tetralogy about the last five years of the British Raj:

> In 1979 Granada TV made a feature film of *Staying On*. Riding the novel's Booker Prize publicity, the venture was also a trial in organizing an Indian shoot, and its success led to a green light for the massively larger venture of adapting the Quartet. (Lennard 2018, Appendix1)

Despite having different scriptwriters and directors, *The Jewel in the Crown* owed its decision to shoot outside and abroad with portable film cameras to *Staying On*'s prior success. Indeed, Jonathan Bignell reminds us how television channels opted for film techniques so as to bypass the 'incompatible technologies of broadcasting' that characterised American and British televisions at the end of the 1970s in order to reach out to non-national audiences and expand their markets: the television choice of the 16mm for *The Jewel in the Crown* gave directors Jim O'Brien and Christopher Morahan the possibility to shoot outdoors and on location, taking advantage of natural light and natural sound and creating more realistic images that had been on display in newsreels and television documentaries and in feature films in theatre halls since WWII (even though many contemporary films used the more costly and heavy 35mm camera). On rather small home screens, the quality of photography, of shooting and sound synchronising was a definite bonus that attracted viewers and their growing taste for more naturalistic outdoor lighting – golden sunsets, blazing sunlight, the shade of trees, dull mists – all of which also inflected the actors' physical appearance and performance (contrary to the artifice of studio lighting).

The Jewel in the Crown could thus boast of showing the Indian district of the town of Mayapore and contrast it with the British cantonment across the bridge, but also with a *puja* scene at a Hindu temple as early as the first episode. All along the miniseries, we cannot but be struck by some visually impressive views such as spanning shots of vast natural landscapes where Sarah Layton and Ahmed Kasim, but also her father, go horse-riding (E04, E11), or where trains rush through (E04, E05, E11, E14), somehow connecting them to North-American landscapes seen in western films. The miniseries caters to aesthetic tastes acquired over the years not only by cinema spectators, but also by television viewers of documentaries and news programmes who relished the possibility they were given to mentally travel through time and space from home. In that respect, the falconry scene (E13) stands as an emblematic scene, reconnecting with ancient hunting aristocratic traditions that are common to India and Europe but that have gradually come to be performed for entertainment and visual pleasure only, as enhanced by Sarah Layton and Guy Perron exchanging binoculars to behold the scene from afar as if they were physically close to it (Figure 2.1 and Figure 2.2).

This growing proximity with film techniques was also illustrated by the filmmaking process, whose total completion lasted about three years, which

Figure 2.1 Watching from afar (E13). Figure 2.2: Watching at close hand (E13).

definitely compares to the duration of an epic film project in those days.[8] What is more, its budget of £5,600,000 (which would be regarded as relatively modest when compared to today's standards[9]) definitely upgraded the amount of money television channels were ready and able to invest in a miniseries,[10] a phenomenon that also contributed to reshaping the vastness of perspective of several miniseries of the period.

Lastly, I would like to point out a few intertextual references that also bind the miniseries with Raj revival films of the time, prolonging its universe towards other stories shot for the big screen before and during the same period.[11] One could think of connections with adventure films made along the lines of *Kim* (Victor Saville, 1950). Hari Kumar himself, whose name was pronounced Harry Coomer during his college years at Chillinborough, explains to Daphne Manners that he had to return to the original pronunciation when he became an orphan and was forced to leave Great Britain and settle with his aunt in Mayapore. He then lightly refers to his name as sounding like that of Mata Hari, the turn-of-the-century Dutch exotic dancer who frequently performed as an Asian exotic: after her death, she was turned into the protagonist of many films (including Greta Garbo's celebrated 1931 role), which recount the French army's accusations of espionage despite the claims made by historians that she was a scapegoat, executed in 1917 to boost morale at a time when France was facing mutinies in the trenches. Here again, this discreet hint to a female character popularised by cinema links Hari Kumar with this other infamous destiny in which cultural merging, spying and treason may foreshadow his fate at the opening of *The Jewel in the Crown*. Closer at hand, the film *Gandhi* (Richard Attenborough, 1982) also provided a filmic entry to the miniseries with the hiring of actress Geraldine James as Sarah Layton. James played Madeleine Slade in this American biopic delving into the waning years of British rule in India. Also known as Mirabehn (or Meera Behn), Madeleine Slade was a famous early supporter of the Indian Independence Movement in Great Britain. She eventually settled in India in the 1920s to live and work with Gandhi, but the latter was wary of their relationship turning into a more personal and intimate bond that would have diverted their collective and political goal.[12] In *The Jewel in the Crown*, Sarah Layton becomes very close with Ahmed Kasim, who, informed of previous scandalous interracial stories (that of the nawab of Mirat with a European woman in Monte Carlo, that of Daphne Manners and Hari Kumar), prefers to maintain a certain distance with the young British woman so that their love remains platonic and he can think of a political alliance through marriage with an influential Muslim family.

Interestingly, the miniseries also foregrounds Muslim characters and their political roles at the time, compensating for a then Western tendency to mix up the variety of confessions and political interests and to favour Hindus as representing the whole of India. Somehow, such a choice also paved the way for the release of *A Passage to India* (David Lean, 1984), in which a variety of complex Indian characters feature, though not as prominently as British characters. In *A Passage to India*, Art Malik is seen performing a minor role as Mamoud Ali, a good friend of Dr Aziz. Here again, the orientalist trope of miscegenation provides a link between miniseries and film as the Muslim doctor is accused of having raped the newly-arrived Adela Quested, a charge that stands even more at the heart of *A Passage to India* than of *The Jewel in the Crown*. Simultaneously, the miniseries and David Lean's film appear to recycle orientalist biases in order to contest them: it is typically the case of the way India is staged as a place of spirituality and timelessness while all religions appear to be failing both in the miniseries and the later film. The Hindu *puja* set into relief as early as Episode 1 does not protect Daphne and Hari, Hindus and Muslims are shown as both resorting to physical violence (patriarchal violence in the case of Daphne Manners' rape in E02 and political brutality in the slaughter of train passengers in E13), without forgetting Western Christian missionaries, who proved unable to change the tragic course of events, whether it be sister Ludmila with Hari or the schoolmistress Miss Crane.[13] Such detailed and nuanced portrayals of an important number of characters in *The Jewel in the Crown* also point to another hybrid connection with a genre that has frequently been described as specifically televisual: the soap opera. If it may be set at the other end of the spectrum of adventure films mentioned here, it is however based on an ensemble set of recurring characters mainly concerned with domestic, sentimental and social issues in a multilayered pattern of narratives that led some critics to question the so-called 'quality' of the miniseries as it appeared to flirt too much with the popular staples typical of soap operas.

Between the miniseries and the soap opera

In spite of the many differences between this fictional show and the format of the soap opera, some comparisons have been made between *The Jewel in the Crown* and the upper-class, women-centric, talkative atmosphere that prevailed in 1970s US soap operas, where the intimate and the private supersede the public and the grand-scale collective approach, where interpersonal relationships, family tensions and family building occupy centre-stage in the narrative arcs and where dialogues dominate as a means to unveil character behavioural motivations. Indeed, even though the miniseries takes place at a crucial time in the history of Great Britain and India and Pakistan, the choice to focus on female Britons (some who followed their husbands because they worked as officers in India, others who are British daughters helping in hospitals or hoping to get married to a young British officer in their turn) reorients the epic tone of earlier adventurous colonial films towards a more domestic narrative.

The overarching plot is driven by the interracial affair between Daphne Manners and Hari Kumar and her rape by an unknown aggressor on the same night Daphne and Hari make love for the first time in the Bibighar gardens. The miniseries could therefore be described as a meandering unofficial investigation into the case, along which several other sets of characters will be introduced and connected to that initial story exposed in Episodes 2 and 3. Several focal viewpoints are used to narrate these entangled subplots: we start with Hari Kumar, and then with Daphne Manners, before the story is taken up by Sarah Layton (Geraldine James), whose perception prevails from E03 to E09, only to be replaced by what is mostly Guy Perron (Charles Dance)'s viewpoint in the last five episodes. Female subjectivity therefore is predominant, even though it is Hari Kumar and Guy Perron's perspectives which introduce and later recapitulate and further investigate the case. In the 1970s, feminist critics tackled the study of soap opera as a 'female genre' from the perspective of emancipation, empowerment or complicity with patriarchy.[14] Richard Dyer, who wrote about *The Jewel in the Crown* in a whole chapter of his famous book *White*, refers to critics 'who disparaged *Jewel* [and who] did so by calling it merely a superior soap' (Dyer 1997, 200). He also provides an analysis of the inefficiency and impotency of the numerous female characters in the miniseries, pointing to the ambivalence of a show in which female agency is nipped in the bud by guilt, by social pressure and by family duty, reinforcing patriarchal and colonial order.

Even though I have mentioned memorable outdoor sequences in the miniseries, the majority of the miniseries' scenes take place indoors, like in a soap opera, in rooms that are crammed with decorative objects, delineated by windows and doors that literally frame the characters, while some of them are more explicitly imprisoned, put in hospital rooms, prison cells or psychiatric wards, insisting on their physical and mental powerlessness.

Thus, the show foregrounds the domestic[15] rather than the epic and appears to reproduce a stereotypical association of femininity with spatial limitation, with care and attention, but also with gossip and surveillance. Indeed, the daily gestures of young and older British women are constantly supervised and discussed by other women, whether it be Daphne Manners' transgressive closeness with Hari Kumar or the number of times Susan Layton (Wendy Morgan) breastfeeds her child, Mrs Layton (Judy Parfitt)'s drinking habit, Barbie Bachelor (Peggy Ashcroft)'s homosexuality, or her embarrassing poverty that prevents Mrs Layton from completely getting rid of this distant relative. Conversations focus on family, be it potential marriages or family duties that drive female characters to travel. The miniseries appears willing to emphasise the banal and mundane behind the seemingly grand order of events, showing that they are two sides of the same coin and debunking the heroic warlike pretence of the show. No male protagonist is glorified as a fighter (the attack of the jeep in E06 is actually shot in a way that makes it fake and gory), but we do see them on toilets, suffering from diarrhoea (E10) or getting washed and dressed (E11), or even getting maudlin in remembrance of the past (E10). Bodies in general are not exalted, whether they be the naked back of Hari Kumar as he is being tortured by Ronald Merrick, or the middle-aged Mrs Layton shown in crude and noisy extramarital sexual intercourse. Private matters rarely remain private: Mrs Layton notices that it has been two months since Sarah last used the sanitary napkins she regularly puts in her drawer, and women openly discuss abortions (still officially illegal but obviously tolerated when carried out away from home); psychiatrist Dr Samuels is heard giving healing sexual advice at a party (E09); and Sarah and the philanderer Jimmy Clark are heard having a long, contrived and explicit conversation about her current virginity and future sexual relationship (E07).

By giving the viewer access to the underbelly of public affairs, the miniseries appears to question the 'prestige' with which it is frequently associated, thus participating in the changing perception of television and filmic genres and their growing crosspollination, to the point that some critics have sustained the idea that the soap opera has become a 'television paradigm' (Wittebols 2004). In a way it joined a new, more inclusive type of program that started to thrive in the 1990s, which attempted to attract both men and women by combining action-driven plots with family plots, i.e. mixing drama with melodrama, self-contained plots and over-arching stories. A sense of intimacy (another trait of the soap) is thus created with the viewer thanks to these issues about women's amorous and sexual lives; however, a certain number of their individual questions resonate on a more collective level, interlacing the domestic and the epic. Indeed, Susan Layton's postpartum depression hints at a more collective dead end for the Britons' role in India – especially when Susan nearly immolates her son at the end of Episode 8 because it is the only means to evade the collective trap in which they find themselves in India. Barbie's gradual mental prostration is also symbolically represented as a blinding blast taking place at the moment when Hiroshima was destroyed by the American atom bomb (E11).

The impression of combined private and public plots is also reinforced when watching the 2004 twentieth anniversary DVD of *The Jewel in the Crown* today. Rapid succession viewing[16] of what was originally intended to be a weekly show creates a proximity reminiscent of watching a soap. In 1994, Laura Stempel Mumford described 'the practice of "daily stripping" [of] older TV shows – that is, airing one episode of a series every week day, five days a week' as a means to 'convert programs that had originally been broadcast once per week into soap operas' (Ford, De Kosnik & Harrington 2012, 10). 'Time-compressed viewing encourages the audience to remember and forge their own narrative linkages to an extent that once-weekly viewing cannot match'

(Ford, De Kosnik & Harrington 2012, 11). In this case, the impression that the miniseries plays with soap opera narrative structure may be magnified by this mode of viewing that changes our relationship to the variety of tones and settings, to the proportion and hierarchy between history and story, and to episode division. Watching *The Jewel in the Crown* all at once reinforces the looming sense of a historical ending conveyed by the miniseries and its finite form, but also highlights the impression that the more personal stories never actually conclude – again paralleling the soap opera 'that never ends' (Ford, De Kosnik & Harrington 2012, 3).

Protracted farewell

The main timeline of *The Jewel in the Crown* is chronological, and thanks to explicit references to precise dates (both in dialogue and the editing of images), we know that the story starts in 1942, when the Quit India campaign launched by Gandhi leads to the imprisonment of its leaders, and that it ends on 15 August 1947, when India and Pakistan are declared independent. But the narrative structure depicts a drawn-out departure mainly characterised by small meandering stories, with the initial Manners case being interpreted by different characters at different moments within those five years / fourteen episodes. The chronology of history is thus regularly undermined by ellipses and analepses. But it is also disoriented by references to two historical events that marked British colonisation in India as we reach the actual moment of India's and Pakistan's independence: the 1919 Amritsar massacre, alluded to in Episode 7 (through its Indian name), and the 1857 First War of Independence, discussed in Episode 12 (through a colonial name, as 'the Mutiny'). By having the narrative move forward in time while simultaneously looking further back, moving from personal stories to history, time limits appear to be regularly contested and over-blown so that a sense of inflated time and protracted farewell gradually overwhelms the show as if this ending of the serial – and of the British Raj – was regularly postponed, even though the spectator knows it is bound to take place.

Richard Dyer commented on this feeling of paralysis and sluggishness elicited by the editing of the series: 'The overall organization is chronological but there is little sense of a drive forward through the narrative; on the contrary, all feeling of momentum is stymied with the series' concern with looking backward' (Dyer 1997, 203). Considerations of structure appeared central to sustain his analysis: 'The lethargic unfolding is in turn reinforced by the handling of breaks in the serial.' Identifying a total of twenty-nine breaking points, he points out eleven cliffhangers – though just one actually functions as such, when at the end of the first episode Daphne Manners is suddenly found to be missing. It is quite true that there is no strict correspondence between the ending of an episode and what we could expect as a significant narrative ending or as a cliffhanger; as such, Richard Dyer describes those moments as 'temps morts' resulting in 'desultory' endings, with 'no one on the screen', 'just a sense of emptiness' (Dyer 1997, 203). Such is the case of Episode 4, which concludes on a quarrel between Sarah Layton and her aunt as they disagree on Lady Manners' adoption of Daphne's child: the conversation comes to an abrupt stop (Lady Manners: 'I worry for you.' Daphne Manners: 'Yes and I worry for myself.') before the editing cuts back to the desert landscape where Sarah and Ahmed Kasim were seen horse-riding earlier in the episode. As the series recalls the circumstances that first seemed to announce a budding romance between the two, we are also reminded of Sarah's comment on Ahmed's awkwardness and coldness on that day, which thwarted any romantic storyline between the two characters. The reminiscence of the young Indian man constantly keeping himself and his horse in check to avoid starting too intimate a relationship with a white woman is left for the viewer to digest as we again behold this barren landscape, which suggests the relationship will bear no fruit and leaves us directionless at this stage of the story. Several episodes also end on dissolves revealing burning flames, which out of context could be interpreted as a tragic cliffhanger – though most of the time, they correspond to imagined flashbacks. At the end of the third episode, Barbie gazes upon the eponymous painting which she received from her dead friend Miss Crane: the contemplation triggers the verbal recollection of Miss Crane's self-immolation, which Barbie can only reconstruct in her mind since she was not there – so that the episode concludes on a fire engulfing a woodshed. If it creates ominous expectations for the viewer who knows about this type of symbolic ending, it does not seem to particularly pave the way for the next episode, which may start somewhere very different and disconnected (which is the case here since we then learn that Sarah Layton's wedding may not take place as planned).

As another significant example illustrating the narrative protraction and lengthening of the miniseries, the very last episode is particularly telling since it ultimately delays its conclusion as much as possible from the very first moments of its opening shots. Indeed, the fourteenth episode opens on an unusual and unique prologue before the opening credits start rolling, as if the episode took its time to start, or as if it were already over. The impression that we are watching a micro episode is strengthened by the relative narrative autonomy of this pre-credits sequence: Sarah is shown as playing matchmaker between Ahmed Kasim and a cousin (so that we understand their own romance is definitely out of perspective) before we move to a discussion between Count Bronowski and Guy Perron about the count's part in the matchmaking, while he denies he has any role in the burning of shops by both Muslims and Hindus in Mirat. As dark smoke rises from several spots in the city, the announcement

Figure 2.3 The culmination of the fire motif (excipit of E14).

of the coming tragedy is made all too clear when the opening credits start to roll over a freeze frame of Shiva dancing before the flames, which will be taken up in the final burning of the 'Jewel in the Crown' painting before the rolling of the closing credits (Figure 2.3).

Shiva, one of the three main divinities of Hinduism, is a complex deity frequently described as the Destroyer (along with the Creator and Preserver). But his dance also symbolises the rhythm of the world, i.e. the cycle of life and death and reincarnation, and his lingam the mastery of the fire of destruction by his female consort Parvati. It is quite symbolic of course that such a figure of renewal should open the last episode of the miniseries, providing a counterpoint to the announcement of a Muslim union between two powerful families and leaving most viewers to marvel at this black enigmatic statue dancing with fire and to feel its portentous meaning.

In between incipits and excipits, the episodes themselves mainly evolve in incremental progressions, which may take several forms. It is typically what happens when the painting entitled 'The Jewel in the Crown' appears on the screen. As the fantasised representation of Queen Victoria receiving a diamond during a ceremony in India, the painting acquires added meaning depending on its owner: if it was a means to teach English for Miss Crane, it becomes a souvenir of her dead friend for Barbie and an embodiment of outdated values of loyalty and protection for Ronald Merrick (in E07 and E08). It also drives the viewer to compare those various interpretations, to go back to the painting's previous apparitions in the miniseries and to form their own appraisal of the painting, which we may construe as a metaphor for the way fictions were transmitted and reshaped during colonisation, as they may serve either as a positive model or as a despised antiquated burden to be replaced by others, or maybe as a more mitigated in-between commentary, like *The Jewel in the Crown* itself.

The narrative use of the Manners case is another means through which the miniseries *pro*gresses by *re*gressing: frequently described as the original trigger of the miniseries, the case is discussed on several occasions and by different characters after the second episode. There is of course the version of events offered by Daphne herself, but there are also the implied accusations of Ronald Merrick, leading the viewer to imagine another potential version of that night at the Bibighar gardens. Later in the middle of Episode 5, we hardly hear Hari's version of that night, as he focuses mostly on the way he was tortured by Merrick to have him confess to a crime he had not committed. Ahmed Kasim's refusal to start a love affair with Sarah Layton may also be interpreted as a commentary on this original interracial romance. Eventually, enigmatic denunciations of the official rape charge crop up in the form of signs, all addressed to Merrick (the bike on his doorstep, the stone thrown at his car, the final chalk sign on the day of his murder). The fact that most of these scenes of delay of the chronology of the story take the form of conversations or monologues about the Manners case also reinforces the impression that the unfolding of the miniseries is held back by those immobile moments during which flashbacks seem to block the linear unfolding of time, as if trying to postpone a historical ending all viewers know is inevitable. The valedictory mood of the show sustains this impression of drawn-out parting which is part and parcel of the hybrid dimension of a miniseries playing with the codes of shorter forms (such as films) or longer forms (such as soap operas). Oddly enough, it is also by resorting to the breaking down of its episodes and subplots that the miniseries creates such an impression of a prolonged ending.

THE FRAGMENT AS A MOTIF UNDERMINING THE UNIT/UNITY OF THE EPISODES?

Newsreel footage breaking up fictional unity

From the first moments of the opening credits, which consist only of documentary film images of the heyday of the British Empire shown at the opening of each of the fourteen episodes, the status of the miniseries is blurred. Relying on 'informative' archive images, the sequence keeps recalling the historical background of the story (in the tradition of 'period dramas'), but it also introduces a visual time rupture between those 'real' shots and those that are subsequently shown in each episode as we move from grainy black-and-white photography to a quality of coloured image that could only be achieved after the British had left India. What is more, as George W. Brandt underlines,

> [n]ot only do these black-and-white news clips provide a factual background to the story – they also reflect period attitudes in their camerawork, editing style and commentaries. Seen four decades later they carry an ironic subtext. Wartime certainties have softened in the light of history; attitudes natural at the time now seem stilted or patronizing. (Brandt 1993, 209)

Indeed, in spite of their proclaimed informative dimension, we understand that these images hide as much as they reveal – but they definitely foreground the domination of colonisation through its visual display of power, be it an impressive official ceremony of troop parade or colonial forces mounted atop elephants on a tiger hunt, followed by a long line of Indians carrying everything required for such an expedition.

In the course of the episodes, news clips are also regularly inserted as if to provide a continuous timeline and a historical backdrop to the more private plots. Such is the case with Episode 1 in particular, opening with a news clip glorifying the 'Empire of the blazing sun' in the early 1940s, before the spectator later discovers another news clip about the threat of a Japanese blitz over Burma (1942), and before tension escalates in the last third of the episode with three newsreels introducing the Quit India campaign (8 August 1942) as a form of betrayal and as the source of troubles in India (with the massive civil disobedience demonstrations and riots that took place in the following weeks of 1942). From the outset, the contrast between these irregular but frequent interruptions (up to five in E01 but only two in E09) and the fictional bulk of the episodes questions this material's status as propaganda since the viewer is constantly buffeted between one 'reality' (documented historical events) and 'another' (fictional narratives, but also censored narratives). For instance, the archive images of Episodes 4 and 5 showing Indian regiments and dead Indian soldiers being honoured for their involvement alongside British troops in WWII, or references to 'gallantry' as shared value (E09) cast a strange light on the narrative of Hari Kumar's ignominious treatment at the hands of Ronald Merrick before and after his arrest. We are therefore regularly led to maintain a critical distance with these historical images, though they are supposedly ingrained with a greater degree of truthfulness than the explicitly fictional narrative of the miniseries.

The regular contrapuntal irony of these 'real images' in the fiction was not lost on 1984 viewers, who could hear the hollowness of the martial music used as soundtrack and the jovial voice-over commentary of the journalist as they discovered a messier version of events in the 'fiction.' The fragmentation of the smooth unwinding of the narrative attracts our attention to the fabrication of those brief news clips and very quickly calls into question the reliability of these images. One may also remember that these newsreels were originally shown in theatre halls before spectators watched a feature film – just like television viewers could watch the evening news on their small screen before watching the miniseries at 9 p.m. The ghostly presence of cinema halls and the implicit suggestion that the heyday of cinema is being replaced by television also participate in a recontextualisation of the miniseries, as it harkens back to other news sources before 1947 and showcases the greater possibility for television viewers to interrogate the nature and contents of images in the 1980s by placing them side by side in several episodes. The retrospective position of 1980s viewers also endowed them with *a posteriori* knowledge that fuelled the dramatic irony pervading the miniseries: introducing archive images in the episodes is not only a means to inform young generations about the last days of the British Raj, it is also a means to appear to control a countdown that all viewers were aware of (though perhaps not in detail). As newsreels become scarcer after Episode 6 (only two interruptions on average), it is as if the miniseries tries to slacken the pace of historical and fictional time once the viewer is hooked on the story, as it takes on the form of subjective approaches to historical and personal events. The return of Colonel Layton from his German POW camp after 1945 (E11) and his supposed lack of engagement with the situation in India illustrate the idea of an officer coming back to his family life and worrying about a former Indian soldier rather than fighting to keep the British Raj.

Thus the regular interruptions of news clips in the first five episodes play with the illusion of History ruling over individual stories, but the fragmentary rhythm they instil in each episode foreshadows the gradual falling apart of the Empire, which is going to be increasingly relegated to the background of history by the rare newsreels of the last episode (with references to more victorious moments in 1945 such as D-Day in Normandy, the liberation of prisoners' camps in Germany, or the return home of Indian soldiers). The fact that these newsreels concentrate exclusively on masculine protagonists and war information also reinforces the jarring impression of two juxtaposed times within the miniseries, even though as wives, daughters and widows of officers, female characters maintain a link between those two timelines. Their forced cohabitation in the episodes exemplifies other tensions that exist in the serial: between epic and domestic, between abroad and home, between what remains foreign and the familiar that threatens to become alienated. As such, a history that originally seems to be framed by famous historical landmarks gives way to a more subterranean type of story that is not so much adventure-driven as atmosphere-driven: linear action-oriented narratives are not what the miniseries is trying to stage, as it instead favours poetic and atmospheric representations of departing rather than showing why and how such a parting takes place. Here again, fragmenting scenes with shots focusing on photos, pictures and paintings undermines linear chronology and reinforces the slow building of an ambiance.

Photos, paintings and engraving as thwarted narratives

As already mentioned, the structure of the episodes does not correspond to the self-contained narrative unit typical of a miniseries. The internal division into identifiable plot-driven episodes is also challenged by the unpredictable intrusion of historical reminders that are gradually exposed as colonial propaganda and pushed back in the wings of an ambivalent account of characters coping with the realisation of the inevitable ending of the British Empire. As they behold old photo albums, paintings or engravings, those micro flashbacks surreptitiously thwart the progression of the narrative arcs and open time loops that come full circle much later and give a sense of stagnancy to the story, as if to both negate and remind us of the passing of time. The presence of the static image within the moving images of the series heightens the pause in both narrative and historical time. We may think of the scene when Mrs Sengupta shows Daphne Manners photos of the places where her nephew Hari Kumar lived in England as a child (E01): they both open and close the possibility of a life as a British Asian for Hari Kumar. This stifled alternative tale can also be traced at the end of the miniseries when, gazing at a recently planted tree in the yard of the Ranpur Government College, the viewer/Hari is brought back to a similar tree when Hari was a student at Chillinborough, which is superimposed as a still shot, photo-like, on the sunny Indian landscape before it fades to a rainy British scenery (E13, see Figure 2.4 and Figure 2.5).

Daphne herself is photographed in a private studio on a day when Hari accompanies the young woman and asks her if he can keep a portrait she was about to throw away (E01). This photo is seen again at the closing of the

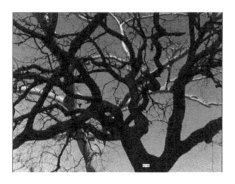 

Figure 2.4–5 Entangled but stifled narrative 'branching out' (E13).

miniseries as Guy Perron imagines Hari working at his desk, with that picture of Daphne by his side (E14). Again, the serial appears to hint at an alternative story that could have taken place, and brings us back to the beginning, in a rondo structure that may fit the closure expected in a miniseries, foregrounding the idea of 'staying on' (even as a ghostly presence) rather than leaving, as embodied by the previous scene when we see Guy taking the plane to go back to Great Britain. Mug shots of Hari also regularly crop up: when Lady Manners secretly attends his interrogation by Captain Rowan, who is investigating Ronald Merrick's suspicious behaviour as Chief Superintendent (E05), or when Guy reads Hari's file (E13), which conjures up the voice of the young Indian man when he was speaking to Captain Rowan about the way Merrick tortured him. These stark black-and-white pictures reactivate stories that could have happened by freezing them at the same time so that they appear to be waiting for some further development, as if in limbo, hoping for another time and another series to take up their characters and imagine a more hopeful story for the two of them.

Several references to painting also open up windows to other narratives that may have taken on a different course and momentarily distract us from the main narratives. I have already mentioned the varying interpretations of the eponymous painting as it is handed down to a new character following the death of its previous owner. Its first educational use by Miss Crane also hints at the role of the miniseries itself and how it works at (re)shaping viewers' representation of these days ('Pictures are so important when instructing the young, don't you agree?' E03), while also encouraging them to take these visual representations with a grain of salt ('Quite absurd, of course, because [Queen Victoria] never came to India. But it's allegorical. Because the jewel isn't the one the prince is offering to his sovereign. The jewel is India – Disraeli's empire' E03). But we may also think of Ronald Merrick showing some of his etchings to Daphne (E01). Contrary to viewer expectations, they are not orientalist erotic etchings that he would use to lure her in, but Henry Moore drawings of Londoners sleeping in the Underground during the Blitz (E01). If this insertion of everyday war scenes involving British civilians may appear to redirect our attention to the constant fright of London dwellers in those days, it also provides a critical echo to Sister Ludmila's opening remark about the British 'who didn't care if people died in the streets' of Mayapore (E01) and their double standard depending on the victims' skin colour. The miniseries therefore constantly undermines its limits by interrupting its linear flow with potential spin-offs. But we understand that they remain encased and trapped within the constraints of history, just like characters in this story are bound by so many visual and mental frames. The result is a proliferation of would-be stories that tentatively appear and disappear, so that the miniseries seems to follow an underlying jigsaw pattern.

Abrupt cuts and parallel editing also point to irreconcilable stories that will never come to fruition. At the end of the second episode, the alternation between scenes where Daphne tells her version of the rape to District Commissioner Robin White and his wife and shots of a silent and worried Hari behind bars, ignorant of Daphne's whereabouts and well-being, of the charges against him and of his upcoming trial, prefigures the untimely termination of their romance. Numerous flashbacks point to fateful choices, or to dead ends, especially when these flashbacks return to investigations that cannot reach their conclusion. When Ronald Merrick is told that a broken lady's bike with a Hindi inscription was found next to his front door, he recalls the night when Daphne's bike was thrown into the river after he had planted it at Hari's house to have him accused of the rape at the beginning of the investigation (E03). As the sunken bike figuratively resurfaces on several occasions in the miniseries, it evokes this (and other) attempts to keep a lid on buried stories that could provide another picture to characters and viewers.

Out of these regular stops and interruptions, a sense of paralysis grows on the spectator, who is sometimes more stricken by sudden flashbacks than by the chronological course of events. We may refer to the flashback in Episode 5, when Ronald Merrick recalls a scene that had been omitted at the opening of that same episode: as newly-wed Susan Layton and Teddie leave the party at the station, Mrs Sengupta throws herself at Merrick's feet, obviously imploring him in Hindi while Merrick wilfully ignores her plea. We deduce that she is begging him to release her nephew Hari, but since many viewers do not understand what she says (and the series chooses not to offer subtitling), it reinforces the improbability of the situation and its disruptive dimension in the episode – these traumatic events take place as Merrick and Sarah are quietly beholding the lake near Ahmed Kasim's house, and as the wedding is coming to a close with friends and family parting at the station. Episode 13 starts with the burial of Ronald Merrick, while Episode 12 ended with a romantic scene between Sarah Layton and Guy Perron as Hari Kumar's file burns. Since we know nothing about the circumstances of Merrick's death and how we can connect the ending of Episode 12 and the beginning of Episode 13, here again we are aware of a missing piece in the jigsaw puzzle. It is only thanks to later conversations between different characters that we begin to understand that Merrick did not, in fact, die in a riding accident, but that he was murdered. His death is not the only one to take place in an ellipsis which is later patched up with flashbacks or conversations about the circumstances of the death: this is also the case for Daphne's death, but also Miss Crane's and Ahmed Kasim's. Paradoxically, these postponed connections for various missing links fragment episodes by imperfectly trying to fill in the original blank since they in turn disrupt the flow of a narrative which is regularly re-routed. More generally speaking, the motif of the double also disperses the main course of the story and somehow dilutes and expands the passage of time within the story as the viewer keeps making connections between episodes that are both constantly drilled and sewed up at rarely expected moments.

The fragmenting and blending motif of the double

Characters may be the most obvious forms of doubles in the miniseries and they create different networks of characters. Hari Kumar and Ahmed Kasim are linked by their more or less successful attempts at resisting the danger of love affairs with white women (respectively Daphne Manners and Sarah Layton, who therefore stand as doubles as well). The two male characters could be described as westernised Indians, being reproached by some other Indians for speaking English only ('the language of your father's jailers', E04) and by some British for being brown. As such, they belong to yet another category, of characters who do not fit, which includes both Indians and Britons, both men and women: because of his low social origins, Ronald Merrick feels he does not belong to the aristocratic group of 'expatriates' in India; because of her lack of money, her absence of a social role and her single status, Barbie is constantly left on the margins of the small community of British colonizers; Teddie and Merrick successively marry Susan Layton, who loves neither of them but conforms to the role of the young lady marrying a British officer. Other doubles people the series: Captain Rowan and Guy Perron both investigate the Manners case and are potential love interests for Sarah; Mohamed Ali Kasim and Colonel Layton both come back home after a stay in prison (because of the Quit India campaign and because of the war against Germany), to find their family radically changed by political and personal choices, so that they may also be regarded as characters having difficulties to reintegrate a group they used to fit in. These underlying ties between characters, regardless of their more obvious attachment to other circles, riddle the miniseries with hidden links that punctuate and counteract the linear progression of time in the episodes.

Places may also be used to superimpose events over one another, and become strongly associated with characters, thanks to a chain of associations provided by the editing, to other places and other moments, as we have already seen with Hari Kumar. One striking example is provided by the name 'Gillian Waller' uttered by Mabel in her sleep (E06), which Barbie misunderstands as being the name of an Englishman whereas Mabel explains in the next episode that it actually refers to 'Jallianwallah Bagh' (E07), i.e. the place where the Amritsar massacre took place in 1919, and recalls that the shooting was ordered against a peaceful demonstration by General Dyer. Her reminiscence is immediately followed by an archive news clip about Japanese soldiers trapped and killed during the battle of Imphal (1944), a landmark in the South-East Asian front of WWII, when the Japanese were definitively pushed back to Burma by the

British and the Indian Army. The images of dead bodies strewn on the ground, and of burning villages accompanied by buoyant military music and a voice-over lauding the British victory, remind us of the violence perpetrated in some Asian countries by those who were fighting Nazi Germany in Europe. Here again, the personal and the historical are gradually more closely knit than the viewer's first impressions of what initially seem to be separate scenes, disparate clips and subplots.

As to Ronald Merrick's obsession with double-dealing and betrayals, it may actually be read as a running thread through the whole of the miniseries: historical events like the Quit India campaign, which Merrick sees as a betrayal at a time when the UK needed to sustain the war effort in Europe, or the Indian general Bose and his INA siding with Japan, eventually bleed in to more individual betrayals, for example by Sayed Kasim and by a former faithful Indian soldier rallying the INA. It may account for Merrick's constant over-achieving persona and his own dissembling attitude when Nigel Rowan and Guy Perron discuss his tendency to play varying roles – that of 'friend of the family' with the Laytons, using his maimed arm as 'an invention', and getting dressed up in Pathan clothes (E11). We may even wonder whether Ronald Merrick's villain is not the most fleshed-out character in the serial, benefiting from a variety of viewpoints and revelations, culminating in the expected revelation of his closeted homosexuality and the vicious extremities it led him to. His being nicknamed Count Dracula by those who are forced to work with him (E13) hints at his nefarious double-sided personality, just like the half-photo of his face that Susan finds in her wedding album (E06) hints at another part of himself that remains a secret in most of the miniseries. Ronald Merrick thus clearly embodies the well-used trope of the queer villain, a stereotype that has frequently been criticised for the way queer characters were regularly boxed-in on the dark side of mankind when they happened to appear in films and TV shows up to the end of the twentieth century.

Through this proliferation of the double motif, *The Jewel in the Crown* reminds us that other stories are there lying in the wings – new beginnings hoping to be born but ending with only tragic impossibilities. As George W. Brandt underlines, '[t]he plot constantly reorganizes itself around new growing points of interest' (Brandt 1993, 209) so that our perception of time becomes pregnant with a multitude of branching out potentialities within each episode, inflating this very same perception of time within the whole miniseries. In the end, the miniseries seems to be inhabited more by those crushed opportunities than by the immobile and powerless lives it stages. When Barbie notices that Sarah seems deeply preoccupied by the story of Hari and Daphne, Sarah's answers provide a meta-commentary that illustrates the sense that the past is more present in the miniseries than the characters' actual lives: 'someone should be haunted by it . . . I suppose we should' (E05).

Uncertainties and regrets seem to constantly pull characters backwards, so that the miniseries is more repetitive than progressive, more atmospheric than narrative and offers a reflection on the way time can be staged by fiction and experienced by the viewer.

A MINISERIES CUT SHORT: A REFLECTION ON THE TELEVISUAL STAGING OF TIME

Subjective time challenging historical time

I have so far discussed the dragging rhythm of the serial, which paradoxically plunges us into a subjective time rather than a time delineated by hours and dates. The references to mental treatments (through hospital wards and psychoanalytic approaches – for Barbie, for Susan Layton, for young soldiers whose files are kept under lock in Dr Samuel's office) draw explicit links between present symptoms and past causes which are lingering and painful to process. Even though Susan cannot be fully rescued by psychoanalysis (no more than by family or social support), her example is a good illustration that, more than history, it is the personal experience of a historical context that is dramatised by the serial. Even though Episodes 1 and 2 may place the story under the aegis of a police investigation, we are quickly led to understand that personal accounts of events predominate, with Merrick's jealousy and bias taking over his rational judgement, for instance. The fact that the focal viewpoint changes on several occasions (from Daphne Manners, to Sarah Layton, to Guy Perron) also sets into relief the situated and limited position of each main observer, especially as we end with that of the historian Guy Perron, who accepts the subjectivity of his position and the partiality of his viewpoint, however open and encompassing it may try to be.

The recourse to private letters, diaries and files frequently read aloud through a voice-over device also momentarily suspends the unwinding of images and focuses our attention on our own visual memories of past moments, or our picturing of moments imagined by the characters themselves – which is to be contrasted with the oral commentaries of the news clips, which appear to impose a one-way viewing of the footage images on the spectators. Thus when Daphne Manners is heard speaking in her mind to Hari (who is in prison) about their newborn daughter, she has decided to view Parvati as their daughter, and not as a baby born out of a gang rape; in so doing, she decides to erase part of what happened to her in this deliberate choice of origins for the little girl. The next shot of a grave with Daphne's name brutally cuts short this new beginning, before another cut transports us to a house where Lady Manners is reading the diary of her dead niece. As we hear this voice of a now dead character, another auditory transition is provided with a shot introducing new characters, Sarah and Mildred Layton, who overhear the newborn girl crying as they stay in a nearby bungalow. The intricate combination of visual cuts and auditory transitions, using the momentary ending of a first plot to 'birth' a second plot centred on Sarah (who will later visit Lady Manners on her own), is a subtle means of illustrating the connection between the departed Daphne and Sarah, though they were not in the least acquainted.

From the first caption in Episode 1, the idea that history is haunted by repressed collective and individual stories that should be unearthed (for example by the miniseries), has been foregrounded by the name of the fictitious town of Mayapore, borrowing from the Sanskrit term 'maya' referring to 'illusion' – and implicitly warning us about hasty and easy interpretations. Much later, in Episode 11, Guy Perron notes that the 'camp servant' that accompanies Ronald Merrick perfectly suits 'the hallucinatory atmosphere' that he has been experiencing since his arrival in India (referring to the incredible British attitudes he has been witnessing). The emphasis laid on the unreliability of what is seen is also ironically highlighted by Daphne Manners constantly fumbling for her glasses as early as E01. The same gesture is taken up in E11 when the Hiroshima bombing is first introduced, as if it were a metaphorical way of referring to Barbie's mental collapse in her hospital room. The cut to a black-and-white shooting of an atom bomb mushroom is immediately followed by another cut, which brings us back outside of Barbie's room with an overexposed shot of vultures lining up on a Tower of Silence, as if they were preying on the reclining old woman. It is only in the next scene, when Captain Coley welcomes Sarah and her father at the Ranpur station, that we learn about the Japanese catastrophe and realise the previous image was also to be taken at face value, and not only as a metaphor of Barbie's mental breakdown – which the small calendar on her bedside table already indicated.

In a sustained metapoetic gesture, the miniseries keeps exploring the unreliability of what is seen and known, cutting short viewers' expectations of a reassuring conclusive show. The original haunting trauma of the miniseries actually takes place offscreen, before the first episode, when Hari Kumar realises that his best friend from Chillingborough did not recognise him when he walked past him in a street in Mayapore – because, even in the eyes of this close friend, Hari had become an Indian among others and was no longer the individual he used to be in Great Britain. The revelation incites his drinking binge before the serial begins. The explanation for this alcoholic excess will be given much later, shedding light on this visual erasure Hari Kumar experienced, and that led to his actual disappearance from the miniseries, though ironically his image remains a haunting presence through photos, memories and renewed investigations. Maybe at the very end of the miniseries, it is his own story as an expatriate that we see Hari Kumar writing. Eventually, the 'Alma Mater' poem Hari reads in voiceover at the end of the penultimate episode conflates in its own terms the tension between the subjective time embodied by lyrical poetry and the historical time *The Jewel in the Crown*'s epic title first appeared to announce. These lines of poetry also dramatise the assumption that, even though time is cyclical and prone to change and repetition, circumstances may bring us to distrust our perception of its movement and promises: the fictional poem laments 'winters when the branches of the trees were bare. So bare that, recalling them now, it seems inconceivable to me that I looked at them and did not think of the summer just gone and the spring to come as illusions, as dreams never fulfilled, never to be fulfilled.' What is arresting in these lines is Hari's *a posteriori* conviction that there is no such thing as hopeful summers and springs, and that he is doomed to remain stuck in this wasteland and limbo, unable to find his way back to the round of seasons, just like the miniseries regularly loses track of its forward narrative impetus because it is hindered by recurrent interruptions.

From the 1940s to the 1980s: fictional time bridging past and present

Having become an outcast in both countries, Hari Kumar remains a crucial but liminal character, who cannot have a central place in the narrative proper, even though his existence stands at the heart of many British characters' guilty consciences. At one stage, Hari is described as a 'loose end', which the various investigations try to tie up – but the failure to wholly rehabilitate him keeps nagging at the narrative. The opening of Pandora's box mentioned by the title of E13 is not so much the result of an individual lapse and Daphne's transgressive attitude is not the one single cause of the tragedy. This easy scapegoating is useful to cover up a more collective and older cause that has to do with greed, colonisation and systemic racism. Broadcast at a moment in Thatcher's Great Britain when some right-wing and conservative political leaders tried to instil the idea that repatriation politics were needed to contain what they perceived as a threatening presence of immigrants from the former colonies,[17] the narrative's depiction of Hari's forced return to India, though not the result of a governmental decision, shows how destructive it can prove for the person rejected by a nation long described as 'the mother country'.[18] The ending of the miniseries may be located in 1947, but when it was broadcast in 1984, it contributed to open up the debate about the contemporary consequences of colonisation 'at home' by having British viewers reflect on Hari Kumar being compelled to remain in India while, ironically, Guy Perron regretfully goes back to Great Britain.

Here again, the miniseries is framed by ambivalence, caught as it is by a somewhat orientalist perception of India as immobile and timeless (Hari contemplating Daphne's photo) and the explicit choice to reinsert viewers in a chronological evolving time (Guy moving on and taking the plane), even though partly defeated by a nostalgia for a failed past (Guy gazing at the receding Indian landscape through the plane's porthole). The miniseries itself is fraught by such an ambivalent approach of time, as it simultaneously stages India's inscription in a dated time and nips in the bud stories waiting in the wings of history (including artistic history) to come out. Daphne's 'bastard' child could thus be read as both a repulsive colonial trope and a postcolonial statement of the reality of underground transformations and hybridisations taking place both in India and in Great Britain.[19] Parvati may indeed be Hari's child, but she may also be the daughter of several anonymous Indian rapists, or even of black-faced Englishmen, as hinted at by Daphne herself (E02). This is how we could finally interpret the constant stifling and repression of potential stories in a miniseries that threatens to burst at the seams of many a scene and many an episode because of a silencing of colonised narratives that yet started to emerge in contemporary fictions in English.

Even though *The Jewel in the Crown* has frequently been associated with heritage films extolling the greatness of the British Empire in a decade when British Asians longed for other role models on British TV screens, the reception of the miniseries has changed as it now appears more as an Empire dis-(re)membering miniseries. The tension it establishes on various scales between duration and brevity, between fragmentation and interweaving (illustrated by the transmission of the butterfly lace shawl), between the epic and the domestic, between what is lost and what is preserved appears to use the relatively short form of the miniseries to enshrine a dense material regularly overflowing the boundaries of the genre. Adapting Paul Scott's 1966 long novel, and choosing a TV format that is both more constrained and freer to accommodate fleshed out plots and characters than a film, *The Jewel in the Crown* appears to embody what Paul Gilroy describes as the 'discomforting ambiguities of the empire's painful and shameful but apparently nonetheless exhilarating history' (Gilroy 2005, 100). Foregrounding the contrasts between what could have been a longer imperial history and the shortening of the British occupation of India, the condensed format enhances the potentiality of more transgressive narrative choices that are kept in the margins of a miniseries which offers many possibilities of branching out and spin-offs. *The Jewel in the Crown*, even though a miniseries, played a major role in the 1980s, which Sarita Malik depicts as characterised by 'institutional and cultural attempts to harness good racial relations' (Malik 2002, 18–19) triggered by the influence of US multiculturalism and the growing 'Race Relations Industry' in the British debates of the time. It brought home the complexity of the eventful era of the decolonisation of India and paved the way for other miniseries, which integrated in their short narratives ethnic characters that were no longer anonymous crowds of exotic peoples or marginal secondary figures – from *The Buddha of Suburbia* (BBC2, 1993) to *A Suitable Boy* (Netflix, 2020).

NOTES

1. 'Limited series, which have grown increasingly popular in recent years, will now all be called limited series instead of miniseries. That's a reversion back to 1974 when the category also was named outstanding limited series until it was changed to outstanding miniseries in 1986 (. . .)' (Albiniak 2015).
2. For a synthetical approach of the critical debates around Raj revival/revisionism films and TV series of the 1980s, see Mendes 2007.
3. 'Attempts to break the duopoly's stranglehold on British television began in the 1970s, gathering momentum throughout the 1980s as cable and satellite became viable commercial options' (Finch, Cox and Giles 2003, 21). For a detailed survey of the BBC rivalry with ITV, see Giddings and Selby 2001, 22 *et sq*.
4. For an analysis of the evolution of the British television landscape in the second half of the twentieth century, see Dawes 2021.
5. 'From the outset, Granada set itself the objective of providing high quality popular programmes that would surpass even the BBC's threshold of quality and standards. The company was against cultural segregation and sought to mix its more popular programming with innovative drama, hard-hitting investigative documentaries and pioneering coverage of political events. It quickly earned itself a reputation as the most socially conscious of all the commercial companies' (Giddings and Selby 2001, 12).
6. *Brideshead Revisited* was divided into eleven episodes of about 50 minutes, except for the 100 minutes of the pilot episode.
7. In 2000, The British Film Institute conducted a poll among British television professionals to rank the top 100 television programmes (among them 'serials') that had been screened in the second half of the twentieth century: *Brideshead Revisited* was number #10 on the list and *The Jewel in the Crown* was number #22. With seventy BBC-produced programmes appearing in the list, Granada ITV came second with seven fictional programmes, among them the popular soap opera *Coronation Street* (1960–), which was number #40. https://en.wikipedia.org/wiki/BFI_TV_100 (Accessed August 2022).
8. For instance David Lean needed three years to complete his *Passage to India* (which was released after *The Jewel in the Crown*, at the end of 1984, when the miniseries was broadcast in the US in December of that year). See Ingersoll 2012, 27.
9. See Brandt 1993, 200.
10. One year earlier, James Ivory and Ismael Merchant had 'only' spent £2,200,000 to shoot the famous *Heat and Dust* (1983, 133 min), which also takes place in India, but was a feature film meant for the big screen (Long 1993, 120).
11. It would be worth devoting a whole chapter to this question, which is the reason why I select only a few pointed film references here.
12. See Sereny 1982, in which the journalist refers to Richard Attenborough's distant contact with Mirabehn herself, who was to die a few months before the release of the film.
13. Typically, in *A Passage to India*, the Christian Mrs Moore is crushed by the trial but also by Miss Quested's accusation and later recanting, as she had benignly

encouraged the interracial bond between Adela and Aziz. Neither Islam nor Hinduism appear to offer any reliable way out for Lean's characters: Islam consists mainly in a legendary and escapist background for atheist Dr Aziz, as he identifies with Moghul emperors on his way to the Malabar Caves; while Hinduism is embodied by the slightly ridiculous Godbole, whose ludicrous mystical explanation of what happened in the cave convinces and helps no one. For a discussion of the way E.M. Forster's atheism is already highlighted in his novel, see Trivedi 1995, 157–8.
14. See Blumenthal 1997.
15. See Cabaret 2012.
16. See what Amanda D. Lotz also calls 'Consecutive viewing' (Lotz 2006).
17. See the historical overview of the question as it developed in Great Britain from the beginning of the twentieth century in Bloch and Schuster 2005, 491–512.
18. As Simon Gikandi questions: 'Does the black subject, then, weave its way in and out of Englishness? And what happens when blacks, through migration, become a physical presence in the heart of Englishness?' (Gikandi 1996, 69).
19. John Thieme has already pointed out the recurrence of this child figure in many postcolonial novels: see Thieme 2001, 8–11.

WORKS CITED

A Passage to India, directed by David Lean, EMI Films, 1984.
A Suitable Boy, adapted by Andrew Davies and directed by Mira Nair, Netflix, 2020.
Albiniak, Paige, 'Rule Changes Open Gates to More Hopefuls', NEXT|TV, 25 May 2015. Available online: https://www.nexttv.com/news/rule-changes-open-gates-more-hopefuls-141149 (Accessed June 2021).
Bloch, Alice and Schuster, Liza, 'At the Extremes of Exclusion: Deportation, Detention and Dispersal', *Ethnic and Racial Studies* 28, no. 3 (May 2005): 491–512.
Brandt, George W., '"The Jewel in the Crown": The Literary Serial, or the Art of Adaptation', in *British Television Drama in the 1980s*, ed. George W. Brandt (Cambridge: Cambridge University Press, 1993).
Blumenthal, Dannielle, *Women and Soap Opera: A Cultural Feminist Perspective* (Westport, Connecticut: Praeger Pub Text, 1997).
Cabaret, Florence, 'Representations of Power Shifts Between Great Britain and India in *The Jewel in the Crown* (ITV, 1984)', *TV/Series*, no. 2 (2012). Available online: http://journals.openedition.org/tvseries/1403 (Accessed February 2024); DOI: https://doi.org/10.4000/tvseries.1403.
Dawes, Simon, 'From Public Service to Public Interest and Beyond in British Broadcasting Regulation', *Revue Française de Civilisation Britannique* n° XXVI-1 (2021). Available online: http://journals.openedition.org/rfcb/7253; DOI: https://doi.org/10.4000/rfcb.7253 (Accessed December 2022).
Dyer, Richard, *White* (London: Routledge, 1997).
Finch, John, Michael Cox and Marjorie Giles (eds), *Granada Television: The First Generation* (Manchester: Manchester University Press, 2003).

Ford, Sam, Abigail De Kosnik and C. Lee Harrington (eds), *The Survival of Soap Opera: Transformations for a New Media Era* (Jackson: University Press of Mississippi, 2012).

Giddings, Robert and Keith Selby, *The Classic Serial on Television and Radio* (Basingstoke and New York: Palgrave, 2001).

Gikandi, Simon, *Maps of Englishness: Writing Identity in the Culture of Colonialism* (New York: Columbia University Press, 1996).

Gandhi, directed by Richard Attenborough, Goldcrest Films, 1982.

Gilroy, Paul, *Postcolonial Melancholia* (New York: Columbia University Press, 2005).

Higson, Andrew, 'Re-presenting the National Past: Nostalgia and Pastiche in the Heritage Film', in *Fires Were Started: British Cinema and Thatcherism*, ed. Lester Friedman (Minneapolis: University of Minnesota Press, 1993), 109–29.

Ingersoll, Earl G., *Filming Forster: The Challenges in Adapting E.M. Forster's Novels for the Screen* (Madison: Fairleigh Dickinson University Press, 2012).

It, directed by Tommy Lee Wallace, ABC, 1990.

Lennard, John, *Reading Paul Scott:* The Raj Quartet *and* Staying On (Indie Books, 2018).

Long, Robert Emmet, *The Films of Merchant Ivory* (New York: Citadel Press, 1993).

Lotz, Amanda D., 'Rethinking Meaning Making: Watching Serial TV on DVD', *Flow*, no. 22 (2006). Aavailable online: https://eprints.qut.edu.au/130984/10/130984.pdf (Accessed February 2024).

Malik, Sarita, *Representing Black Britain: A History of Black and Asian Images on British Television* (London: Sage Publications, 2002).

Mendes, Ana Cristina, 'The Empire on Film: Recasting India from the Raj Revival to *Lagaan*', in *In A Tangled Web: Ideas, Images, Symbols*, eds J. Carlos Viana Ferreira and Theresa de Ataída Malafaia (Lisbon: Colibro, 2007), 65–80.

Monk, Claire, *Heritage Film Audiences: Period Films and Contemporary Audiences in the UK* (Edinburgh: Edinburgh University Press, 2011).

Roots, created by Marvin Joseph Chomsky et al., ABC, 1977.

Said, Edward, *Orientalism, or Western Perceptions of the Orient* (London: Penguin Classics, 2019 [originally published 1978]).

Sereny, Gitta, 'A Life with Gandhi', *The New York Times Magazine*, 14 November 1982. Available online: https://www.nytimes.com/1982/11/14/magazine/a-life-with-gandhi.html (Accessed August 2022).

Staying On, directed by Silvio Narizzano, Granada ITV, 1980.

The Jewel in the Crown, directed by Christopher Morahan, Granada ITV, 1984.

The Buddha of Suburbia, adapted by Hanif Kureishi and directed by Roger Mitchell, BBC2, 1993.

The Raj Quartet, written by Paul Scott, 1966–75.

Thieme, John, *Postcolonial Contexts: Writing back to the Canon* (London: Continuum, 2001).

Trivedi, Harish, '*Passage* or *Farewell*? Politics of the Raj in E.M. Forster and Edward Thompson', in *Colonial Transactions: English Literature and India* (Manchester: Manchester University Press, 1995), 139–73.

When They See Us, created by Ava DuVernay, Netflix, 2019.

Wittebols, James H., *The Soap Opera Paradigm: Television Programming and Corporate Priorities* (Oxford: Rowman and Littlefield, 2004).

CHAPTER 3

Short Middle Ages: Comic Dramatisation of Rhythm in French Shortcom *Kaamelott*

Justine Breton

The French TV series *Kaamelott* was first broadcast on the public channel M6[1] from early 2005 to 2009, and reruns of the show still appear weekly on different channels of M6 group to this day.[2] This rewriting of the Arthurian legend started off as a short humorous program made for a wide family audience, a 'shortcom' centred on the character of King Arthur, his Knights of the Round Table and their courtly life in the castle of Kaamelott – a mock rewriting of the famous 'Camelot'.[3] Created by Alexandre Astier, the show is one of the earliest and most popular series belonging to the exclusively French televisual genre of the shortcom (Bihel 2012, Conseil Supérieur de l'Audiovisuel 2013, 6),[4] a genre characterised by 'its short format (less than 10 minutes), its recurrence (it is broadcast daily) and its comic intent, but also by its function in the scheduling grid', as shortcoms are usually placed 'before or after the evening news' and are meant to 'preserve the audience's attention before the prime time program' (Delaporte 2019, § 2).[5]

The legend of King Arthur, with the Quest for the Holy Grail and the love-triangle between Arthur, his Queen Guinevere and the knight Lancelot, has been known and developed since the twelfth century in Europe, and remains to this day one of the recurring topics for movies and TV adaptations of medieval stories (Harty 2002).[6] However, with the tragic outcome of its love-triangle and the importance of dark themes like fighting and violence, the story is usually presented as an epic, and rarely appears as comic material. One of the major specificities of *Kaamelott* lies in its comic reading of the legendary epic and its irreverent treatment of the Middle Ages. Of course, Astier's shortcom is not the first adaptation to attempt this original presentation – or indeed to succeed in it. A range of media have had similar successes, from Mark Twain's novel *A Connecticut Yankee in King Arthur's Court* (1889) to Terry Gilliam and

Terry Jones' famous movie *Monty Python and the Holy Grail* (1975) (Breton 2021). However, *Kaamelott* offers a renewal of the legendary themes by making them more accessible to a wider French audience, and by establishing narrative and aesthetic links to other media. After the poor reception of *Lancelot du lac* (1974) by Robert Bresson and *Perceval le Gallois* (1978) by Éric Rohmer, this comedy is one of the first audiovisual appropriations of the legend to bring the story to a broad audience, leaving aside the seriousness of the two previous 'auteur' films to favour the provocative mood of Monty Python, to whom *Kaamelott* obviously pays a tribute.[7] What is more, by recycling the legend and transposing it to a short format rather than going back to the tradition of the long epic form, Astier appears to be following in the footsteps of previous storytellers who, since the Middle Ages, have contributed to bringing a well-known story to new audiences by combining it with other genres. Indeed, the show is not restricted to the limitations of television, as it regularly uses key features of the theatre and of music as a way to broaden its diegetic horizons. As such, *Kaamelott* appears as a dense musical play, humorously rewriting and adapting a traditional epic in a particularly short time.

Given its contract with the for-profit channel M6, and its producers CALT and Robin & Co., *Kaamelott* was legally obligated to be a short program, of no more than 10 minutes, made for a family audience: this association of format and target audience traditionally implies a comedy program (Duthoit 2016, 12–13 and 37–8), as was requested from *Kaamelott* – at least in its early days. In its first three seasons, *Kaamelott* was indeed broadcast every weekday in two episodes of 3 and a half minutes, while the fourth season gradually changed to present one 7-minute episode every day. From the start, the Arthurian series also had to be written as a comedy *because* of its extremely short format, which appears as a contrast with its medieval origins that tended to expand on the story of Arthur by adding the stories of his numerous knights – Percival, Lancelot or even Tristram. The length and genre requirements given to *Kaamelott* derive from the series' predecessor on the channel, *Caméra Café* (2001–2004), a very successful shortcom of 3-minute episodes, devoted to typical corporate life and the social implications of coffee breaks. This program was broadcast every weekday at 8:30 pm, that is to say, right between the news segment and the prime-time movie or show, which usually started – at the time the series first appeared – at 8:50 pm. This time slot, the easy-to-follow narrative and the archetypal characters from the workplace – the trade unionist, the naïve secretary, the mean boss, et cetera – were obvious ingredients that contributed to the popularity of *Caméra Café* and somehow paved the way for the type of humour in *Kaamelott*, even though the change of context and characters was quite a challenge, which M6 willingly embraced so that no comparison could be made between the two programs. Nowadays, this slot tends to expand, with prime-time movies starting on for-profit channels at 9 or 9:15 pm, because channels quickly realised the potential of keeping the viewers between the news and the prime-time movie or show. But, in the 2000s, the slot and its brevity deeply contributed to *Caméra Café*'s success and, subsequently, to *Kaamelott*'s.

As a consequence, this shortcom makes us wonder how it is possible to make a traditionally tragic topic available – and interesting – to a large family audience, and to create laughter from it. The answer chosen by Alexandre Astier might lie in the traditional literary theory of genres. In his *Poetics*, Aristotle defines the main principles of tragedy and comedy.[8] Even though the second part of his text, dedicated to comedy *per se*, is now lost, we can infer Aristotle's ideas on comedy from what remains of his thesis on tragedy. Indeed, it seems that the main difference between Greek tragedy and comedy resides in the characters depicted on stage. While tragedy depicts virtuous, noble and serious heroes, comedy mostly presents weak and inferior characters (Heath 1989, 344–54). A different interpretation can be made about Roman comedy, which relies less on characters and more on the juxtaposition of superiority and incongruity, the bases for the burlesque genre (Duckworth 1952; Golden 1984, 283–90). *Kaamelott* proposes a generic compromise by presenting socially superior characters – kings, knights and wizards – who are depicted in incongruous situations *because* they happen to be weak. In most cases, their weakness manifests as their stupidity and incompetence, which is definitely a means to debunk the prestige attached to the Arthurian legend as well as to its famous heroic deeds and supposedly noble characters. By having them speak in contemporary French and situating them in colloquial everyday situations, the series creates comedy from its undermined characters, as well as from a change in the tone of the traditionally tragic story. But what is striking is that this description of characters and the generic shift from epic to burlesque can only be achieved through a precise use of timing.

According to a popular saying, the formula for comedy is 'tragedy plus time', to borrow a quote originally attributed to American actor Steve Allen (Wilson 2017). In the case of *Kaamelott*, the 'time' factor consists in a brief and dynamic rhythm: to play with rhythm variations, the series uses a paradoxical static narrative, which highlights the creation of each episode as a condensed play.[9] As we will see, this theatrical context is punctuated by musical cues, which showcase both the dramatic structure and the humorous tone of *Kaamelott*.

As a shortcom of 3 and a half minutes, *Kaamelott* does not have a lot of on-air time in order to present its narrative. As a result, the show is based on a particularly static narrative and aesthetics. Its first three seasons, out of a total of six, aim to introduce the setting, the characters and the stakes of the main story. These essential narrative elements are progressively built over the course of almost 300 standalone episodes, thus following a traditional sitcom structure over the first seasons. Indeed, nothing major really happens to the characters besides everyday life: marital disputes, family arguments at the dinner table about food and wine, growing teenagers, troubles with the neighbours, et cetera. This diegetic stillness results from a general cyclical sitcom structure, where each episode's news or mishap has an influence which is limited both in time and effect: the adventure of the episode ends with said episode, and nothing remains from it in the next episode broadcast the following day. In *Kaamelott*, the military invasion of Attila the Hun is, for instance, easily defeated in a 3-and-a-half-minute episode, and does not have any consequences in the long term. Although the series sets the scene for its subsequent diegetic developments, such as the secret love of the knight Lancelot for Queen Guinevere, a plot line which is at the heart of Season 4, the first three seasons remain mostly static in their narrative.

This diegetic aspect is emphasised by the very limited movements of the characters onscreen, who remain stationary for most of the episodes. No walking around for the characters implies very limited camera movements. Most of the time, *Kaamelott*'s episodes consist of a juxtaposition of still shots of mainly still actors. This reduction of narrative and physical action, especially compared with traditional sitcom series, first derives from the need to limit production costs. From its beginnings, *Kaamelott* was shot with several high-definition cameras, which was a novelty in France at the time for this kind of television short program. The show first used several settings inside a film studio and, starting with the second season, included scenes shot on location. Moreover, because of its period nature – insofar as the Arthurian legend can be associated with a legendary image of the Middle Ages – *Kaamelott* implies an important number and variety of historical costumes and props, including plate armours and horses, all of which considerably raise the production costs. This high production value is especially impressive when compared with the short format of the series, and with its predecessor *Caméra Café*, a single-camera and single-setting TV series with a limited number of recurring characters – although *Caméra Café*, like *Kaamelott*, included frequent cameos from famous guests. The restricted physical action in the first seasons allowed *Kaamelott* to partly reduce its production costs. Following the success of the first seasons, the adventures of King Arthur and his knights were also developed after 2006 in a series of comic books, created by Alexandre Astier and Stephen Dupré.[10] The characters' movements and the narrative arcs are far wider in the comic books than in the television series since, on paper, drawing a whole army or a fire-breathing dragon does not cost more than drawing a single static character. For example, *L'Armée du Nécromant* (the first instalment) includes a zombie army, and *Le Serpent géant du lac de l'ombre* (volume 5) presents the Knights of the Round Table facing a giant aquatic snake.

In the television series, the stillness of the characters is regularly justified within the narrative, in order to avoid the strangeness of the situation. The characters are presented while they are waiting, which allows for important dialogues and contributes to explaining the lack of physical action. Very often, King Arthur and his knights and family are seen eating and drinking – thus, sitting around a table –, having a meeting – thus, sitting around a table –, or chatting in bed – thus sitting on the bed, as a discreet setting variation. The

Round Table not only becomes symbolic of the Arthurian legend – it also becomes the material representation of the key role of dialogue in *Kaamelott*. In other occurrences, stillness invites itself into the adventures of the knights errant, which forces them to settle and discuss the next plan of attack. For instance, the heroes' inability to defeat or even find their enemies in several episodes implies a necessary change in tactics, and justifies the narrative use of conversation. Many episodes are built on a wandering principle, where the characters are supposed to advance – in a forest, in a labyrinth, in a cave – but where they quickly become lost and have to find their way out by talking about their route. Typically, a sequence where the knights encounter a closed door gives a diegetic opportunity for discussions about lock picking or the probability of finding a dangerous creature hidden behind the obstacle.[11]

Kaamelott confronts its characters with numerous obstacles, thus slowing down their narrative progression in the course of the episode, but simultaneously reinforcing the characters' psychology through the constant use of dialogue. As a consequence, most of what happens during the first seasons of the show is established through conversation and not through action. For example, the episode 'Les Exploités' (S02E36) presents two famous Knights of the Round Table, Perceval and Karadoc,[12] who come to see King Arthur at night to complain about their social and political status within the royal court (Figure 3.1). Most of the episode's comedy is created by the use of the closed door, added to the knights' inability to clearly explain what they want, thus preventing the characters from really hearing or understanding each other.

Figure 3.1 'But we're just here to complain' ('Mais nous, on venait juste se plaindre') – Perceval and Karadoc as medieval precursors to modern-day workers' rights protesters ('Les Exploités').

Part of the show's humour is also based on the discrepancy between the noble characters and their familiar language, as well as between the medievalist setting and the contemporary dialogues and sometimes thoughts of the characters. Here, echoing the famous anarcho-syndicalist peasant of *Monty Python and the Holy Grail* (1975), the knights demand to be regarded with higher respect by the King. The use of repetition and distorted vocabulary creates a series of misunderstandings between them and King Arthur, and gives the impression of a dynamic episode, where paradoxically nothing happens. The short format, which bans long silences and breaks in the dialogue, partly compensates for the static narrative. Perceval and Karadoc find it unacceptable that they are only 'used' by the sovereign in his quest for the Holy Grail, failing to understand that the quest is the very reason for the existence of their order of chivalry. As Jonathan Bocquet explains,

> They feel exploited but can't manage to formulate their grievances. The King tries to explain that their situation is eminently advantageous, but finally loses his patience and prefers to simply acquiesce that he's 'using them'. The two friends get nothing but the King's forced confession – and that's enough for them. (Bocquet 2018, 108)[13]

The King's words are enough to create an illusion of change for the knights, just as the dialogue is enough to create the illusion of action throughout the scene. The short episode ends on the knights' feeling of accomplishment: they leave happy and satisfied, even though their situation did not improve or change in any way during their discussion with the King. Similarly, the episode gives the viewer the impression that something happened, even though it only consisted in a vain 3-minute conversation and did not have any repercussions on the overall story.

The illusion of action brought by dialogue highlights the use of theatrical mechanisms in *Kaamelott* (Delaporte 2019). Since comedy mainly relies on rhythm and timing, the first seasons of the show are conceived of as a series of extremely short plays, originally broadcast in pairs every weekday – except during the holidays – from January 2005 to November 2006, for the first four seasons, on which we focus for this study. The very brief 3-and-a-half-minute format necessarily implies tight plot structures in order to have a full narrative structure during the episode, with a beginning, a development and a strong ending. Far from the long epic texts known since the Middle Ages, which proposed complex adventures for King Arthur and his Knights, *Kaamelott* focuses on everyday life in King Arthur's court. The name of the series, which parodies the name of Camelot, is a first indicator of this shift in narrative focalisation. Even though the characters sometimes appear in war contexts or are seen fighting supernatural creatures, they spend most of the episodes addressing trivial issues, such as what to wear during a Round Table meeting or how to survive a dinner with your in-laws. Contrary to clan wars, these topics can be developed and concluded in a few minutes. This reduction of the narrative scale is also made for the twenty-first-century viewer, who is presumably more familiar with daily struggles like family quarrels than with political negotiations. Here, Astier wants to address a broad audience by describing a familiar environment, partly distorted by the 'exotic' setting of the Middle Ages. As a result, the comedy that is thus developed can move quickly because it is partially built on familiarity and shared experiences. The new time setting, namely the medieval and fantasy context, also has an important comedic potential. Many episodes of *Kaamelott* mention the Holy Grail or political conflicts, which become comical topics because they are treated in an irreverent way – exactly like the familiar topics (see for instance in 'Les Exploités', the comic repetition of the knights' grievance about the Grail in particular: 'Le Graal par ci, le Graal par là. Le Graal par ci, le Graal par là. Le Graal par ci, le Graal par là. Le Graal par ci, le Graal par là.'[14]) The episodes with foreign enemies, such as Attila the Hun (S01E05, 'Le Fléau de Dieu') or the Viking chief (S03E42, 'Le Dialogue de Paix II') are based upon the same principles of miscommunication as most of the courtly episodes.

However, the 'serious' topics progressively took up more and more narrative space within the series, and therefore deserve to be treated at greater length. This evolution in the themes and atmosphere of *Kaamelott* is reflected in the use of the short format during the first seasons. Indeed, each season presents an increasing number of double episodes. Whereas the first season only includes short and light-themed episodes, the second one maintains the format while announcing deeper issues: the end of the second season consists of Lancelot, the bravest and most famous knight, embezzling the realm's money (S02E100, 'Les Comptes'). Later episodes show that this misappropriation was a first step in the knight's attempted military rebellion. The third season includes three double episodes, focusing on a literary discussion (S03E12–13, 'La Poétique'), on political debates (S03E26–27, 'L'Assemblée des Rois') and on a tense argument between Arthur and Lancelot (S03E99–100, 'La Dispute'), thus announcing the upcoming fall of the realm.

By writing two-part episodes, Astier kept the dynamic short format while finding new opportunities to tackle graver issues in the narrative. This way of lengthening the episodes is made obvious by the fourth season of *Kaamelott*, which includes nine double episodes of 7 minutes: 'Tous les Matins du monde' (S04E01–02), 'La Faute' (S04E08–09), 'Duel' (S04E17–18), 'L'Échange' (S04E23–24), 'Les Curieux' (S04E41–42), 'Les Tacticiens' (S04E47–48), 'La Poétique II' (S04E61–62), 'Le Face-à-face' (S04E80–81) and 'Le Renoncement' (S04E93–94). To these must be added one longer episode, which concludes the season: the 7-minute episode entitled 'Le Désordre et la Nuit' (S04E99) is twice as long as the others, as a way to slowly prepare both the narrative and the viewer for the longer episodes of Season 5. It starts with a discussion on betrayal and fear of punishment, which is treated without parodic intent despite a few jokes, then develops the theme of Lancelot's paranoia from the relatively detached perspective of Arthur and his spy, before showing Lancelot's discovery of Guenièvre's absence and his meeting with the mysterious 'man in black' in an entirely serious way, ending on a cliffhanger as the man, ordering him to stand up, announces that they are going to 'secretly rejoice at the return of long nights'.[15] Thus, the last season of *Kaamelott* to use short format progressively abandons it in order to develop longer and darker episodes (in that sense, the last words of Season 4 have a reflexive prophetic ring), which deal with both personal and political issues, and build the tensions that will lead to the destruction of the realm in the fifth season.

Kaamelott describes a general evolution towards more serious themes and thus towards longer episodes, which implies a change in the airing time of the series: Seasons 5 and 6, constituted of 40 to 50-minute episodes,[16] were first broadcast during prime-time. The comedy aspect of *Kaamelott*, in its first seasons, slowly prepared this narrative shift, by being very meticulous in the composition of the short episodes. As indicated earlier, these are written like a series of short plays, following a precise and regular construction. Although most of the first four seasons are made of stand-alone episodes, they all share a dynamic structure inherited from classical theatre. Each episode, in spite of – or because of – its brevity, is divided into five more or less equal parts, which echo the composition of Greek tragedy as well as highlighting the central and humorous parts as the very core of the episode. *Kaamelott* is thus based on a traditional dramatic composition:

Kaamelott read as a tragedy	*Kaamelott* read as a comedy	Role within the narrative
Act I	Introduction	Exposition
[opening titles]		*Musical transition for information purposes*
Act II	Act I	Disruptive element
[cut]		*Thematic musical cue*
Act III	Act II	Event (centre of the episode)
[cut]		*Thematic musical cue*
Act IV	Act III	Resolution
[closing credits]		*Musical transition for information purposes*
Act V	Epilogue	Final outcome and consequences of the resolution – with a humorous or tragic twist

The consistent partition gives a precise structure to every episode, but leaves enough freedom to allow for narrative variations. Astier's shortcom uses two traditional divisions of story, theorized by Aristotle, and which insist on the key role of the three central acts. For each episode, *Kaamelott* uses a structure that can be read as a five-part tragedy or as a three-part comedy. In this perspective, while the exposition and the consequences can be read as the paratext of the episode, the central acts unfold the story with its beginning, middle and end. This structural choice is all the more important to underline the program's comical principle in its first seasons, since comedy is frequently built on three successive units. Indeed, the first two parts, usually called 'setup' and 'reinforcement', create a dynamic and a logical association, i.e. they develop an impression of regularity and thus of rationality (Attardo and Pickering 2011; Yus 2017). The third part, the 'payoff', breaks this association by subverting the expectations built by the setup, thus creating laughter. Following this structure, the viewer discovers, for example, the enchanter Merlin repeatedly failing to craft jokes for an upcoming meeting of druids, before finally hearing Arthur put an end to his enchanter's comical attempts by forbidding him to go to the sacred meeting (S02E07, 'Le Rassemblement du Corbeau'). This format can be developed through repetition, exaggeration or escalation, thus amplifying the length of the comical composition.

The Aristotelian structure is even discussed in several episodes of *Kaamelott*, when King Arthur tries to explain to his knight Perceval how he is supposed to tell a story during their Round Table meetings. Indeed, the knights are supposed to go on adventures before coming back to court to share their experience and have their stories written down by the court's scribe, Père Blaise – a character inherited from the medieval tradition and the legend of Merlin. In two two-part episodes entitled 'La Poétique', as a reference to Aristotle's *Poetics*, the traditional dramatic structure is both explained and twisted by the impatient King (Catellani 2018, 39–51). After explaining at length to Perceval that any story should have a beginning, a middle and an end, but should also make sense, Arthur loses his patience and delicately dunks the knight's head in some sort of *fromage blanc* (S03E13, 'La Poétique – 2e partie'). In an unexpected twist, the literary discussion between the two characters ends with physical comedy typical of the slapstick tradition both on the stage and on the screen. But this metatextual silent commentary is also quite in keeping with the mixture of high and low references in the show, as well as with the carnivalesque pleasure Astier finds in 'cutting short' stories that could become too long-winded and inflated.

As a consequence, from the outset, *Kaamelott* includes structural references to both tragedy and comedy, with a traditional five-part tragic composition encompassing the three-part structure dedicated to comedy. Although this structure does not imply that the introduction and the epilogue are inherently tragic elements within the narrative, it nevertheless highlights the fact that

Astier has chosen a hybrid theatrical basis for his television series. From its first seasons, built on short and humorous episodes, *Kaamelott* hence comprises the potential for a tragic evolution, which happens progressively in the fourth season and is then made obvious in the fifth and sixth seasons of the program (Breton 2020).

The dramatic composition is made evident thanks to clear visual cuts between the acts, and to the use of musical transitions within each episode. Music and auditory cues are not incidental in *Kaamelott*, since they establish the dramatic structure of the episodes, as if each one was a short play created for the screen. We must recall that, before being a director, Astier, who was born to a family of actors and playwrights, was trained as a musician and a composer. This personal background actively contributed to the artistic atmosphere of the show, which maintains strong connections with both music and the theatre. As a consequence, the themes and titles chosen for this adaptation of the Arthurian legends frequently deal with these two arts. For example, the episode 'Cuisine et Dépendances' (S03E57) uses the title of a humorous French play by Agnès Jaoui and Jean-Pierre Bacri, presented in 1991, and 'Beaucoup de bruit pour rien' (S04E73) is a direct reference to Shakespeare's comedy *Much Ado About Nothing*. Similarly, the episode 'La Répétition' (S04E76) depicts rehearsals for a courtly performance. As for music, besides its recurring use during opening and closing credits, as we will see, it is mentioned as an important art in several episodes about singing and musical instruments, such as 'Le Oud' (S01E45). Music theory is even discussed in the famous episode 'La Quinte Juste' (S02E55), in which knights and members of the church alike sing and examine the medieval evolution of music (Lakits 2018, 241–52).

The fusion of these two complementary arts in the short format of *Kaamelott* appears clearly as soon as the first episode begins: the sound of three horn blows accompanies the initial credits appearing in white letters on a black background. This process, repeated at the beginning of each episode, is conceived of as a dynamic reference to the 'trois coups', the three blows struck before every play in French classical theatre, a traditional auditory cue – nowadays replaced by a discernible, long ringing – informing the audience of the beginning of the play. The same ritual is applied to *Kaamelott*: it is only after the three blows that the virtual curtain rises and that the characters are made visible for the viewers. Moreover, the three acts of each episode are 'framed' by two musical sequences, presenting the opening title and the closing credits. These consist in dynamic music with a cheerful tone, which establishes slight variations from season to season, thus creating its own musical – and visual – identity for each season. As a consequence, the musical credits were completely changed in the fifth and sixth seasons, as the tone of the show was deeply altered. Music thus became part of the identity of *Kaamelott*, both as a complete program and as a series of independent seasons.

But the auditory structure of the short episodes is not restricted to the preliminary sequences. Each act is separated from the other by a thematic musical cue which reinforces the visual cut. In the first seasons of the show, *Kaamelott* proposed a diegetic and auditory classification of its episodes through brief sound effects. The sounds of percussion and horn, echoing the instruments mainly heard in the opening title, are used to characterise a general conflict happening in the royal court (S01E18, 'En Forme de Graal'). The drum roll is associated with military sequences within the episode (S01E01, 'Heat'); the violin is heard before acts presenting the royal family (S02E27, 'L'Ancien Temps'); a few harp notes announce scenes with King Arthur's mistresses, and thus with a love interest (S02E17, 'Les Jumelles du Pêcheur'); combined sounds of harp and chiming appear in episodes about magic (S02E80, 'Les Parchemins Magiques'); and church bells, of course, are the sign of a religious theme in the following act (S02E45, 'Amen'). The narrative is also built around these brief sounds between each act, which help create an unconscious structure for the episode. Indeed, these elements are barely noticeable for the viewer, since they are not emphasised and since this auditory process is abandoned in the third season. However, in the first two seasons of *Kaamelott*, these transitions are essential to understand the dynamic of each act: the choice of the musical instrument for a transition announces the main theme of the following sequence. As a result, if we follow the comedy reading of the show, the transition between Act I and Act II can be different from the transition between Act II and Act III in the same episode, since the themes developed in each act may vary. Here, Astier brings musical variations into the precise dramatic structure of his short episodes in order to say more in a very brief period of time.

Each episode also ends with the audio-visual equivalent of a full stop, highlighted both by an auditory cue and by a black screen. This association of musical sound and absence of image helps the comic tone of the episode as a form of punctuation for the last sentence – as would a drum and cymbal sound at the end of a joke in stand-up comedy. Through this conclusive element, the director signals the end of the episode: the curtain falls and the brief play is over. In *Kaamelott*, music is not a mere subsidiary element; it is a way to narrate a story. This clever and discreet use of music in the first seasons became a real advantage in telling a long story – based on the Arthurian legend – in such a short format.

The first seasons of *Kaamelott* present a static narrative which is kept dynamic by a light tone and by the importance of dialogue. With very little action, the series is mainly built around its use of language. It also forges its own comic rhythm by applying a traditional dramatic structure to each episode, and thus conceiving each of the first seasons as a juxtaposition of 100 microplays. Here, comedy is for the most part built on regularity and variation. This process is evidenced by the use of music and melody in each episode as a way to structure and to narrate. According to Aristotle, poetic creation mainly depends on language, rhythm and melody, three structural elements which, as we have seen, play a key role in *Kaamelott*'s episodes. The show twists the literary and theatrical use of language, rhythm and melody in order to create comical episodes in less than 4 minutes out of a traditional epic story. It proved a fruitful attempt at renewing a 'sacred' genre by combining legendary and heroic stories, which tend to favour the long film format, with the 'shortcom' genre as well as a form of derogatory humour that had been successfully promoted by French cable channel Canal+, whose evening shows launched such artistic teams as 'Les Nuls' (from 1987 to 1992) or 'Les Robins des bois' (from 1999 to 2001), which had spectators laughing their heads off with short and ludicrous intermissions between TV news and serious programs. The 2021 release of the long-awaited film version of *Kaamelott* (whose title, *Kaamelott: premier volet*, announces that it is only the first film in a trilogy sequence) definitely raises questions as to the changes of rhythm, tone and techniques imposed by a 2-hour-long version catering both to old-time fans attached to the original short format and to newcomers who may expect the kind of sweeping grandeur displayed more clearly in *The Lord of the Rings* or *Game of Thrones*.

NOTES

1. M6, for 'Métropole Télévision,' started broadcasting in 1987, after Hertzian channels were opened to private companies in France at the beginning of the 1980s (Sepulchre 2011, 32). M6 is one of the two main commercial broadcasters, with TF1 (the leader in terms of audience shares; privatised in 1987), and the fourth most watched channel in France, in a television landscape where public-service channels France 2 and France 3 hold strong positions (as second and third) (see Alcaraz 2023). M6 especially aims its programs at teenagers and young adults. Its programming has historically included musical content (one of the main components of the schedule at the beginnings); American series – M6 is famous for introducing *The X-Files* (Fox, 1993–2002) and *Buffy the Vampire Slayer* (WB, 1997–2003) to a wide French audience; flagship magazines *Zone Interdite*, *Capital* and *Culture Pub*; reality TV shows, starting with the controversial *Loft Story* in 2001; and 'shortcoms' such as *Caméra Café* (2001–4), *Kaamelott* or *Scènes de ménages* (2009–present). M6 Group is the owner of M6 and several other channels such as W9, Série Club (specialising in television series), Paris-Première, Téva (targeting women with children) or Gulli (aimed at children). M6 Group also owns radio stations as well as film and television production companies.
2. Most of the episodes can still be watched on the channel's replay website: www.6play.fr/kaamelott-p_888

3. The written form 'Kaamelott', with its initial 'k', modernises the name of the famous Arthurian castle and guarantees its rightful pronunciation from a French-speaking audience. The final double 't' invites the pronunciation [kamǝlɔt], which copies the English pronunciation, and thus differs from the French word 'camelot', designating a peddler and pronounced [kamǝlo]. Simultaneously, the [kamǝlɔt] pronunciation clearly points to another French word, 'camelote', i.e. junk or rubbish, which immediately foregrounds the desecrating 'cheap' dimension of the show. As for the central double 'a', it is frequently said it was a subtle way to include the creator's initials, Alexandre Astier, into the name of the show. It may also be a reference to the double 'a' of the word 'Graal' (Grail) in French.
4. M6's *Caméra Café* and France 2's *Un gars, Une fille* (1999–2003) are two other early examples of this genre that does not seem to have equivalents on English-speaking broadcast TV (the very short format is more a web-series format in the Anglo-Saxon world).
5. 'La shortcom se caractérise par son format bref (moins d'une dizaine de minutes), sa récurrence (diffusion quotidienne) et sa vocation comique, mais aussi par sa fonction au sein des grilles de programmation: généralement diffusées en *access prime-time*, avant ou après le journal télévisé du soir, les shortcoms ont pour but de conserver l'attention des téléspectateur·ices jusqu'à la diffusion du programme en *prime-time*.' In English-inflected French television parlance, the term 'shortcom', a contraction of English words 'short' and 'comedy' coined on the model of 'sitcom', is used as such to designate this typically French genre.
6. The Arthurian legend is frequently pictured in movies, such as John Boorman's *Excalibur* (1981), Antoine Fuqua's *King Arthur* (2004), and Guy Ritchie's *King Arthur: Legend of the Sword* (2017), to name only a few; but it also regularly appears in TV series, like *Merlin* (BBC, 2008–12) or *Camelot* (2011). For a particularly long bibliography on the topic, see Harty 2002.
7. For further details of the recycling of the Arthurian legend by French writers, comics authors and filmmakers, see Blanc 2021.
8. *Kaamelott*'s first seasons are clearly based on these principles, as is openly stated in two two-part episodes entitled 'La Poétique' and directly referencing Aristotle's *Poetics*. See Catellani 2018, 39–51.
9. *Kaamelott* develops a theatrical tradition deeply present in shortcoms, as evidenced by Chloé Delaporte (Delaporte 2019).
10. Ten volumes of *Kaamelott*'s comic books are currently published by Casterman, and an eleventh volume entitled *Arthur contre le Soldat-Silence* is planned. Although they follow the humorous principle of the show and depict the same characters, the comic books also present more epic and magical adventures, independent from one another, and which occur during the first season of the show.
11. This 'closed-door setting' is also used outside knightly adventures, in courtly episodes where characters try to talk to the King, who refuses to open his bedroom door, such as 'Le Tourment' (S01E98) or 'Les Exploités II' (S04E15).

12. We chose for this paper to maintain the spelling used in *Kaamelott*, despite the fact that these characters traditionally have an English spelling.
13. 'Ils se sentent exploités mais ne parviennent pas à formuler leurs revendications. Le roi tente de leur expliquer que leur situation est plus qu'avantageuse mais finalement perd patience et préfère reconnaître qu'il "les utilise". Les deux compères n'obtiennent rien si ce n'est l'aveu volé au roi et cela leur suffit [. . .].'
14. 'The Grail here, the Grail there. The Grail here, the Grail there. The Grail here, the Grail there. The Grail here, the Grail there.'
15. '[. . .] nous allons secrètement nous réjouir du retour des longues nuits.'
16. While the first three seasons are made of 100 episodes of three and a half minutes each, Season 4 is composed of 99 episodes – since the last one is longer and thus counts as a double episode –, Season 5 has 8 episodes and Season 6 has 9. Thus, the total running time of each season remains approximately the same, with 350 minutes, be it cut into 100 or only 8 episodes.

WORKS CITED

Alcaraz, Marina, 'Audiences 2022: TF1 et M6 souffrent, les chaînes d'info se distinguent', *Les Echos*, 3 January 2023.

Aristotle, *Poetics*, translated by Anthony Kenny (Oxford: Oxford University Press, 2013).

Attardo, Salvatore and Lucy Pickering, 'Timing in the Performance of Jokes', *Humour* 24, no. 2 (2011). Available online: https://doi.org/10.1515/HUMR.2011.015 (Accessed February 2024).

Bihel, Ingrid, 'L'explosion des programmes comiques courts (shortcoms) en France', *Web-revue des industries culturelles et numériques* (2012). Available online: http://industrie-culturelle.fr/industrie-culturelle/lexplosion-des-programmes-courts-comiques-shortcoms-en-france-ingrid-bihel (Accessed February 2024).

Blanc, William, 'Kaamelott ou la lente réintroduction d'Arthur dans la culture française', *Le Point* (22 July 2021). Available online: https://www.lepoint.fr/pop-culture/kaamelott-ou-la-lente-reintroduction-d-arthur-dans-la-culture-francaise-22-07-2021-2436483_2920.php (Accessed July 2021).

Bocquet, Jonathan, '"Des chefs de guerre, y en a de toutes sortes": De l'idéal de la Table Ronde à la pratique du pouvoir', in *Kaamelott, un livre d'histoire*, eds Florian Besson and Justine Breton (Paris: Vendémiaire, 2018), 103–16.

Breton, Justine, 'Quand les chevaliers dépassent les bornes: l'enfermement dans *Kaamelott*', in *Voyages intérieurs et espaces clos dans les domaines de l'imaginaire (littérature, cinéma, transmédias), XIXe–XXIe siècles*, eds Delphine Gachet, Florence Plet-Nicolas and Natacha Vas-Deyres (Université Bordeaux Montaigne, Le Fil à retordre, 2020). Available online: https://hal.archives-ouvertes.fr/hal-02882492 (Accessed February 2024).

Breton, Justine, *Monty Python: Sacré Graal !*, coll. (Contrechamps, Vendémiaire, 2021).

Caméra Café, created by Bruno Solo, Yvan Le Bolloc'h et Alain Kappauf, M6, 2001–4.

Catellani, Nathalie, '"C'est Aristote, ça!" Perceval et la *Poétique* d'Aristote', *Kaamelott, un livre d'histoire*, eds Florian Besson and Justine Breton (Paris: Vendémiaire, 2018), 39–51.

Conseil Supérieur de l'Audiovisuel, *Étude sur la fiction de journée & d'avant-soirée*, Les études du CSA, June 2013. Available online: https://www.csa.fr/Informer/Collections-du-CSA/Thema-Toutes-les-etudes-realisees-ou-co-realisees-par-le-CSA-sur-des-themes-specifiques/Les-etudes-du-CSA/Etude-sur-la-fiction-de-journee-et-d-avant-soiree-2013 (Accessed December 2022).

Delaporte, Chloé, 'Aux marges de la fiction sérielle télévisuelle: sémio-pragmatique de la shortcom familiale,' *TV/Series*, no. 15 (2019). Available online: http://journals.openedition.org/tvseries/3661 (Accessed February 2024); DOI: https://doi.org/10.4000/tvseries.3661

Duckworth, George E., *Nature of Roman Comedy: A Study in Popular Entertainment* (Princeton: Princeton University Press, 1952).

Duthoit, Juliette, 'Laugh With Me: Effects of Shortcoms on Students' Motivation, Confidence, and Cultural Understanding in the French Classroom', Graduate thesis (Eberly College of Arts and Sciences, West Virginia, 2016).

Golden, Leon, 'Aristotle in Comedy', *The Journal of Aesthetics and Art Criticism* 42, no. 3 (Spring 1984).

Harty, Kevin J. (ed.), *Cinema Arthuriana*, 2nd edition (Jefferson: MacFarland & Co., 2002).

Heath, Malcolm, 'Aristotelian Comedy', *Classical Quarterly* 39 (1989).

Kaamelott, created by Alexandre Astier, Alain Kappauf et Jean-Yves Robin, M6, 2005–9.

Kaamelott.1. L'Armée du Nécromant, created by Alexandre Astier and Steven Dupré, Casterman, 2006.

Kaamelott. 5. Le Serpent géant du lac de l'ombre, created by Alexandre Astier and Steven Dupré, Casterman, 2010.

Lakits, Matthias, '"Une petite sixte, et c'est joli…" Quand les chevaliers se mettent à chanter', in *Kaamelott, un livre d'histoire*, eds Florian Besson and Justine Breton (Paris: Vendémiaire, 2018), 241–52.

Monty Python and the Holy Grail, directed by Terry Gilliam and Terry Jones, National Film Trustee Company and Python Pictures, 1975.

Sepulchre, Sarah (ed.), *Décoder les séries télévisées* (Bruxelles: De Boeck, 2011).

Twain, Mark, *A Connecticut Yankee in King Arthur's Court* (London: Penguin Books, 1976 [originally published 1889]).

Wilson, Nathan. 'Tragedy Plus Time', *The Critical Comic*, posted on 1 July, 2017. Available online: https://thecriticalcomic.com/tragedy-plus-time/ (Accessed February 2024).

Un gars, une fille, developed by Isabelle Camus and Hélène Jacques, France 2, 1999–2003.

Yus, Francisco, 'Incongruity-resolution cases in jokes', *Lingua* 197 (2017): 103–22.

CHAPTER 4

Short but Serious? Slimming Down the Episode in 'Prestige' Drama *Homecoming*

Sylvaine Bataille

At a time when shows like *Westworld* (HBO, 2016–22) or *The Romanoffs* (Amazon Prime Video, 2018) occasionally expanded episode runtime well beyond an hour, the brevity of *Homecoming*, 'a half-hour *drama*' as one reviewer insisted (Stuever 2018), was a curiosity when its first season was released in 2018 on Amazon. In this series directed by Sam Esmail, Julia Roberts plays Heidi Bergman, a newly appointed therapist and administrator of Homecoming, a private facility welcoming war veterans and preparing their return to civilian life. Created by Eli Horowitz and Micah Bloomberg, and adapted from their podcast series of the same name that was released on Gimlet from 2016 to 2017, *Homecoming* was described in reviews as 'a cerebral thriller' (Poniewozik 2018), 'an artfully absorbing government-conspiracy drama' (Stuever 2018), as well as 'the latest series with prestige TV bona fides' (Watercutter 2018). However, with its ten 24-to-37-minute episodes,[1] it was different from its fellow 'prestige'-branded dramas in conspicuously 'slimming down' the episode and attempting to dissociate a number of highly valued features, such as seriousness, complexity or high production values, from length. In this chapter I will argue that even in the context of post-television and the transformation of viewing habits induced by streaming platforms, choosing to preserve the original podcast's half-hour format and to adapt the 'regular' hour-long format of the quality drama model rather than fully conform to generic expectations had the potential to delegitimise the series as serious drama. As it negotiated the contradictory claims of today's high-profile drama series and the half-hour episode format, implicitly associated with lower televisual genres in cultural hierarchies, *Homecoming* not only counterbalanced its reduced episode length with strong 'quality' markers, but also endowed the short form with artistic legitimacy, ennobling it rather than simply compensating for it. Ultimately the show's creative engagement with 'smallness' was an effective distinction tool, enabling *Homecoming* to affirm its legitimacy and visibility in a context where 'quality' drama's own distinction strategies regularly came under fire for coalescing into a predictable formula and a set of unquestioned assumptions.

Genre, episode runtime and scheduling have had a long-standing relationship in the American television industry, where network programmers 'learned to think of television in relation to the rhythms of the household and in terms of audience flow' (Curtin and Shattuc 2018, 60) as they organised content according to 'the half-hour matrix of the television schedule' (Mittell 2004, 63), which includes commercials on broadcast television. The sitcom, 'originally made to fit into a broadcast schedule's 30-minute time slot' (Butler 2020, 23), became a staple of early evening schedules, intended for an audience expected to comprise the whole family, all of them at home at this time of day but their attention also potentially engaged by other domestic activities. However, '[l]ater in the evening, after young children went to bed, audience composition shifted towards mature viewers who were presumably less distracted by household responsibilities and therefore willing to invest in longer, more complex and perhaps more serious programmes' (Curtin and Shattuc 2018, 60). While half-hour western series, crime series and soap operas were common before the end of the 1970s, the longer 1-hour format then began to be the norm for drama series. Thus network television programming solidified generic conventions and expectations concerning fiction series, associating 'comedy' with half-hour episodes, whereas 'seriousness' and 'complexity' became tightly linked to a longer, 1-hour episode runtime (both formats including advertisements on broadcast television). As Jason Mittell has shown, programming practices 'often communicate generic assumptions' (Mittell 2004, 58) and, along with other industrial practices, are instrumental in 'linking [genres] to cultural hierarchies and systems of difference' (Mittell 2004, 20).

From a technical point of view, considerations of episode runtime seem obsolete in the case of series 'dropped' all at once on Amazon Prime Video. There are no such things as time slots or a daily schedule on a streaming platform, since it is 'a database [from which] you can pull up what you want to watch at any time' (Bianculli, quoted by Volpe 2017). However, in social and discursive practices, the technical possibilities offered by streaming platforms, notably thanks to the absence of scheduling and commercial breaks, obscure rather than obliterate the conventional associations between genre and episode duration. Linear television's cultural hierarchies between longer and shorter episode formats, which intersect with 'intergeneric' as well as 'intrageneric hierarchies' (Mittell 2004), are actually perpetuated, and even exacerbated, by streaming platforms.

For all the talk, both from Netflix and from critics, about Netflix 'revolutionizing television' (Tryon 2015, 105, 107), Netflix did not set out to break all existing norms of television, but rather to rival a certain type of television – cable television, more specifically HBO – thus 'implicitly defin[ing] itself as television rather than an online broadcaster like YouTube' (Jenner 2018, 5). Using a strategy of cultural legitimation itself borrowed from HBO (Tryon 2015, 104), Netflix relied on a discourse of distinction that insisted on 'quality' and 'prestige', constructing the platform as a 'superior form of entertainment' compared with more traditional forms of television – including HBO (Tryon 2015, 110). Although the scholarship on Amazon Prime Video, the uncontested second to Netflix in 2018 (Shattuc 2020, 150), is much sparser than that about Netflix, the same rhetoric of 'quality' has been noted in the promotional material for Amazon's original shows (Barker 2017). Thus despite Netflix and Amazon's emphasis on the specific viewing experiences they provide, allowing in particular an 'instant mode' of viewing (Tryon 2015, 106) and binge-watching, often presented as 'a mode of audience behavior that improves upon traditional television's liveness and linear scheduling' (Wayne 2018, 730), the existing associations between genres and episode lengths, and the implicit hierarchies accompanying them in the cultural field of television, were preserved rather than levelled or seriously disrupted by the streaming platforms. The half-hour format is still a strong distinctive feature of comedy (Butler 2020, 2), even though there is technically no such thing as a 30-minute time slot in non-linear television, while drama has remained an overwhelmingly long form (Volpe 2017).

The traditional associations between longer episodes and more 'serious' content aimed at the 'mature', 'invested' audience of network television's later primetime hours have persisted in more or less explicit evaluations of comedy and drama, but also in the differential attribution of cultural value to varieties of the same genre. The category of drama has traditionally been more highly considered than the sitcom, 'often regarded contemptuously as among the most conservative, formulaic and artless of the narrative forms' (Newman and Levine 2012, 77), but within the drama genre, extended episode runtime (the full hour or more instead of the actual 42 minutes plus commercials of network television) has been a marker of 'quality' in the intrageneric hierarchies and discourses of legitimation initiated by HBO's distinguishing itself from 'TV': as M. Jenner points out, 'time (meaning episode length) and notions of "quality" are linked. Largely, it indicates how "commercial" a text is by how much time it allows for advertising messages. HBO started to develop series that could take full advantage of the hour of television they were given' (Jenner 2018, 143). This has also been the case within the category of comedy, with single-camera 'quality comedy' taking the full half-hour (Jenner 2018, 143; Newman and Levine 2012, 86). Streaming platforms were able to introduce variations in episode runtime (Jenner 2018, 143) and to go beyond the 1-hour or half-hour limit. The deregulation of episode length on streaming platforms thus mainly led to an expansion of traditional episode durations. Especially for heavily serialised drama, longer episode runtimes coincide with the 'promise of plenitude' delivered by Netflix, a promise that does not simply hinge on the sheer number of shows available on the platform, but also on 'the ability of that content to keep its subscribers engaged for hours on end' (Tryon 2015, 105, 112). More generally, in the now well-rehearsed discourse of revolutionised television tightly interwoven with Quality TV, longer episodes are more than ever thought to provide 'creative scope'[2] and are seen as fully respecting the showrunner's artistic vision (see Jeff Wachtel, quoted in Sandberg and Rose 2017). With streaming platforms 'putting pressure on the rest of the industry to match the freedom', fierce competition over 'prestige' content has resulted in 'supersized' episodes not only across streaming platforms and premium cable, but also on basic cable channels (Sandberg and Rose 2017).

The context of *Homecoming*'s first season was thus marked by an increase in televisual content in two ways: not only could individual episodes contain longer portions of television narratives, but the number of scripted original series produced had also reached several hundred and was still growing – a trend called Peak TV by John Landgraf in 2015 (Rose and Guthrie 2015). In such a competitive context of 'too much TV', *Homecoming*'s choice of swimming against the tide with shorter episodes was not only original and surprising but also implied taking the risk of being easily eclipsed by longer shows and depriving the series of the positive associations linking the long episode with quality, instead courting connections with lesser-valued forms of television fiction. The comments made by both Esmail and Roberts on the half-hour format convey a sense of resistance to and even transgression of norms regarding the drama episode (see Miller 2018). They are also revealing for the legitimising strategies of 'prestige' dramas that *Homecoming* risked forgoing when it sought to preserve the short format imported from the podcast. For instance, Julia Roberts acknowledged being initially averse to the half-hour format: 'to me, drama is an hour. Only teenagers can get drama done in 30 minutes. [. . .] We're tall. We need an hour' (quoted in Miller 2018). Such a parallel suggests how difficult it is to disassociate 'adult', 'serious' content from long episode runtime and attests to the persistence of discourses of distinction that elevate television series characterised as 'sophisticated and adult (rather than simplistic and juvenile)' (Newman and Levine 2012, 50), even inside the genre of drama. Shortening rather than extending the conventional duration of the drama episode, even reducing it to the length typical of comedy, seriously challenged entrenched intrageneric and intergeneric hierarchies.

Homecoming cleverly contested these hierarchies without removing itself from the genre of serious, 'prestige' drama, benefiting from its legitimacy while subverting some of its norms from the inside. The associations of the shorter episode format with lower televisual genres were countered with strong 'prestige' markers,[3] most notably the involvement of big names in both the acting and the direction; constant references to cinema; and complex, even confusing storytelling.[4] These markers appear prominently in the show's trailer – a characteristically condensed short form.[5] Recombining fragments from the whole season in a bewildering montage that reconstructs passages or dialogues in an often-misleading way more than it offers a sample of scenes,[6] the trailer overcomplicates the story and alludes to as-yet-undecipherable metaphorical meanings. As the editing of the trailer brings together shots, or images and dialogue, that can be episodes apart in the show, it also encourages the audience to have an eye for echoes or parallels and adopt a non-linear reading of the show. The trailer features some of the show's signature overhead shots, of geometrical, Hitchcockian stairwells or precisely arranged interiors, visually striking images that advertise the cinematic nature of the series.[7] The mention 'Directed by the creator of *Mr. Robot*' is superimposed on a shot of an empty lounge area in the Homecoming facility whose arresting composition is characteristically symmetrical and strongly structured by vertical and horizontal lines. Sam Esmail is designated by a periphrasis announcing *Homecoming*'s connection with an already established prestige drama and putting forward Esmail's credentials as a *creator* – presenting the showrunner as an *auteur* with a personal artistic vision is typical of quality television's discourses of distinction (Newman and Levine 2012). The names of the cast flicker in and out over a whirling shot of a spiral staircase, some of them eminently recognisable (Julia Roberts of course, but also Bobby Cannavale, Shea Whigham and Sissy Spacek). What transpires both from the text presented onscreen and the images shown in the trailer thus secures *Homecoming*'s affiliations with cinema and prestige television.

In fact, the series is so visibly steeped in cinema that an annoyed critic derogatively called it 'an exercise in postmodern pastiche' (Patten 2018). The references to Hitchcock, De Palma, Kubrick and the thrillers of the 1970s are not only visual but also aural, with a soundtrack exclusively made of pre-existing scores previously composed by Bernard Herrmann, Ennio Morricone, Vangelis, Pino Donaggio or Michael Small among others (O'Falt 2018). These 'really big scores' (music supervisor M. Phillips, quoted in O'Falt 2018) play an important part in the show's efforts to dissociate its smaller format from the traditional implications of triviality, lack of amplitude and 'televisual' style that go with the half-hour episode. So do the long takes that are characteristic of Esmail's directorial style (he famously directed *Mr. Robot*'s Episode 5 of Season 3 as one continuous shot): *Homecoming*'s first episode has three continuous takes in its first 10 minutes, among them a tour of the Homecoming facility as Heidi talks with her boss Colin (Bobby Cannavale) on the phone in just one almost-three-minute shot (2 minutes 47 seconds).[8]

Do these strongly cinematic choices mean that each season of *Homecoming* should be considered as a several-hour-long film, in line with the now clichéd but still laudatory assimilation of high-profile drama series with very long films?[9] The duration of the whole first season (approximately 4 hours and 35 minutes) would certainly make the comparison with a film less far-fetched than is the case with longer dramas like *Game of Thrones* (HBO, 2011–19). The release of all the episodes on Amazon Prime on the same date, and the widespread practice of binge-viewing, encouraged on streaming platforms by the Auto Play and the 'Next up' window, are also contextual factors that would seem to make it all the easier to consume or at least envisage the season as a continuous narrative flow, whose only significant boundaries would be the beginning and the end of the series, where breaks between episodes become negligible divisions not carrying much greater meaning than short interruptions decided by the viewer would be. *Homecoming*'s serialised narrative, and its aesthetics inspired by classic films, would then not only work as prestige markers counterbalancing the lesser value assigned to the half-hour episode in televisual hierarchies, but they would effectively tend to obliterate the very notion of its (shorter) length altogether.

What is particularly striking in the specific case of *Homecoming*, however, is that the series, rather than taking advantage of these opportunities to gloss over its unusual episode length, made it entirely and intrinsically relevant to its artistic project, reaffirming the value of episodic division and working brevity and smallness into its very fabric. Thus the show actively counters the industrial and contextual incentives potentially leading to a dissolution of the episode as a unit in the bigger whole of the season. Like *In Treatment* (HBO, 2008–10; 2021) – an earlier example of a non-comic series told in roughly half-hour episodes – and the other adaptations of *BeTipul*,[10] the series uses the interactions between the therapist (Roberts) and the patient (in this case, Walter Cruz, played by Stephan James) to structure its episodic framework, although it does so in a much looser way, rapidly altering the paradigmatic correspondence between therapy session and episode introduced in the first two episodes.[11] The narrative unit of the episode is also occasionally reinforced in traditional but rather discreet ways. The construction of Episodes 2 and 9 involves echoing sequences at the beginning and at the end which frame the episode.[12] Episode 5 playfully evokes the connections of the half-hour format to the comic genre by introducing a lighter, funnier subplot in the 2018 timeline: Walter plays a prank on Heidi; Heidi retaliates; Walter and his friends' mysterious preparations result in the final prank of the episode. More systematically and visibly, however, the limits of the episode are foregrounded through the series' 'intrinsic norms' (Mittell 2007, 166) in the presentation of the episode opening and ending.

The series dispenses with opening credits and has no recurring title sequence, but each of the season's ten instalments is given a title and is explicitly designated as an 'episode': the words 'Episode One – Mandatory'; 'Episode Two – Pineapple'; 'Episode Three – Optics', et cetera appear in capitals a few minutes into the episode, printed on a shot that lingers for a few seconds (see Figure 4.1). The episode endings are particularly marked: in all the episodes of the season except the very last one, the last scene is prolonged so that the last shot(s) serve(s) as a backdrop to the end credits for over a minute, most often without any music, before the screen goes black for the remainder of the credits.[13] The ambient sound however can often still be heard up to the very end of the credits. This uneventful moment – Carrasco gathering his belongings at the end of Episode 1, Shrier pacing up and down in his locked room in Episode 2, people politely chatting at a cocktail party in the lobby of the Geist building in Episode 4, or everyday activities on a quiet suburban street in Episode 7 – offers a lull after a revelation, a surprise, a decision or a twist of fate – Heidi stating in 2022 that she does not know Walter Cruz (E01), Heidi in 2018 discovering a pelican on her desk (E05), or Heidi (in a flashback) finding the right words to convince Colin to hire her for the Homecoming program in the last instants of an otherwise dull job interview (E09). Because of their unusual length, these 'ambient scenes' (Herman 2018) or 'lingering endings' (Esmail, quoted in Zoller Seitz 2018) visibly break with the conventions of traditional television narratives in which every 'beat' must have a 'dramatic function' (Newman 2006, 17).[14] They also create an effect that is conspicuously the opposite both of the cliffhanger or other devices used in heavily serialised dramas to encourage the viewer to watch the next episodes,[15] and of the freeze-frame that traditionally closed sitcoms until the beginning of the 1990s.[16] Instead, they are a nod to the 'dead time' moments in Michelangelo Antonioni's films (Elsaesser and Hagener 2010, 74). While 'bingeable' series have accustomed viewers to episode endings that leave us at a crucial moment in the action, the episode conclusions in *Homecoming* stay with us instead, waiting for us to leave, making us feel the time passing rather than forget about it. They thus strongly punctuate the break between two episodes, forcefully slowing down the rhythm of consumption of narrative content. These protracted endings reflexively draw attention to their own narrative status as 'borders': when does the episode end? Does it end when there is no longer any action or dialogue? Or when the screen goes black? Or when there is no sound anymore? The show thus replaces the effacement of episode boundaries that has become customary in drama series with an invitation not only to notice these frontiers but also to observe them and question our viewing habits.

The series' slight distortions of the 'normal' use of time in television episodes can also be found during the episodes themselves. For instance at the beginning of Episode 3, Carrasco spends what seems to be a considerable amount of time in front of his computer, pensively 'clicking' on the top of his pen, deciding whether he will 'click to confirm' that he recommends the anonymous complaint about Homecoming to be 'dismissed', resolving he will not, looking for an archive bin number in a database, jotting down the number on a post-it note and deliberately removing his glasses (a model that 'clicks' open and closed in the middle) before getting up. At the end of the episode, his determination to investigate is demonstrated when he remains reading files in the archive much longer than the automated lights would allow and has to trigger the lights' motion sensors at short intervals. These noticeable lengthened segments of the narrative[17] obviously serve characterisation and thematic development, but they also participate in the series' constant play with long and short durations, putting forward the human experience of time both for the characters and the viewers.

How time feels is one of the recurring themes in Walter's sessions when he talks about his life 'over there': the series' work on rhythm thus translates in perceptible terms for the audience the expansion and constriction of time reported by Walter. At the beginning of his treatment, Walter recalls the intense feeling of boredom during his deployment (E02 and E03). In the army, time felt circular: Walter wanted to escape 'the pointlessness' and 'be in a place where the days build on each other' (E04). Although Homecoming's avowed goal is to help him 'think about what comes next' (E08), it turns out that 'it's all about durability, added use' (as Colin reveals in Episode 7): the real objective is actually to keep Walter in the circle, 'rebooting' his memory thanks to the medication administered in his food, in order to get him ready for another tour of duty. During his last session (E09), Walter, who is 'excited' about the news that he will soon be redeployed, expresses a perception of time during service that is radically altered: 'The point is this will all go by really quickly. I mean, my last deployment felt like a long day.' Ironically enough, Heidi will use the same medication to extract Walter and herself from the cycle of repetitions that imprisons them both: as Walter is now 'fixed up' (E09) and ready to go back to war, Heidi is supposed to welcome and 'fix' new soldiers who have just arrived at the facility. Heidi's intentional misuse of the treatment results in a massive memory loss for both of them, enabling them to start over with no memory of their time at Homecoming.

Walter's thoughts obviously contribute to the series' critical discourse on the US army, its wars and its contracts with private companies. His words and story also reflexively echo *Homecoming*'s own negotiations between cyclic and linear storytelling, as its serialised narrative, where the episodes 'build on each other' and rely on the viewers' memory, retains strong episode delimitations that mark the recurrence of the same narrative unit and resorts to an episode format traditionally used for heavily episodic storytelling in sitcoms or in halfhour procedurals from the 1950s and the 1960s like *Dragnet* or *Peter Gunn*, which 'systematically reboot after each half-hour' (Wells-Lassagne 2017, 20).

Just as it chooses to underline its reduction of the drama episode format in its handling of the boundaries of the short episodes, *Homecoming* also makes reduction highly visible in its visual choices. Just as the series' work on rhythm makes us aware of duration, its work on the borders of the frame, on image ratio, on shot scale and camera angle draws our attention to size, playing on and sometimes troubling or even deconstructing our notions of 'small' and 'big'. Esmail linked the choice of keeping the podcast's half-hour format with his artistic project for this specific story: 'the unique thing about this story is that it was a thriller about intimate relationships[.] I wanted it to feel small' (quoted in Miller 2018). The series builds an organic connection between the content of the narrative and the perception of it by the audience, temporally but also spatially and metaphorically. Esmail's comment only hints at the polysemy of 'smallness' that unfurls in the show, where 'small' can be understood as 'short', but also 'insignificant', 'narrow', 'confined', 'reduced' or 'truncated'.

While the importance of 'intimate relationships' is reminiscent of *In Treatment*, as a thriller *Homecoming* has common points with Ben Ketai's *Chosen*, whose three seasons of six 21-to-23-minute episodes each were first released on the streaming platform Crackle between 2013 and 2014. In *Chosen*, Ian Mitchell (Milo Ventimiglia) and other people are selected by an all-powerful, mysterious organisation called The Watchers – an evil in-diegesis version of the series' viewers – to participate against their will in a cruel game: they are forced to kill the other players on pain of being killed themselves. Ian is given three days to commit the murder assigned to him. *Chosen*'s short episode duration emphasises the sense of time running out for Ian in a fast paced, action-packed narrative that relies on an inexorable countdown and end-of-episode cliffhangers – in *Homecoming* the action unfolds much more slowly, especially as each half-hour episode skips from one timeline to the other, presenting scenes happening in 2018 in alternation with others taking place in 2022, so that one conversation or short sequence of events can be split into several parts distributed over the whole episode or even into the next: thus the crucial phone call during which Heidi and Colin discuss the effects of the medication on Walter spans Episodes 7 and 8, as Episode 8 repeats the conclusion of the conversation that was shown in Episode 7, now filmed in a slightly different way, before showing its immediate effect on Heidi, in two separate sequences placed at the beginning and at the end of the episode. Although *Homecoming* and *Chosen* greatly differ in terms of rhythm, *Homecoming*'s characters are, like the victims of The Watchers in *Chosen*, ensnared in the web of the obscure but omnipresent Geist company that runs the Homecoming project.[18] Mr Geist himself, true to his name, is talked about but never actually seen throughout Season 1 (he will be embodied by an actor, Chris Cooper, only in Season 2). Heidi, a middle-aged woman embarked in a professional adventure she does not control – and hired precisely because of her lack of experience for the job; Walter, the soft-mannered young Black soldier with whom she develops a close relationship; Thomas Carrasco, the unassuming, scrupulous DOD investigator, are 'small' in front of the Geist corporation, a smallness that is reflected in

Figure 4.1 The barrel distortion of the shot makes the wall of boxes even more imposing and is a visual nod to the title of the episode.

the episodes' diminished length (Herman 2018). This is occasionally stated in the dialogue – Carrasco acknowledges that he is 'just a cog' (E07) and is called 'a good little clerk [. . .] so eager to forget the truth – that you're insignificant' by Colin in Episode 8 – but smallness is generally expressed by the images rather than the words, through *mise-en-scène* and cinematic choices. Examples of visual evocations of Carrasco's 'smallness' include a long shot where only his head can be seen, lost in a grid of half-height partitions in a big DOD office, or wide-angle shots of the archive shelves producing slightly distorted images of the stacked boxes towering over him as he starts looking for documents about the Homecoming initiative (see Figure 4.1). More generally the numerous overhead shots reduce human figures to the size of 'insects under a microscope' (Esmail, quoted in Hazelton 2018) and metaphorically imply that the characters are crushed by forces beyond their control.

The unusually narrow delimitations of the episode are also echoed in the general sense of confinement that pervades the show. The labyrinthine set of the Homecoming centre, revealed at length by the walk-and-talk sequence shot in the first episode, offers an abundance of vertical lines and frames that confer a vaguely sinister, prison-like dimension overshadowing the warm colours and muted tones of the 'hip but masculine' decorated interiors (Colin's words in Episode 1). The facility, located in Florida, is supposed to free veterans from their war traumas and provide them with the comfort of 'home', but the set was designed as a building that is 'contained and looking inward' (production designer Anastasia White, quoted in Stamp 2018). The decor

Figure 4.2 Heidi (Julia Roberts) in her office at the Homecoming centre, inside the frame formed by the vertical curtains and the horizontal windowsill (E01).

exudes 'a menacing midcentury aesthetic' (Syme 2018) that accords with the distant recollections of 1950s television brought by the half-hour format of the show. Heidi's silhouette is seen within architectural frames that visibly restrict the space surrounding her. In her office, the longer-than-wide windows, placed in an uncommonly high position, offer a limited view on the outside and lead to dimly lit shots of Roberts, dulling the star's usual radiance (see Figure 4.2).

The very first minutes of the series, while presenting a seemingly ordinary and innocuous scene (Heidi welcoming Walter for his first session), already allude to a subtext of confinement and deceiving appearances thanks to a sequence shot that starts with a trompe l'oeil: palm trees gently swaying in a starry night turn out to be a miniature décor inside a fish tank in Heidi's office. After the camera glides out of the aquarium and reveals the office, it moves towards the window. The next shot shows the exterior of the glass pane, before lingering on the palm trees in front of the Homecoming building – a full-scale, natural version of the tiny plastic trees in the fish tank. The visual parallels establish a synecdoche that will recur throughout the season, where the microcosm of the aquarium cryptically reflects the macrocosm of the centre. The Russian doll effect suggests the presence of outward layers hiding a deeper meaning, insinuating that the Homecoming centre is itself an artificial set – which it actually is, both in the diegesis and in the real-world context of the series' production (see Stamp 2018). Even as it establishes the place of the action, the sequence creates a sense of disorientation, manipulating the viewers' perception of size and scale as well as their apprehension of interior vs exterior spaces, so that when the space outside the building is finally presented – in a progression that goes against conventional procedures for setting the scene – its openness finds itself curtailed.

Continuing this play on the notions of big vs small, and open vs enclosed, the elaborate handling of the borders of the frame itself is one of the distinctive features of the series' first season. The recurring use of rectangular or square patterns and frames-within-the-frame reflexively signal *Homecoming*'s formal attachments to both the small and the big screens and allow the series to allude to its own negotiations between the two forms of audio-visual narrative. Not only does the series make generous use of the split screen, but it also alternates between two ratios, switching to a square 1:1 ratio for the events taking place in 2022, which has the effect of creating two black margins on the sides of the screen (see Figures 4.1 and 4.3). These black bars are the visual representation of the incompleteness of Heidi's memory (Esmail, quoted in Hazelton 2018) and of the information gap that the viewers as well as the characters try to fill to get 'the full picture', but they also constantly present Heidi (as well as other characters, like Carrasco) as locked up inside a square box. The sense of confinement elicited by the images of the 2018 timeline thus becomes exacerbated and permanent in the 2022 timeline, at least until Episode 8, when Heidi suddenly recovers her memory: the ratio changes until the shot fills the screen. This expansion visually illustrates Heidi's mind pushing back the borders of the frame that restricted her

Figure 4.3 Carrasco (Shea Whigham) in the stairs leading to the archive: the geometrical overhead shot uses architectural elements to embed rectangular and square frames within its reduced square boundaries and may evoke the absurdity of M.C. Escher's stairs through its flattening effect (E03).

memory until she heard the once-familiar grunt of the pelican, triggering her complete recollection of what happened at Homecoming.[19]

Once the mysteries have been solved and Heidi decides to go to California in search of Walter, the last episode uses the split screen in an upbeat fashion, in a montage of moments from Heidi's long road trip, compressing over 2 minutes her whole expedition across the country. The multiple frames and ellipses stress Heidi's determination despite her tiredness and the repetitiveness of the trip, the sequence also tapping into the American myth of the reparative and redemptive powers of going West. The smaller, black-framed screens expanding and wiping laterally or vertically within the screen offer images that dynamically match with each other or look similar, the little frames no longer evoking confinement or loss but the pieces of a jigsaw puzzle being assembled and reassembled as Heidi comes to terms with her past and her fragmented identity (see Figures 4.4 and 4.5). Even if Heidi still looks very small, or even invisible, in these cropped shots, even if the expanse of forest and the straight line of the road are cut short in framed aerial shots, the sequence, with the help of Eels' energetic rock song 'Tremendous Dynamite', conveys a sense of freedom and renewed hope. Ultimately, then, Heidi and the other 'small' characters find their own unspectacular ways to resist the oppression of the system in which they are caught, even if Colin's demise at the very end, after the Homecoming centre has been closed, causes no real damage to the hydra-like Geist corporation, and instead opens up perspectives for the second season. Both Heidi and Walter eventually manage to secure spaces where they can

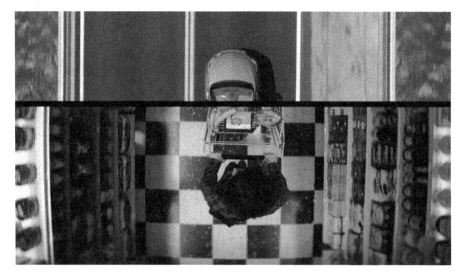

Figure 4.4 A shot of Heidi's car gradually replaces the matching overhead shot of Heidi shopping, creating continuity between the two shots separated by a black horizontal line (E10).

Figure 4.5 All in one: Heidi's road trip as a way for her to start putting together the pieces of her splintered identity (E10).

regain personal freedom – Heidi's leap of faith when giving the powerful dose of medication to herself and Walter is validated as the right course of action by Walter's mother's words ('He's finally back to who he was before this whole mess', 'He's finally where he belongs', E10) and by the very end of the season that shows Walter building a wooden deck in front of a cabin in the woods, apparently leading a happy new life where 'the days build on each other'.

Ultimately the series' legitimation of 'smallness', both as an aesthetic and an ethical value, became an effective strategy of distinction in the context of Peak TV. *Homecoming*'s first season was unique in its articulation of short episode length, reduced ratio and embedded frames, all combining to support the narrative themes of confinement and memory loss but also to make noticeably perceptible the material conditions of the narrative's representation both in time and in space. With its singular work on time, rhythm and episodic division, it continued the experiments in 'narrative spectacle' (Mittell 2006, 35) previously carried out by shows such as *In Treatment*, but also *The Affair* (Showtime, 2014–19), with its *Rashomon*-style narrative and its episodes' explicit two-part structure, or even *24* (Fox, 2001–10; 2014) and its 'real-time' storytelling. Rather than being swallowed in the mass of television content, *Homecoming* was the object of much critical attention and praise. It reaffirmed the value of episodic division at a moment when critic Alan Sepinwall had written two pieces 'in defence of the episode' (in 2015 and 2017) and when the expression 'Netflix bloat' had been coined to express irritation at overly long dramas (see for instance Miller 2018). *Homecoming*'s reconfigurations of the prestige model, despite a certain amount of ambiguity as the series consistently tried to get the best of both worlds, worked in the show's favour at a time when the 'quality' drama had become criticised for its solidification into a predictable formula, even as it was supposed to be more creative than other TV content (see Hill 2013 and VanArendonk 2017). In a 2018 piece, *Vulture* critic VanArendonk wrote that 'overly long TV episodes feel like self-important prestige signaling, more about muscle (and budget) flexing than they are about the best way to serve a story' (VanArendonk 2018).[20] Such criticisms suggest that the time was ripe for shorter forms of drama,[21] and *Homecoming*, in its own paradoxical way, with both its arguably 'self-important' cinematic style and references, and its ethics and aesthetics of smallness, successfully shook up the prestige recipe.[22]

NOTES

1. The second season was released on 22 May 2020. It has seven episodes, ranging from 25 to 38 minutes in length. The narrative of the first season is to a large extent self-contained, with an ending that has uncertainties, but is not suspenseful. Although Season 2 offers a sequel to the events of Season 1, it introduces a new female lead character (Jacqueline Calico/Alex Eastern), played by Janelle Monáe, and a new plot involving memory loss. The cast, but also the crew, were thoroughly renewed, most notably the director, cinematographer and production designer (see IMDb, 'Homecoming [TV Series 2018–2020] Full Cast & Crew'). For all these reasons, this contribution will solely focus on Season 1.
2. This is what John Landgraf explained about the extended episodes of the fifth season of FX's *Sons of Anarchy* in 2012 (Levine 2012). See also VanArendonk 2018.
3. See VanArendonk (2017) for a gleefully sarcastic 'Vulture list' of these markers that perceptively distils the distinction strategies at work in today's discourses and practices of prestige television. On prestige television, also see Friedman and Keeler 2022.
4. See Mittell 2006, 31, 37, 39.
5. Available here: https://www.youtube.com/watch?v=9WJSdpE-sJQ
6. For instance at the end of the trailer, one of Roberts' lines from a dialogue about Shrier in Episode 4 was truncated so that it took a much more general meaning, as 'You're worried about him' became 'You're worried.'
7. See Bastién 2018, Zoller Seitz 2018 and Grobar 2019 for examples of the series' multiple references to films.
8. In return, one can assume that, in terms of costs, securing the stellar cast as well as the technical expertise, amount of work and budget necessitated both by the cinematographic style and this unusual choice in the composition of the soundtrack was facilitated by the short length of the episodes and of the ten-episode season as a whole.
9. For instance, *Game of Thrones* was called a '73-hour movie' by its creators: see VanArendonk 2017.

10. *In Treatment* was based on Israeli series *BeTipul* (HOT3, 2005–8), which was adapted in many countries: see Vincent Poymiro's interview in the present volume.
11. For instance the 'Week 3' session is replaced by off-session encounters in Episodes 3, 4 and 5; 'Week 4' is in Episode 6 and is interrupted by Walter's mother's arrival; 'Week 5' and 'Week 6' are respectively in Episodes 7 and 9.
12. For instance, flashbacks to Heidi's job interview in Episode 9.
13. The last episode of Season 1 ends with a cut to a black screen presenting the credits. However there is a short post-credits scene ending on Audrey rubbing a mysterious roll-on on her wrists, a teaser for the second season.
14. See Florent Favard's contribution in the present volume for a discussion of Newman's article.
15. While they do fulfil a function in narrative terms (Esmail's intention was to suggest 'a meditative, dreamlike state' and to create an unsettling sense of menace), they were also a way for Esmail to play with the binge-watching model, because '[he] knew it would all be dropped on Amazon in one day' (see Zoller Seitz 2018).
16. See TV Tropes, 'Every Episode Ending' (I thank Shannon Wells-Lassagne for pointing this out to me). The freeze-frame (which was often accompanied by the applause from the audience) offers a clear signal that the episode is now concluded, returning the televisual image to its two-dimensional nature.
17. Another example is in the long 'walk-and-talk' phone conversation between Heidi and Colin in Episode 1, when Colin can be heard admonishing other people for a little while, leaving Heidi (and the viewer) unsure whether the conversation is actually over.
18. The 'faceless conglomerate' is also found in *Mr. Robot*: see Herman 2018, for this parallel and others.
19. The 2018 timeline contains the symmetrical reduction of the image ratio in Episode 10, figuring the effect of the massive dose of medication ingested by Heidi on her last day at the Homecoming centre.
20. In this article, VanArendonk interestingly addresses the overlapping of gender hierarchies with assumptions about episode length. It is beyond the scope of the present contribution to discuss *Homecoming*'s own paradoxical challenging of 'masculinised' drama and the differences between the first and the second season (which replaces the muted heterosexual attraction between Heidi and Walter with the same-sex relationship between Alex and Audrey).
21. Later examples include *Limetown* (Facebook Watch, 2019), *A Teacher* (FX on Hulu, 2020) or *Keep Breathing* (Netflix, 2022).
22. Several colleagues gave me precious feedback on earlier versions of this chapter: I warmly thank them.

WORKS CITED

24, created by Joel Surnow and Robert Cochran, Fox, 2001–10; 2014.
A Teacher, created by Hannah Fidell, FX on Hulu, 2020.

Barker, Cory, '"Great Shows, Thanks to You": From Participatory Culture to "Quality TV" in Amazon's Pilot Season', *Television & New Media* 18, no. 5 (2017): 441–58.

Bastién, Angelica Jade, '*Homecoming*: Every Major Pop-Culture Reference and Influence', *Vulture*, 12 November 2018.

BeTipul, created by Hagai Levi, Ori Sivan and Nir Bergman, HOT3, 2005–8.

Butler, Jeremy G., *The Sitcom* (New York: Routledge, 2020).

Chosen, created by Ben Ketai and Ryan Lewis, Crackle, 2013–14.

Curtin, Michael and Jane Shattuc, *The American Television Industry* (London, New York: Bloomsbury, 2018 [originally published by Palgrave Macmillan, 2009]).

Dragnet, created by Jack Webb, NBC, 1951–9.

Elsaesser, Thomas and Malte Hagener, *Film Theory: An Introduction through the Senses* (New York: Routledge, 2010).

Friedman, Seth and Amanda Keele, eds, *Prestige Television: Cultural and Artistic Value in Twenty-First-Century America* (New Brunswick: Rutgers University Press, 2022).

Game of Thrones, created by David Benioff and D.B. Weiss, HBO, 2011–19.

Grobar, Matt, '"Homecoming" Cinematographer Tod Campbell Finds His "Kubrick Shot" For '70s Paranoid Thriller', *Deadline*, 3 June 2019.

IMDb, 'Homecoming (TV Series 2018–2020) Full Cast & Crew', available online: https://www.imdb.com/title/tt7008682/fullcredits/?ref_=tt_cl_sm (Accessed February 2024).

In Treatment, developed by Rodrigo Garcia, HBO, 2008–10; 2021.

Hazelton, John, 'The Story behind Amazon's New Drama "Homecoming" Starring Julia Roberts', *Screendaily*, 16 October 2018.

Herman, Alison, '"Homecoming" is a Victory for Amazon – and Sam Esmail', *The Ringer*, 5 November 2018.

Hill, Logan, 'The 13 Rules for Creating a Prestige TV Drama', *Vulture*, 15 May 2013.

Homecoming, created by Eli Horowitz and Micah Bloomberg, Amazon Prime Video, 2018–20.

Jenner, Mareike, *Netflix and the Re-Invention of Television* (Cambridge: Palgrave Macmillan, 2018 [eBook]).

Keep Breathing, created by Martin Gero and Brendan Gall, Netflix, 2022.

Levine, Stuart, '"Sons of Anarchy" stretches episode length – 90 minutes becomes the norm for hot FX series', *Variety*, 26 November 2012.

Limetown, created by Zack Akers and Skip Bronkie, Facebook Watch, 2019.

Miller, Liz Shannon, 'From "Homecoming" to "Maniac," 30-Minute Episodes Solve TV's Pacing Problem', *IndieWire*, 15 November 2018.

Mittell, Jason, *Genre and Television: From Cop Shows to Cartoons in American Culture* (New York and London: Routledge, 2004).

Mittell, Jason, 'Narrative Complexity in Contemporary American Television', *The Velvet Light Trap*, no. 58 (Fall 2006): 29–40.

Mittell, Jason, 'Film and Television Narrative', in *The Cambridge Companion to Narrative*, ed. David Herman (Cambridge: Cambridge University Press, 2007), 156–71.

Mr. Robot, created by Sam Esmail, USA Network, 2015–19.

Newman, Michael Z. and Elana Levine, *Legitimating Television: Media Convergence and Cultural Status* (New York: Routledge, 2012 [eBook]).

Newman, Michael Z., 'From Beats to Arcs: Toward a Poetic of Television Narrative', *The Velvet Light Trap*, no. 58 (Fall 2006): 16–28.

O'Falt, Chris, '"Homecoming": All the Classic Movie Soundtracks in the Series – and Why Sam Esmail Used Them', *IndieWire*, 5 November 2018.

Peter Gunn, created by Blake Edwards, NBC, 1958–60; ABC, 1960–1.

Patten, Dominic, '"Homecoming" Review: Julia Roberts Series is Too Much Style, Little Substance', *Deadline*, 1 November 2018.

Poniewozik, James, 'Review: "Homecoming" is Military, Industrial and Complex', *The New York Times*, 31 October 2018 (online).

Rashomon, directed by Akira Kurosawa, 1950.

Rose, Lacey and Marisa Guthrie, 'FX Chief John Landgraf on Content Bubble: "This Is Simply Too Much Television"', *The Hollywood Reporter*, 7 August 2015.

Sandberg, Bryn, and Lacey Rose, 'TV's Age of Entitlement: Why Episodes Are Now So Damn Long', *The Hollywood Reporter*, 8 June 2017.

Shattuc, Jane, 'Netflix, Inc. and Online Television', in *A Companion to Television*, 2nd Edition, eds Janet Wasko and Eileen R. Meehan (Hoboken: Wiley Blackwell, 2020), 145–64.

Stamp, Elizabeth, 'How the Sets of Amazon's *Homecoming* Helped Julia Roberts Get Into Character', *AD*, 1 November 2018.

Stuever, Hank, 'What's More Enticing than Julia Roberts Starring in a TV Drama? How About Half-hour Episodes?', *The Washington Post*, 1 November 2018.

Surrey, Miles, 'In Praise of the 30-Minute Drama', *The Ringer*, 6 November 2018.

Syme, Rachel, 'The Menacing Midcentury Aesthetic of Prestige TV', *The New Republic*, 12 November 2018.

The Affair, created by Sarah Treem and Hagai Levi, Showtime, 2014–19.

The Romanoffs, created by Matthew Weiner, Amazon Prime Video, 2018.

TV Tropes, 'Every Episode Ending', available online: https://tvtropes.org/pmwiki/pmwiki.php/Main/EveryEpisodeEnding (Accessed February 2024).

Tryon, Chuck, 'TV Got Better: Netflix's Original Programming Strategies and the On-demand Television Transition', *Media Industries Journal* 2, no. 2 (2015): 104–16.

VanArendonk, Kathryn, '13 Signs You're Watching a "Prestige" TV Show', *Vulture*, 28 March 2017.

VanArendonk, Kathryn, 'Overly Long Episodes Are the Manspreading of TV', *Vulture*, 22 April 2018.

Volpe, Allie, 'The One Thing That Isn't Evolving With Netflix & Hulu's Takeover of TV', *Thrillist*, 16 October 2017.

Watercutter, Angela, 'Sam Esmail's *Homecoming* Is Nothing Like *Mr. Robot*', *Wired*, 2 November 2018.

Wayne, Michael L., 'Netflix, Amazon, and Branded Television Content in Subscription Video-On-Demand Portals', *Media, Culture & Society* 40, no.5 (2018): 725–41.

Wells-Lassagne, Shannon, *Television and Serial Adaptation* (New York: Routledge, 2017).

Westworld, created by Jonathan Nolan and Lisa Joy, HBO, 2016–22.

Zoller Seitz, Matt, 'How Sam Esmail Directed the Hell Out of Homecoming', *Vulture*, 14 November 2018.

CHAPTER 5

Twin Peaks, 25 Years Later: Whatever Happens Happens Now, and Nothing Else Matters

Benjamin Campion

The overall trend in American television is 'continuum' scheduling (Thompson 2003, 6), opening seasons conceived as 'pilots' (VanDerWerff 2015) or 'supersized movies' and extended episodes which can be compared to full-length features in extreme cases. Dramas, and even serialised cable and SVOD comedies, are running faster and faster after the promise of a conclusion that is supposed to justify any narrative prevarication. Loops have been superseded by arcs.

However, some concerns have begun to be raised about this blurring of boundaries between TV series and movies, criticising it for neglecting the major asset that is segmentation between continuous yet autonomous units within the TV season. In a two-part column posted in 2015 and 2017, Alan Sepinwall notably objected to the ongoing 'novelization' of storytelling, advocating for a reconsideration of episodes as independent objects instead of mere elements of a larger whole. A few months later, while scrutinising the narrative stratagems of the third season of *Twin Peaks* (ABC, 1990–91; Showtime, 2017), Stéphane Delorme made a statement worth discussing in more detail: 'The show reasserts the importance of individual scenes'[1] (Delorme October 2017, 17). Making every episode relevant, and allowing each scene to find its own logic, are two unconventional gestures in the current television landscape that will be examined in reference to *Twin Peaks*' long-awaited comeback, referred to hereafter as 'The Return', as officially promoted since 2017.

To this end, I will first analyse the journey through a mushroom cloud as depicted in S03E08, questioning this fictional fragment, itself reminiscent of avant-garde cinema, and its relationship to seriality and to micro/macro storytelling. Subsequently, I'll pursue Stéphane Delorme's reflection on scenes as coherent and complete entities, allowing David Lynch – as the director and sound designer of the eighteen episodes of *The Return* – to reintroduce 'time' as characterised by a 'rapid succession of short segments' (Newman 2006, 17), often associated with a highly debatable notion of narrative 'efficiency', along with the disruption of consumption patterns (Lotz 2007) in the era of peak TV (Rose and Guthrie 2015). To do so, I will examine the short scene in S03E12 showing Dougie's son launching a baseball directly into his father's thorax, with no apparent reaction from the latter. Simultaneously, I will study a significantly longer scene from the same episode in which Gordon Cole (played by David Lynch) asks a glamorous and mannered French female friend to go and wait for him in the lobby bar. The juxtaposition suggests that, as 'dispensable' as these two scenes may appear from a diegetic perspective (removing them from the final cut would not prevent us from understanding what is going on, as long as one can make sense of *Twin Peaks*' nebulous story . . .), their presence in the same episode dialectically enlightens us about the formal (thus substantive) purpose of such an iconoclastic revival.

Due to the 'elliptic nature of many of their plotlines', Willem Strank considers that 'neither *Twin Peaks* nor David Lynch's work in general have been particularly famous for their narrative achievements' (Strank 2023, 47). Yet this elliptical nature can be countered by a desire to meditate on the notion of the moment, regardless of what comes before or next, without delving into memories or trying to anticipate the outcome. In a way, *Twin Peaks* borrows the serial form to better emancipate itself from the redundancy associated with seriality. It is certainly a 'returning television series comprising eighteen episodes' (Hills 2020, 97), but one that seeks to place itself in a 'liminal, auteurist class of its own' (Hills 2020, 99). In this chapter, I'll argue that this quest for singularity meets a desire to restore serial fragments (episodes, scenes) to their full integrity. Beyond simple narrative comprehension, *The Return* is a sensorial experience of every moment.

ONE EPISODE TO MAKE HISTORY

A purely aesthetic experience

As Alan Sepinwall emphasised in his two-part column in defence of the episode (against the 'threat' of novelisation on the one hand, against the assimilation of TV with film on the other), if a given episode of a TV show looks like any other, we may consider that segmentation no longer really matters; if resolution rhymes with satisfaction, it can by no means compensate for the boredom engendered by superfluous detours and false leads aiming to fill a few more hours of fiction (Sepinwall 2015). This is especially true since, according to the TV critic, 'an episode doesn't have to be standalone in story to stand alone in form and function' (Sepinwall 2017). From *Breaking Bad* (AMC, 2008–13) to

The Leftovers (HBO, 2014–17), from *Mad Men* (AMC, 2007–15) to *Fargo* (FX, 2014–present), from *Mr. Robot* (USA Network, 2015–19) to *You're the Worst* (FX/FXX, 2014–19), modern serialised TV series have the precious ability to escape from themselves and from their own seriality, once their fictional world has been implanted in our brains. This is of course a radical change from the episodic narrative template of procedurals like *Columbo* (NBC, 1968–78; ABC, 1989–2003) or *CSI* (CBS, 2000–15). Walter White may well suspend his methamphetamine production for three quarters of an hour, chasing a fly that is getting on his nerves ('Fly', S03E10), but the viewer remains cognizant of his past struggles and the uncertainty of his future.

Words in parenthesis aren't isolated from the rest of the sentence; similarly, while segments breaking with seasonal or even series patterns are often called 'bottle episodes', every episode of a TV series ultimately shares the same DNA, regardless of its specific features. The eighth episode of *The Return*, 'Gotta Light?',[2] exemplifies this observation, combining a unique sensorial experience with more or less fleeting intertextuality.

Its mushroom cloud scene opens as a somewhat conventional flashback, with a degree of contextualisation that had rarely been achieved by *Twin Peaks* beforehand. We are in White Sands, New Mexico, on July 16, 1945, 5.29 am – i.e. the exact location and time of the (real life) first detonation of a nuclear weapon, Trinity, conducted by the United States Army as part of the Manhattan Project (Figure 5.1). The accompanying atonal music chosen by David Lynch is – as mentioned in the end credits – *Threnody for the Victims of Hiroshima*, a piece written by the Polish composer Krzysztof Penderecki to

Figure 5.1 A mushroom cloud in White Sands, New Mexico, on 16 July 1945 (S03E08).

pay tribute to the residents of Hiroshima who were killed or injured by the atomic weapon.[3] As surreal and indescribable as this turning point in the history of mankind may be, it can hardly be qualified as fictitious or phantasmagorical. Facts are dated, located and inscribed in all our minds.

Then everything goes awry. We penetrate the heart of the mushroom cloud (which means literally going *inside* a picture so frequently invoked for its intolerable plastic beauty that it can't extend beyond a diluted cliché), and ink clouds invade the screen as if they were projected by giant octopuses, plagues of frantic blank patches spread over an invisible prey, and black and white (to be considered here as fully-fledged colours) are joined by other vivid and ever-changing hues, inner fireworks that emerge from a succession of shimmering explosions, as flames rain down upon rock walls like lava flows, before an asynchronous musical transition takes us to the next scene: the (no less staggering) convenience store sequence, which will later play an important part in the rest of the story.

What is striking at this stage of the analysis is the insistence with which this eighth part of *The Return*[4] refuses to give us any explanation, or any way of understanding what is happening on the screen. From the 16th to the 57th minute of the episode, long cryptic scenes keep flashing before our eyes, which are largely unspecifiable in the absence of a strictly formalist rhetoric. Nonetheless, *our immersion is genuine*, for the 'purely aesthetic experience', the 'poetics of absolute mystery' (Hatchuel 2016, 244–5) do not equate to a denial of our need to figure out what we are being told; on the contrary, they are a revelation of *Twin Peaks*' deepest meaning – that evil is out there, and that it would be pointless to pretend otherwise.

Through duration, *The Return* thus gives new strength to the supposedly unitary and ephemeral object we call a television episode. 'Gotta Light?' is a performance that can be watched over and over again; considering the first two seasons of *The Sopranos* (HBO, 1999–2007) were repeatedly screened at the Museum of Modern Art (MoMA) in February 2001 (James 2001), it's not difficult to imagine the journey through a mushroom cloud depicted in *The Return* being played on a loop between the walls of the prestigious New York museum. The episode manages to extricate itself from the relentless televisual flow (and even more so, from SVOD's 'streamed at-your-disposal' images), rotating instead on its own axis like a self-sufficient piece of art. In the same way that a movie is reborn every time a new screening begins, this episode aims to leave a mark on the viewer's mind beyond its material existence.

Intertextuality and macro storytelling

However, autonomy does not always mean independence. And although *The Return*'s episodes may be watched in a random order – the final blasphemy for seriality's apostles – it does not prevent them from dialoguing, sharing and interacting over time. We should note that 'Gotta Light?' resumes the story exactly where the previous episode left off (Mr. C and Ray escaped from prison, driving by night), and that it does not shrink from serial repetition, in so far as it begins with the season's unchanging opening title sequence. Besides, this eighth episode anticipates – but does not neglect – the live musical performance that usually concludes each episode (or so) of *The Return*: in this case, we watch the American industrial rock band Nine Inch Nails playing 'She's Gone Away', just before the beginning of the pre-apocalyptic countdown.

Let's also emphasise that early warning signs of the forthcoming deflagration had started to emerge in previous episodes, such as a large painting of a mushroom cloud that featured prominently in S03E03 (Figure 5.2) and S03E07, inside Gordon Cole's office (we note how the characters' gaze, whether they have their eyes open or not, is directed towards the starting point of our strange journey to come). Cole's office also includes a portrait of Franz Kafka (Figure 5.3) and a photograph of corn cobs that leave room for a great deal of interpretation – a 'forensic fandom' (Mittell 2015, 52) approach I will voluntarily avoid, only highlighting that those subliminal images, as well as

Figure 5.2–3 Early signs of the forthcoming deflagration: a painting of a mushroom cloud and a portrait of Franz Kafka (S03E03).

the ink clouds, the golden orb (S03E03), the gas station (S03E14, S03E15) and, of course, the recurring portrait of Laura Palmer, flow between episodes like stimuli of a weird eerie world to which we now belong. More than ever, *Twin Peaks* replays – and sometimes reconfigures – its own images and its own sounds, thus mixing the characteristics of film (one director, the ability to shoot and edit the whole feature before airing) with those of television (a nearly 18-hour running time, with separate episodes aired weekly).

Therefore, the episode stands by itself as it stands by its relationship to a bigger project; micro storytelling blends with macro storytelling, which is precisely the kind of hybridity that enables modern TV series to be more than supersized movies. Making every episode special, enjoyable, festive, without rejecting any pleasure to come, is one of the major challenges that peak TV's (online or broadcast) series will have to face in the coming years, in order to continue their artistic rise and to engrave more than a few evanescent recollections in our memories. Although I have focused so far on matters of integrity and autonomy from an *episode* point of view, this arguably applies even more to *scenes*.

TWO SCENES SHARING BURLESQUE VIRTUES

Twin Peaks: a 'full-length feature'?

The sharp and provocative spirit of the *Cahiers du cinéma*'s 'young Turks' is definitely not dead.[5] In a typically 'Godardian' divisive gesture, Stéphane Delorme and his editorial staff chose to elect the 18 hours of *Twin Peaks*' third season 'Movie of the year 2017' (Anon. December 2017, 6–7), without taking into account any time limitation nor any division into separate episodes, contrary to film festival programmers, members of financing programs and selection committees tasked with awarding prizes. David Lynch is a (cinema) auteur, thus *The Return* is an auteur movie: QED. And to finalise this assimilation/reappropriation process, the film journal – which increasingly tends to address TV series in recent years, albeit focusing more specifically on 'signature' pieces of work like *True Detective* (HBO, 2014–present) 'by' Cary J. Fukunaga, *Stranger Things* (Netflix, 2016–present) 'by' the Duffer Brothers, *Mindhunter* (Netflix, 2017–19) 'by' David Fincher – takes a malicious pleasure in honouring what it specifically refers to as '*Twin Peaks* by David Lynch' (Anon. December 2017, 6). This makes it even harder to know what is being rewarded: the third season, or the whole series? Labelling a TV series consisting of multiple episodes – and even more so, of multiple seasons – as a 'movie' apt to compete with strictly cinematographic and sometimes very brief pictures by Philippe Garrel or Hong Sang-soo is an example of how the (French) film press fulfils its self-centred fantasy of conscripting 'auteur TV series' into a global cinematic landscape.

It seems unnecessary to argue that, apart from *Fire Walk with Me* (David Lynch, 1992), *Twin Peaks* is not a 'full-length feature' (Lynch 2017, 14): that is just good common sense, though the fact that the debate about the relationship between television and film rages on nearly seven decades after TV series appeared onscreen raises its own questions. Let's just emphasise a few more incongruous facts that show the amount of work required if we are to consider TV series as an art form in their own right. As if they were trapped in an unsettling time paradox, the *Cahiers du cinéma* have notably opted for episode guides in two separate issues (Anon. July–August 2017 & October 2017); entitled one of their articles dedicated to *The Return* 'Developing a TV Series' (Béghin 2017), then named it 'number one of our Top Ten movies list' (Delorme December 2017, 5); used in the same editorial words like 'series', 'film' (supposedly with David Lynch's blessing, 'in his own words'), 'cinema coming to television' (again, apparently repeating after Lynch), and 'films [. . .] produced by television' (Delorme December 2017, 5). One would be tempted to think that words have lost any meaning, that lines may blur as long as critics are not prevented from taking any opportunity to appropriate the 'greatest event of the decade'. Stéphane Delorme goes so far as to explain to the reader that, since David Lynch has chosen to express himself through 'poetic logic' (quite a paradoxical choice of words) instead of 'storytelling' intended to keep viewers breathless, he manages to bring the magic of cinema to television and, incidentally, to free the 'box' from its coercive tendency towards pure action.

May the scene find its own way

Rather than pursuing the auteurist 'series as a movie' approach, this analysis will attempt to build a bridge between cinema and television without denying each medium's structural and formal specificities, as a way of demonstrating that dissimilar artistic forms may nevertheless share the same techniques of expression in the short and medium term, and thus intermittently speak the same language. When Stéphane Delorme affirms that *Twin Peaks* – and more specifically its third season – 'reasserts the importance of individual scenes' (October 2017, 16), we can ultimately consider that he opens the door to a constructive dialogue between film critics and TV scholars. Since scenes – and, to a greater extent, shots – tend to drown in the ocean of relentless images that shape a full-length movie, this is especially true in the case of TV series lasting tens, hundreds or even thousands of hours intended to satisfy the hunger of those insatiable ogres: the viewers.

I propose to study two seemingly 'dispensable' scenes of S03E12 as a response to this supposedly 'foregone conclusion': one short baseball 'interaction' between Sonny Jim Jones and his catatonic dad, Dougie

(Figure 5.4), and one very long hotel room scene in which Gordon Cole asks a 'French woman' (as mentioned in the end credits) to go and wait for him in the lobby bar (Figure 5.5). The two scenes appear as a study in contrasts: brevity (30 seconds) versus lengthiness (3 minutes and 10 seconds, which feel much longer); muteness and minimalist gestures (the players' entrance under the leadership of Sonny Jim, the pitch, and the marked absence of a reaction from Dougie) versus functional speech (a swaggering police story told by Gordon Cole, a seduction catchphrase – 'I'll call you in the bar' – said twice by the same Cole as a way of convincing his one-night stand not to walk away), blended with moves so slow and refined one can't help but suspect they deliberately confront us with the 'experience of (serial) repetition' (Verevis 2023, 61); closure versus an open-ended conclusion leading to a more serious debate between Cole and Albert Rosenfield (typically the kind

Figure 5.4 Sonny Jim Jones tries to play baseball with his catatonic dad, Dougie (S03E12).

Figure 5.5 Gordon Cole has a great time with an exquisite French lady dressed in red (S03E12).

of discussion a traditional TV series or theatrical feature would have opened the scene with).

Everything seems to oppose these two scenes, yet they share the same completeness, the same taste for micro closure (an absolute lack of reaction from Dougie on the one hand, David Lynch alias Gordon Cole's look at the camera and complicit smile on the other), the same balance between duration, pace and fulfilment resulting from their symbiosis. Dougie is here to play baseball in the family home's garden with his only son, and that means more than any futile 'chit chat' shared through the speaker of a smartphone from the other side of the country. Likewise, since a chic style 'à la française' is not dead, Gordon Cole seems determined not to miss any part of it, even if that means slowing his ongoing investigation and incidentally exasperating one of his closest collaborators, the poor Rosenfield. Once again, *Twin Peaks* demonstrates that the comedy of the absurd does not follow a given order; it comes to life as the scene unfolds before our eyes.

This also applies to editing – a task assigned to the American film director and editor Duwayne Dunham in the case of *Twin Peaks*. Our first scene consists of a single shot (apart from two short opening establishing shots), which is explicit enough to testify to a re-established harmony between the father and his son-in-charge. Conversely, the second scene uses cuts to isolate and make fun of Rosenfield's downcast face, as the miserable sidekick holds the role of an unwanted guest who is anything but pleased to have to play third wheel to the two lovebirds. As an ideal comic counterpart to Cole and his facetious conquest playing seductive games in front of him, Rosenfield constantly appears alone on screen (Figure 5.6) once the object of contention has been visually materialised: I mean the French 'femme fatale', the disturbing tip of a triangle that is anything but loving.

Figure 5.6 Albert Rosenfield appears alone onscreen, in front of Gordon Cole and his French conquest sharing intimacy (S03E12).

On the one hand, Cole and his girlfriend's straightforward shared intimacy systematically takes form through the presence of one's body in the foreground of the other's medium shot, and vice versa. Furthermore, as a counterpoint to the glamorous French lady's way of dragging out each of her movements (slowly donning her black cardigan, adjusting her breasts, retrieving her red and black stiletto, raising a leg like a cabaret dancer, applying lipstick one more time, slowly sipping red wine, pulling down her skirt a little bit, blowing her suitor a promise-filled kiss, and at long last posing like Ava Gardner before leaving the hotel room), we see Rosenfield's low-key but at the very least explicit facial expressions. By successively blinking quickly, frowning, raising his eyebrows, sweeping his bald head and letting out a long sigh synonymous with extreme exasperation, Gordon Cole's disgruntled underling makes no secret of his deep discontent. Like any slow-burn gag, this one reveals itself over time through subtle variations, the kind which only (intrinsically serial) repetition can provide.

Each one of the two scenes just analysed therefore has its own grammar, its own logic, its own dialectic (coming together/remaining separated), in a word, its own *life*. For, to quote Walter Murch (Francis Ford Coppola's long-time film editor and sound designer): 'Editing is not so much about putting pieces together as finding a path' (Murch 2011, 26). Whether or not you have seen *The Return*'s behind-the-scenes, whether or not you know when it was decided this scene would contain just one shot and that one, a dozen, what *does* matter is that the scene finds its own path (through writing, directing, editing) and conveys emotions – even, dare I say, pleasure – to us. That is where the truth lies, beyond any attempt at interpreting a TV series as consciously indecipherable as *Twin Peaks*. Some might end up convincing themselves they have uncovered the meaning of 'Blue Rose' or the role of Judy in this whole story, but this will never replace the delight of savouring the genuine taste of each scene like sweets randomly grabbed in a box of chocolates.

CONCLUSION

This analysis examined only one episode (though admittedly an iconic one) and two scenes relying on the slow-burn technique created by exploiting episode duration and slowly (albeit briefly) turning the ordinariness of a daily situation into pure nonsense. Yet there is no shortage of choices, between the meticulous never-ending sweeping at the Roadhouse (S03E07), the 'game of liar's poker' between Lucy and Andy Brennan arguing over whether to shop for a red or a beige chair online (S03E09), the pink-clad Candie's fly hunt ending up with her boss Rodney being smacked with a remote control (S03E10), the endless domestic talk between Audrey Horne and her 'indoor' husband Charlie (S03E12), and the (literal) loop of a boxing match displayed on Sarah

Palmer's TV screen (S03E13). As to the French lady's power of seduction, it is far from being *The Return*'s only erotic appeal, if one refers to Busby Berkeley-like leg shots and to multiple female rolling gaits caught by Lynch's playful camera throughout the season.

Consequently, far be it from me to suggest that the apocalyptic episode and the two dialectical scenes I've chosen to focus on are 'unique' and exempt from any recurrence obligation in relation with seriality. But what is striking when studying *Twin Peaks*' third season is the extent to which the series' move to premium cable evidently freed it from the constraints of narrative 'efficiency' and the unnatural cliffhangers intended to make viewers more or less consciously want to tune in again the following week. TV series are not just a matter of postponed delight and 'oh-now-all-is-clear' resolution; they also – and above all – engage perception and comprehension of images full of life, spontaneity and, in Lynchian cases, mystery.

Perhaps it is time to consider TV series as a contemporary art form instead of systematically underlining their legacy – serial literature, radio dramas, daytime soap operas – as has become customary for many scholars over the past decade, in television and elsewhere. For, as indisputable as such a statement may be, TV's new era (as initiated by HBO in the late 1990s) should not cause us to forget that there is still a window for synergy between episodic and serial television – whether the latter is told through a 'flexi-narrative' (Nelson 1997, 24), a 'multistrand narrative' (Corner 1999, 57–8) or a 'long-term television narrative' (Lavery 2009). In any case, what counts the most is right here, right now. The future can wait.

NOTES

1. Every French-to-English translation is carried out by the author.
2. A title chosen by Showtime rather than David Lynch, according to the director's 'feature-length' theory.
3. The same piece would thereafter be heard in *Black Mirror*'s robot episode, 'Metalhead' (S04E05), triggering a comparable feeling of atonal vertigo as its fictional world falls into a state of horror.
4. David Lynch uses the term 'part', obviously a more cinematographic expression than 'episode'.
5. In the 1950s, challenging traditional cinema was a way for French critics and aspiring filmmakers like François Truffaut, Jean-Luc Godard and Claude Chabrol to make their own place in a tightly closed environment (hence the nickname 'young Turks'). As explains Robert B. Ray: 'The one major exception to this rule, *auteurism*, or the view that film ought to express the unique sensibility of the individual filmmaker, may owe its long life to its origins in a particular problem: the young Turks at the *Cahiers du cinéma* were, after all, trying to figure out how to break into the French film industry' (Ray 2006, 107).

WORKS CITED

Anon., 'Résumés', *Cahiers du cinéma* 735, July–August 2017, 34–5.
Anon., 'Résumés', *Cahiers du cinéma* 737, October 2017, 34–5.
Anon., 'Top Ten 2017 de la rédaction', *Cahiers du cinéma* 739, December 2017, 6–7.
Béghin, Cyril, 'Faire une série', *Cahiers du cinéma* 735, July–August 2017, 14–15.
Breaking Bad, created by Vince Gilligan, AMC, 2008–13.
Columbo, created by Richard Levinson and William Link, NBC, 1968–78; ABC, 1989–2003.
Corner, John, *Critical Ideas in Television Studies* (Oxford: Clarendon Press, 1999).
CSI, created by Anthony E. Zuiker , CBS, 2000–15.
Delorme, Stéphane, 'Le réveil', *Cahiers du cinéma* 737, October 2017, 16–18.
Delorme, Stéphane, 'Mystère', *Cahiers du cinéma* 739, December 2017, 5.
Delorme, Stéphane and Tessé, Jean-Philippe, 'Mystery Man', *Cahiers du cinéma* 739, December 2015, 8–18.
Fargo, created by Noah Hawley, FX, 2014–present.
Fire Walk with Me, directed by David Lynch, CIBY Pictures, 1992.
Hatchuel, Sarah, *Rêves et séries américaines. La fabrique d'autres mondes* (Aix-en-Provence: Rouge profond, 2016).
Hills, Matt, 'Understanding *Twin Peaks: The Return* as a "Film Reboot" via Anti-Franchise Discourses Within Media Franchising', in Daniel Herbert and Constantine Verevis (eds), *Film Reboots* (Edinburgh: Edinburgh University Press, 2020), 97–110.
James, Caryn, '"Sopranos": Blood, Bullets and Proust', *The New York Times*, 2 March 2001. Available online: http://www.nytimes.com/2001/03/02/movies/tv-weekend-sopranos-blood-bullets-and-proust.html (Accessed July 2021).
Lavery, David, '*Lost* and Long-Term Television Narrative', in *Third Person: Authoring and Exploring Vast Narratives*, eds Pat Harrigan and Noah Wardrip-Fruin (Cambridge and London: MIT Press, 2009), 313–22.
Lotz, Amanda D., *The Television Will Be Revolutionized* (New York: New York University Press, 2007).
Mad Men, created by Matthew Weiner, AMC, 2007–15.
Mindhunter, created by Joe Penhall, Netflix, 2017–19.
Mittell, Jason, *Complex TV: The Poetics of Contemporary Television Storytelling* (New York: New York University Press, 2015).
Mr. Robot, created by Sam Esmail, USA Network, 2015–19.
Murch, Walter, *En un clin d'œil. Passé, présent et futur du montage* (Paris: Capricci, 2011).
Nelson, Robin, *TV Drama in Transition: Forms, Values and Cultural Change* (Houndsmills and New York: Palgrave Macmillan, 1997).
Newman, Michael Z., 'From Beats to Arcs: Toward a Poetics of Television Narrative', *The Velvet Light Trap* 58 (Fall 2006): 16–28.
Ray, Robert B., 'Film Studies and the Problems of the New Century', *New England Review* 27, no. 4 (2006), 106–20.
Rose, Lacey and Marisa Guthrie, 'FX Chief John Landgraf on Content Bubble: "This Is Simply Too Much Television"', *The Hollywood Reporter*, 7 August 2015.

Available online: https://www.hollywoodreporter.com/live-feed/fx-chief-john-landgraf-content-813914 (Accessed July 2021).

Sepinwall, Alan, 'Why Your TV Show Doesn't Have to Be a Novel: In Defense of the Episode', *What's Alan Watching?*, 24 November 2015. Available online: http://uproxx.com/sepinwall/why-your-tv-show-doesnt-have-to-be-a-novel-in-defense-of-the-episode (Accessed July 2021).

Sepinwall, Alan, 'Your TV Show Doesn't Have To Be A Movie: In Defense Of The Episode (Again)', *What's Alan Watching?*, 14 March 2017. Available online: http://uproxx.com/sepinwall/in-defense-of-the-episode-again (Accessed July 2021).

Stranger Things, created by Matt and Ross Duffer, Netflix, 2016–present.

Strank, Willem, 'Singing the Body Electric: Myth and Electricity as Both Sides of a Metaphorical Coin in *Twin Peaks: The Return*', in *Networked David Lynch: Critical Perspectives on Cinematic Transmediality*, eds Marcel Hartwig, Andreas Rauscher and Peter Niedermüller (Edinburgh: Edinburgh University Press, 2023), 47–60.

The Leftovers, created by Damon Lindelof and Tom Perrotta, HBO, 2014–17.

The Sopranos, created by David Chase, HBO, 1999–2007.

Thompson, Kristin, *Storytelling in Film and Television* (Cambridge: Harvard University Press, 2003).

Threnody for the Victims of Hiroshima, composed by Krzysztof Penderecki, 1961.

True Detective, created by Nic Pizzolatto, HBO, 2014–present.

Twin Peaks, created by David Lynch and Mark Frost, ABC, 1990–91; Showtime, 2017.

VanDerWerff, Todd, 'Netflix is Accidentally Inventing a New Art Form – Not Quite TV and Not Quite Film', *Vox*, 30 July 2015. Available online: https://www.vox.com/2015/7/29/9061833/netflix-binge-new-artform (Accessed July 2021).

Verevis, Constantine, 'The W/hole David Lynch: *Twin Peaks: Fire Walk with Me*', in *Networked David Lynch: Critical Perspectives on Cinematic Transmediality*, eds Marcel Hartwig, Andreas Rauscher and Peter Niedermüller (Edinburgh: Edinburgh University Press, 2023), 61–77.

You're the Worst, created by Stephen Falk, FX/FXX, 2014–19.

Part 2

New Media and New Forms: Web-series, Streaming Platforms and the Short Form

CHAPTER 6

Orders of Magnitude: Fractality and Granularity in Contemporary Television Series

Florent Favard

Allow me to start this chapter with some considerations about physics (from the limited point of view of a media scholar, of course). What is the smallest particle in the universe? The atom, literally 'which cannot be divided', was long hailed as the *elemental particle*, the fundamental building block of molecules, which in turn are required to build bigger structures – a cell, a grain of sand, a planet, a galaxy. Yet, this matryoshka doll was, and still is, incomplete, unfurling smaller and smaller elemental particles in what is colloquially referred to as a 'particle zoo', from the electron at the end of the nineteenth century to the vast families of subatomic particles discovered or theorised about throughout the twentieth century (Greene 1999, Chapter 1).

Whether you know about them all or not, we can infer that, unless you're a physicist, the most fundamental units of your daily life will be atoms and molecules, as you rely on chemical and physical processes – from cooking to washing the dishes – that can be understood at these microscopic levels, without the need to go further down – with the exception of the electron, an elemental particle carrying an electric charge, which comes in handy when you want to turn your computer or television on and watch your favourite series.

A similar question sparked the following chapter: what is the most fundamental unit of *television series narratives*? A possible – and logical – answer would be the *film frame*, at the heart of the process first engineered by Edison and the Lumière brothers, and the latter's now-ubiquitous cinematograph. It could be argued that the frame in audiovisual works, just like a picture, already possesses narrativity, the quality of being a narrative (Steiner 2004). But unless you hit pause – generally, to take a break from the narrative, or to look for clues in a still image as forensic fans do (Mittell 2009) – the frame is not the basic unit of your understanding and experience of a television series narrative. Jacques Aumont sees the pause as disrupting the cinema *dispositif* (apparatus) in a Foucaldian sense (Aumont 2012, 84), because it goes against a cinematographic experience socially, institutionally, architecturally and mechanically defined (and even *constrained*) as 'the production of a sustained viewing in time' (my translation). He is of course focusing on the cinematographic experience within a theatre, where the viewer *cannot* and *should not* hit pause. According to him, 'any presentation of a movie that lets me interrupt or modulate the experience is not cinematographic in nature' (my translation, 84). Aumont, however, does not wish to blame viewers watching movies on VHS or DVD, only to underline the fact that their experience belongs to another frame of reference, another apparatus that has become ubiquitous as we consume media on a variety of devices that allow us to interrupt or modulate the experience at will. I don't intend to deny the pause button its effective value in interpreting an audiovisual text such as a television narrative; yet, while all viewers of television series also produce a specific and modulated 'sustained viewing' of any given episode, hitting pause in order to uncover clues or admire a specific frame composition remains a peculiar operation that not all viewers will undertake – generally, we are more likely to hit pause to take a break from the narrative.

The shot may appear to be a better candidate, an ensemble of frames captured by the camera in one continuous period of time; yet in both mainstream cinema and television, it has continuously been stealthily merged into a bigger unit through invisible editing: the scene. The scene is remarkable for its capacity to encapsulate a fragment of time and space from the diegesis; each scene in a conventional audiovisual narrative may jump in time, if only for a few seconds, and/or show a different region of the storyworld. Within television series, scenes may be called *beats*, as they are carefully manipulated by the writers, especially on network television, where time is of the essence. Just like the atom, the scene, or beat, while not being the most fundamental particle, is the one that writers and viewers alike will manipulate and understand – it is the basic level of granularity needed to interpret the narrative – with the shot being an equivalent to the electron, discernible only through specific 'chemical reactions' – a continuous, long shot, or an unconventional one, that will spark through a scene just like static electricity.

The aim of this chapter is to keep in mind this analogy of a matryoshka doll and the fundamental mise-en-abyme of the real, physical world, to question whether television series follow such a strict and rigid succession of orders of magnitude, from the microscopic to the macroscopic, especially in the context of post-network TV (Lotz 2014) and the advent of subscription-based video-on-demand platforms like Netflix. The level of granularity required to understand the narrative, along with the fractal structure of television series, will thus be dissected. The goal of this chapter is not to uncover the 'God particle' of television series and discover the ultimate truth about their structure, but rather to (re)open a discussion about the possible evolution of their granularity and fractality, mostly within the context of the American television industry.

THE 'PARTICLE ZOO' OF TELEVISION SERIES NARRATIVES

Fifteen years ago, Jason Mittell started to build what would become a major thread of television series studies, the now-ubiquitous notion of 'narrative complexity', in a paper published in *The Velvet Light Trap* in 2006 (Mittell 2006). The same issue happened to feature another paper by Michael Z. Newman, entitled 'From Beats to Arcs: Toward a Poetics of Television Narratives'. Both papers were focused on a growing trend in the 1990s and 2000s: the blending of episodic and serialised plots, of micro- and macro-narratives, in television series, which has become a standard of the industry. Both shared the same assumptions about the origins of these trends and the way they were reconfiguring viewers' interpretation of long-term narratives. But while Mittell detailed an ambitious – and successful – program that would take the next ten years of his career to unravel, Newman, more frequently jumping between media in his previous and subsequent publications, and trying not to 'isolate the text from its makers and users' (16), focused on one specific structural aspect of television series. Nowhere in his paper is the word 'fractal' ever used, and yet, when analysing the structure of the 'prime time serial', Newman is precisely describing a fractal structure:

> Looking at the PTS [Prime Time Serial]'s narrative form, we may consider it to have three storytelling levels for analysis: a micro level of the scene or 'beat,' a middle level of the episode, and a macro level of greater than one episode, such as a multi-episode arc. On all three levels the commercial and aesthetic goals of television's storytellers are held in a mutually reinforcing balance. (Newman 2006, 17)

The first level described is that of the scene, or 'beat' as most writers call it – especially on network television; it works as 'television's most basic unit' since 'situation comedies, episodics, and serial dramas all organize their stories into rather short segments', with 'long, drawn-out beats' being 'exceedingly rare' (Newman 2006, 17). Newman notes that, because of 'the commercial imperative of keeping the audience interested', no beat is 'without a dramatic function' (17–18). This in turn helps writers craft the perfect balance between plotlines A, B, C and so on, along with constant reiteration of the names and roles of characters – a form of diegetic retelling (Mittell 2015, 181) at the microscopic level. *The beat is our atom.*

The episode is Newman's second level, with its varying length, and the required balance of closure and ongoing narrative tension typical of narratively complex television series according to Mittell: while an episodic plot might end with an episode, cliffhangers and serialised plots will have audiences waiting for the next iteration. *The episode is our molecule.*

If we are to keep up this analogy, though, we must take the act into account: Newman ignores it, and yet it is a fundamental unit, made of numerous beats, and designed to generate tension before each commercial break within a single episode on network television. Viewers watching pirated shows, or consuming them on DVD or a streaming platform, won't feel the act break as intensely as live viewers do – instead of an ad, they'll only see a brief cut to black – but it is always there. *The episode may then be seen as a complex molecule presenting itself in varying shapes and sizes*: the symmetrical structure of the forty atoms composing sucrose (a procedural with a rigid, familiar structure), the spiral of DNA (an episode of *Twin Peaks: The Return*, Showtime, 2017), or, for smaller serial forms, the elegant couple of sodium chloride (the 10-minute episodes of *State of the Union*, Sundance TV, 2019).

In his paper, Newman also decides to ignore the series as an obvious macrostructure to focus on arcs, which he defines as being tied to characters demanding 'an investment in time' (23) for both writers and viewers. While 'life-span arcs operate on the level of the series', Newman spends more time describing shorter, six-to-eight-episode arcs (24). Research focused on visualising these plot arcs confirms the existence of blocks within a network season, sometimes influenced by even shorter breaks of two to three weeks (Örnebring 2007; Favard 2017). The growing importance of the 'midseason finale' in network television also emphasises the bilateral structure of September-to-May seasons, usually consisting of twenty to twenty-four episodes (whereas cable television usually focuses on shorter, ten-to-thirteen-episode seasons). *The arc, defined as a group of episodes within a season, is our grain – of sand, of salt, of snow.*

Although Newman's contribution was of the utmost importance in the 2000s, some matryoshka dolls are missing. It is possible to take the argument further – and it is, nowadays, extremely important that we do so, since television is going through a revolution on all fronts, in terms of economics, technology, reception and aesthetics.

Just as beats, acts, episodes and arcs are fundamental units, the season appears to be another obvious component of television series narratives, pacing production and fiscal years as well as offering a narrative unit with a beginning (the season premiere) and an end (the season finale). But just as seasonal arcs may be of varying length and structure – the six-to-eight-episodes structure, the half-season – seasons themselves may be very different depending on which broadcasting platform we are looking at. The season is first and foremost 'a prototypical network-era concept' structured around the school year and allowing for reruns and breaks devoted to sport or holiday programs for example (Lotz 2014, 115); the network season, and its arcs, are also influenced by the 'sweeps' of the Nielsen institute, gathering 'national audience data' (Lotz 2014, 116). Cable television's shorter seasons are usually built as a whole, produced before being broadcast, as opposed to network television series, usually the product of ongoing work, with writers and directors desperately racing against the clock. Hence cable television's ability to propose seasons with a more concrete unity, 'a more finite narrative range' (Lotz 2014, 119), and season finales, which are 'often treated as potential series wrap-up' (Mittell 2015, 320, paraphrasing). *The season can be anything from a chunk of salt crystal to an entire beach or mountain*: it is the product of the fundamental 'segmentivity' of serial storytelling, repeated across micro- and macro-levels in order to create what may be a 'new and significant unit of meaning' (O'Sullivan 2010, 60).

Pushing this 'segmentivity' beyond the seasons themselves, and before the macroscopic unit that is the series as a whole, it would be interesting to isolate 'movements', specific blocks of a length equal or superior to one season, separated by 'tilts' than can be intradiegetic (plot points reconfiguring the entire storyworld) or extradiegetic (the departure of a lead actor or actress, a change of shooting location, a new showrunner . . .) (Favard 2019, 172). Although initially focused on serialised television series, these movements can also describe specific 'eras' of an episodic television series, building on the classification of eras characterised by different 'production signatures' in *Doctor Who* (BBC, 1963–89; 2005–present) by various scholars (Hills 2010, 148; Chapman 2013; Booth 2014). Such movements animate *The X-Files* (Fox, 1993–2002), with the move from Vancouver to Los Angeles and the departure of David Duchovny as irreversible aesthetic and narrative tilts impacting reception of the series; or *Lost* (ABC, 2004–10), in which the end of the third season goes from one movement to the next because of a tilt that was both extradiegetic (ABC scheduling an end date three years in advance in an unprecedented move) and intradiegetic (the subsequent use of flash-forward, increasing non-linearity, seriality and complexity). Movements are units that frequently appear in long-running television series, when seasons start to structure blocks of a superior order of magnitude while the series itself is still on the air: the infamous 'jump the shark' identified by fans of long-running television series since *Happy Days* (ABC, 1974–84) and its S05E03 is indeed a tilt which brings an 'era' to a close, from a more or less subjective viewpoint; Rachel lamenting that her move from Monica's apartment is the 'end of an era' in *Friends* (NBC, 1993–2003, S06E02) is a reflexive nod to such perceptions of macroscopic units of narrative time beyond seasons. *The movement can be an entire country; it can be an entire continent. Beyond lies only the series itself, akin to a planet the viewer may never fully explore.*

From the beat to the series, from the microscopic to the macroscopic, all these units structure and influence each other in a fractal way (Favard 2019, 113), generating dense, intricate narratives over the past three to four decades. Yet Newman's three levels are deeply rooted in network television, as may be, to an extent, the additional units listed here. A revolution is happening, decades in the making and still underway (Lotz 2014, 10), and it is even more relevant nowadays, as subscription-based video-on-demand platforms are exploring new territories, with network and cable television following their lead and trying to compete for the better part of the last decade. Most surprisingly, the unit most affected by these changes appears to be not a macroscopic one such as the arc, or the season, but one of the microscopic variety: the act.

THE SHRINKING ACT AND THE *BRUCKHEIMERISATION* OF TELEVISION

Among the many interviews writers give to various journalists and critics, Tara Bennett's book on showrunners gives us an interesting peek behind the curtain of both network and cable television. While Bill Prady, showrunner of *The Big Bang Theory* (CBS, 2007–19), explains that 'You have to develop the ability to live in the micro and not the macro', referring to a 'tunnel vision' focused on 'this scene or this joke or this moment' (97), Terence Winter details the difficult work of 'breaking' an episode into acts and beats, with an episode usually containing '25 to 33 beats' (Bennett 2014, 98).

But what is even more interesting is to learn how writers react to the steadily increasing time allotted for commercial content, a 'clutter' that ironically proves to 'decrease the effectiveness of [the advertisers'] message' (Lotz 2014, 121). Acts themselves have gone from four to five, six, even seven on network television as the number of commercial breaks increases as well. It follows that narrative tension must rise more frequently, as each shrinking act is supposed to end with a mini cliffhanger that will keep the audience glued to the screen during commercials. Jane Espenson explains:

> There's this inflation because they want to put more commercial breaks in, so you end up having to turn your story more often. You [write] six pages and you stop for a commercial break. Now you need that next six-page chunk when you come back to feel a little different in flavor than the first six pages, or that act break will feel like it didn't quite land. You

end up having to make all these little turns in the story. The problem is you end up with a very shallow, twisty story. (Bennett 2014, 71)

Robert King, co-showrunner of *The Good Wife* (CBS, 2009–16), is even more pessimistic:

> The six-act structure will destroy storytelling, only because, even though the network or the studio will say, 'Oh, don't worry about having a strong act-out,' when they come down to it, they want a strong act-out, which usually means some bullshit nonsense explosion in there of some kind. [. . .] The problem is that you have to create strong act-outs that will pull people back, so it's not very friendly to storytelling; it's friendly to more 'Bruckheimeresque' explosion storytelling. (Bennett 2014, 71)

For a drama episode on network television, with an allotted time of 60 minutes – including in general 16 to 18 minutes of commercials, and 42 to 44 minutes of fiction – the four-act structure allowed each act to go beyond ten minutes; with a seven-act structure ('and a teaser' at the beginning, as Jane Espenson explains), acts are reduced to under six minutes, barely time for three to four beats, unless they become shorter and shorter in their own right – as they seem to be on every episode of *Law and Order* (NBC, 1990–2010). One could suggest that Robert King is specifically referring to the fast-paced movies Bruckheimer produced with Michael Bay as director in the late 1990s and early 2000s, such as *Bad Boys* (1995), *Armageddon* (1998) or *Pearl Harbor* (2001). While the protagonists of *Law and Order* do not walk away from explosions every single episode, the series' fast editing is reminiscent of Bay's shots, always full of movement and action, never taking a break.

These problems do not concern premium cable television programs, or at least not in an obvious way: HBO and Showtime do not need commercial breaks, being 'subscription cable services [that] rely on viewers desiring to watch their programming so much that they are willing to pay for it' (Lotz 2014, 235), and allowing 'creators to develop episodes at a length determined by the story' (236). Even then, when they are sold to syndication, episodes of premium cable may be trimmed down to allow for the insertion of commercial breaks – a reediting that may go along with the use of alternative, more family-friendly scenes, as with *Sex and the City* (HBO, 1998–2004) (237).

The jumps between A stories, B stories, even C or D stories in an increasingly intricate structure, and the twists at the end of each act, thus seem even more frequent on network and basic cable television, whereas premium cable tries to emulate auteur cinema and take its time to unfold each beat, each act, whether it is about mafiosi in New Jersey or dragons in Westeros. The rhythm of one episode of *CSI* (CBS, 2000–15) feels very different from that of *Boardwalk Empire* (HBO, 2010–14), not because the beats are essentially shorter in the former (such a claim would require a global, quantitative measuring) but because network television is compressing increasing numbers of shorter acts – and thus commercial breaks – into the 60 and 30 minutes formats of dramas and sitcoms, leading to the impression that *CSI* has to twist and turn every few minutes. 'Context can dictate content' (Sodano 2012, 29).

This foregrounding of narrative tension for the sake of narrative tension is caught in legitimating discourse on writing and genres, as Raphaël Baroni argues: suspense, curiosity and surprise, the three components of narrative tension, are considered to be too rough and demeaning for highbrow literature (Baroni 2007, 236), an idea that the French narratology wave of the 1960s did not challenge because at the time, the Nouveau Roman helped literary theorists to shape a model based on 'the sanitized [*aseptisé*] form of a structural opposition or the consequences of an action', ignoring the fact that between a set-up and a denouement, the narrative aims to produce a tension, an emotion, that needs to be resolved (Baroni 2007, 29–30). In short, the endless twists and turns of shorter acts of network television may seem ideal for a superficial reading of the action, while the slow acts of premium cable allow for a deeper meaning – an opposition between plot and theme that, indeed, lacks nuance (VanArendonk 2019, 75). But the writers interviewed by Tara Bennett seem right in pointing out that there may be a limit to these 'industrial ritual[s] with commercial and artistic ramifications' (Lotz 2014, 115), whether it be the season or the act: one can only 'twist and turn' a story so often before it breaks. It remains to be seen if the act as a narrative unit is bound to disappear completely on network television, becoming one with the beat. In the last part of this chapter, however, I argue that the commercial break is not the only factor in the effacement of the act and the global evolution of the narrative matryoshka doll that is a television series.

NETFLIX SERIES AS A SOUP OF BEATS

While SVoD platforms such as Hulu still use commercial breaks, at least as an incentive to pay for a subscription plan allowing the viewer to bypass them, the dominant, content-creating platforms that are Amazon, Disney+ and Netflix are generally ad-free and subscription-based. Netflix may be the most innovative, as it started releasing full seasons at once during the mid-2010s, eschewing the fundamental gaps between episodes that 'define the serial experience' (Mittell 2015, 27). Following Mittell, it could be argued that Netflix only took note of the broader, earlier remodulation of televisual experience, as VHS, DVD and digital video recording allowed the viewer to watch multiple episodes at once, helping 'establish more momentum and continuity' (39) in the narrative. It should also be noted that the rise of 'cable channels' unconventional scheduling and season organization contributed to [the viewers'] changing expectations of broadcast programming' (Lotz 2014, 119). Netflix thus capitalises on viewers' current ability to maximise their relationship to television series, what Lisa Perks calls 'marathoning' instead of 'binge-watching', putting the emphasis on the physical and mental investment: 'Rather than viewing these media experiences as mindless indulgences, media marathoning connotes a conjoined triumph of commitment and stamina' (Perks 2015, ix).

Binge-watching a Netflix original production (by that I mean a 'true' original production, not the misleading label applied to series produced by other studios) is thus a peculiar experience, encouraged by the platform, which automatically plays the next episode before the current one finishes unrolling the credits. Not only do the acts become unobtrusive since there is no need for commercial breaks, but the unit that is the episode is likewise eschewed. It is interesting to note that while these microscopic units of television narratives are put aside to facilitate the consumption of content, they also orient a reading of the narrative on a macroscopic scale – they 'displace the "complete unit" pressure onto the television season as a frame' (VanArendonk 2019, 74).

This redefinition of the fractal structure owes as much to the economic imperatives of this fourth era of television – characterised by a new technological shift according to Mareike Jenner – as the one described by Newman in 2006 owed to the network: 'Binge-watching (...) has become more than a mode of viewing to Netflix. It has become a publishing model that dictates how content is supposed to be watched on Netflix' (Jenner 2018, 109). For VanArendonk, the episode becomes 'a gesture, a pause – a convention fulfilled' (75). Following Renata Salecl, Jenner goes as far as to claim that the episode unit (and its narrative unity with a beginning, middle and end) is a threat to Netflix, a platform built around the impossibility for viewers to make choices without the help of the algorithm; the automatic playing of the next episode thus 'mitigate[s] the paralysis viewers might feel in the face of too much choice' (Jenner 2018, 109).

Ri Pierce-Grove offers an in-depth analysis of how critics defined binge-watching during the 2010s, focusing on both positive and negative effects (Pierce-Grove 2017). For example, talking about *Breaking Bad* (AMC, 2008–13) for the *New York Times*, James Poniewozik claims that:

> The live viewer saw Walter White's change distended, in slow-motion; little by little, he broke badder and badder, in a way that emphasized the gradual slope of moral compromise. The binger saw him change in time-lapse, in a way that suggested that the tendency to arrogance and evil was in him all along. Neither perception is wrong. In fact,

both themes are thoroughly built into the show. But how you watch, in some way, affects the story you see (Poniewozik 2015, quoted in Pierce-Grove 2017).

Whether the narrative is still watched with gaps or binge-watched, the primary focus is on long-term storytelling and macroscopic units, with the gaps, the 'segmentivity' reduced to a 'slow' motion effect (note that a slow motion is still understood as a *continuous* motion). Rather than the beat or even the episode, the season becomes the standard and most fundamental unit of Netflix television series as the platform is 'accidentally inventing a new art form – not quite TV and not quite film' (VanDerWerff 2015), a storytelling logic that is now contaminating cable and network television, according to Alan Sepinwall.

Sepinwall also references an interview with Jill Soloway, the creator of *Transparent* (Amazon, 2014–19), in which she explains that she's 'started to look at the individual episodes as almost interchangeable in terms of where [she] can place scenes, and that [her and her writers] think of the whole season as a five-hour movie'. Such a claim, in line with the endless comparison of contemporary television series with '*n*-hour long movies', completely redefines the fundamental granularity necessary (according to the writers) to understand and create such narratives. The level of granularity required to experience such series is of a lesser degree of detail, focusing on macroscopic units. This 'hypernovelisation' of television transforms first seasons into the equivalent of pilot episodes, with, for example, the opening credits of *The OA* (Netflix, 2016–19) appearing near the end of the first 'episode' (Campion 2019), if it can still be called an episode.

While television series have claimed to be 'novel-like' for decades (for example, see McGrath 1995), this new 'art form' that critics and academics struggle to define (since the form itself is gradually finding its footing) is slowly transforming the episode into a continuous chapter, with more or less unnoticeable act divisions. Meanwhile, movements may not have enough time to appear, as Netflix and Amazon economic models may favour shorter series of two or three seasons (Andreeva 2019).

Beats, however, are too fundamental a unit to be swept away: this redefinition of the classic fractal structure (beats > acts > episodes > arcs > seasons > movements > series), gives us an intriguing new structure where the most important particles happen to be the following: beats > seasons > series. The jump from micro to macro is akin to the one separating the atom from the beach, with the grain of sand being nowhere to be seen. The fact that beats can be rearranged on demand in the writing room of *Transparent*, and that the length of episodes is even more variable than it is on cable television, essentially means that the beat, this microscopic unit, has to carry an important amount of narrative material on its shoulders; individual episodes are barely discernible on some Netflix shows, thanks to the inevitable cliffhanger at the end which pushes the viewer to watch the next episode. This phenomenon, that I call hypergranularity, may explain why, in this new 'art form' that is the SVoD season (especially on Netflix), some series tend to fall prey to what critics called 'the Netflix bloat', a 'looser, emptier storytelling' (VanArendonk 2019). Alan Sepinwall explains:

> When the material is interesting enough, and there's enough story to comfortably stretch out over however many episodes and hours, this isn't an issue. [. . .] But when the story's not quite there, then those formless blobs intended as episodes become a real drag: necessary viewing to understand the overall plot, but not interesting viewing in the meantime, even as part of a day-long binge. (Sepinwall 2015)

Netflix itself is ready to acknowledge this bloat, going so far as to explain – through its VP of Original Programming, Cindy Holland – that this new structure requires shortening seasons, from the standard thirteen-episode seasons imposed by third-party studios to their new convention of seasons (or parts) of no more than ten episodes (Sepinwall 2018). Their goal, however, might be more to reduce costs than to avoid creating the 'big, lumpy, 10- to 13-hour ball of plot arranged in chronological order' described by Sepinwall (Sepinwall 2018), further shortening a standard season already abbreviated by cable television in the 2000s.

Although I agree with Sepinwall with regard to the appearance of this 'formless blob', I think it has more to do with a shifting storytelling structure: beats, atoms, have to create entire beaches and mountains without first agglomerating into molecules and grains of sand. The result, one that may be temporary as SVoD platforms are still experimenting, is a soup of atoms, a soup of beats, trying to take on the shape of a mountain, a season, a series. We may be looking at a complete overhaul of television series narrative, or at the difficult birth of new narrative norms requiring that the traditional fractal structure be deconstructed first, before being reassembled. Only time will tell.

CONCLUSION

The aim of this chapter was to (re)open a discussion on the fractal nature of television series narratives, and the level of granularity required to understand and interpret them. Following in the steps of Jason Mittell and Michael Newman, among others, I proposed a typology of fundamental units which act like matryoshka dolls, with the first two akin to elemental, almost invisible particles:

[frame> shot >] beat > act > episode > arc > season > movement > series.

I then described how post-network television shortened the act, leading to the 'twisty' episodes described by writers, before arguing that SVoD platforms, by shortening series and using the season as their basic level of granularity, have eschewed the episode and proposed a new fractal structure:

$$\text{beat} > (\text{acts?}) > (\text{episode?}) > \text{season} > \text{series}$$

I surmised that the 'bloat' perceived by critics may have less to do with the quality of content and more with the fact that beats, the microscopic units, now have to structure entire seasons by themselves. Not only might series be contracting on SVoD platforms, but microscopic units are on a collision course with macroscopic ones, with almost nothing in between. Of course, not all Netflix and Amazon series resemble a soup of beats; the analogy is subjective, and its only purpose is to open a debate. It would be interesting to explore the relationship between the most 'bloated' SVoD series and the degree of control of a third-party studio, for example. Measuring narrative tension, we are also venturing into storyology, 'the study of the logic that binds events into plots' (Ryan 2009, 73), and the way in which what is defined as 'good' storytelling is influenced by time and culture. It would be useful to devise a specific protocol to measure the way in which narrative tension may have shifted from network television to SVoD series, but that would require another chapter, another episode.

Finally, it could even be argued that series themselves may be diminishing, not just in length, but in scope, integrated into vast transmedia systems, with revivals and reboots also redefining the transfictional system (Saint-Gelais 2011), the ultimate macroscopic unit within which each series is interpreted: if television series are planets, transmedia franchises might be stellar systems, perhaps even galaxies, in an ever-expanding fractal composition.

WORKS CITED

Andreeva, Nellie, 'Feeling The Churn: Why Netflix Cancels Shows After a Couple of Seasons & Why They can't Move to New Homes', *Deadline*, 18 March 2019. Available online: https://deadline.com/2019/03/netflix-tv-series-cancellations-strategy-one-day-at-a-time-1202576297/ (Accessed February 2024).
Armageddon, directed by Michael Bay, Touchstone Pictures, 1998.
Aumont, Jacques, *Que reste-t-il du cinéma* (Paris: Vrin, 2012).
Bad Boys, directed by Michael Bay, Columbia Pictures, 1995.
Baroni, Raphaël, *La Tension narrative: Suspense, curiosité et surprise* (Paris: Seuil, 2007).
Bennett, Tara, *Showrunners: The Art of Running a TV Show* (London: Titan Books, 2014).
The Big Bang Theory, created by Chuck Lorre and Bill Prady, CBS, 2007–19.
Boardwalk Empire, created by Terence Winter, HBO, 2010–14.

Booth, Paul, 'Periodising *Doctor Who*', *Science Fiction Film and Television* 7, no. 2 (2014): 195–215.
Breaking Bad, created by Vince Gilligan, AMC, 2008–13.
Campion, Benjamin, 'Regarder des séries sur Netflix: l'illusion d'une expérience spectatorielle augmentée', *TV/Series*, no. 15 (2019). Available online: URL: http://journals.openedition.org/tvseries/3479; DOI: https://doi.org/10.4000/tvseries.3479 (Accessed February 2024).
Chapman, James, *Inside the TARDIS: The Worlds of Doctor Who* (London and New York: I.B. Tauris, 2013).
CSI, created by Anthony E. Zuiker, CBS, 2000–15.
Doctor Who, created by Donald B. Wilson, Sydney Newman, BBC, 1963–89; 2005–present.
Favard, Florent, 'Mapping Macroscopic Plots in Narratively Complex Television Series', *Revues française d'études américaines*, no. 151 (December 2017): 72–85.
Favard, Florent, *Écrire une série TV : La Promesse d'un dénouement* (Tours, Presses Universitaires François Rabelais, 2019).
Friends, created by David Crane and Marta Kauffman, NBC, 1993–2003.
Happy Days, created by Garry Marshall, ABC, 1974–84.
Hills, Matt, *Triumph of a Time Lord: Regenerating* Doctor Who *in the Twenty-First Century* (London and New York: I.B. Tauris, 2010).
Greene, Brian, *The Elegant Universe* (New York: W. W. Norton, 1999).
Jenner, Marieke, *Netflix and the Re-invention of Television* (Cambridge: Palgrave McMillan, 2018).
Law and Order, created by Dick Wolf, NBC, 1990–2010.
Lost, created by Jeffrey Lieber, J.J. Abrams and Damon Lindelof, ABC, 2004–10.
Lotz, Amanda, *The Television Will Be Revolutionized*, Second Edition (New York: New York University Press, 2014).
McGrath, Charles, 'The Triumph of the Prime-time Novel', *The New York Times*, 22 October 1995. Available online: http://www.nytimes.com/1995/10/22/magazine/the-prime-time-novel-the-triumph-of-the-prime-time-novel.html (Accessed February 2024).
Mittell, Jason, *Complex TV: The Poetics of Contemporary Television Storytelling* (New York: New York University Press, 2015).
Mittell, Jason, 'Sites of Participation: Wiki Fandom and the Case of Lostpedia', *Transformative Works and Cultures* 3 (2009).
Mittell, Jason, 'Narrative Complexity in Contemporary American Television', *The Velvet Light Trap*, no. 58 (2006): 29–40.
Newman, Michael, 'From Beats to Arcs: Toward a Poetic of Television Narrative', *The Velvet Light Trap*, no. 58 (2006): 16–28.
Örnebring, Henrik, 'The Show Must Go On . . . And On: Narrative and Seriality in *Alias*', in *Investigating Alias: Secrets and Spies*, eds Stacey Abbott and Simon Brown (London and New York: I.B. Tauris, 2007).
O'Sullivan, Sean, 'Broken on Purpose: Poetry, Serial Television, and the Season', *Storyworlds: A Journal of Narrative Studies* 2 (2010): 59–77.
Pearl Harbor, directed by Michael Bay, Touchstone Pictures, 2001.
Perks, Lisa Glebatis, *Media Marathoning: Immersions in Morality* (Lanham: Lexington Books, 2015).

Pierce-Grove, Ri, 'Just One More', *First Monday* 22, no. 1 (January 2017).

Poniewozik, James, 'Streaming TV isn't just a New Way to Watch. It's a New Genre', *The New York Times*, 16 December 2015. Available online: https://www.nytimes.com/2015/12/20/arts/television/streaming-tv-isnt-just-a-new-way-to-watch-its-a-new-genre.html (Accessed February 2024).

Ryan, Marie-Laure, 'Cheap Plot Tricks, Plot Holes, and Narrative Design', *Narrative* 17, no. 1 (2009): 56–75.

Saint-Gelais, Richard, *Fictions transfuges: La Transfictionnalité et ses enjeux* (Paris: Éditions du Seuil, 2011).

Salecl, Renata, *The Tyranny of Choice* (London: Profile Books, 2010).

Sepinwall, Alan, 'Why Netflix Dramas Sag Midseason – and How They're Fixing It', *Rolling Stone*, 18 August 2018. Available online: https://www.rollingstone.com/tv/tv-features/why-netflix-dramas-sag-midseason-cindy-holland-interview-707986/ (Accessed February 2024).

Sepinwall, Alan, 'Why Your TV Show doesn't Have to Be a Novel: In Defense of the Episode', *Uproxx*, 24 November 2015. Available online: https://uproxx.com/sepinwall/why-your-tv-show-doesnt-have-to-be-a-novel-in-defense-of-the-episode/ (Accessed February 2024).

Sex and the City, created by Darren Star, HBO, 1998–2004.

Sodano, Todd M., 'Television's Paradigm (Time)Shift: Production and Consumption Practices in the Post-Network Era', in *Time in TV Narrative: Exploring Temporality in Twenty-First-Century Programming*, ed. Melissa Ames (Jackson: University Press of Mississippi, 2012).

State of the Union, created by Nick Hornby and Stephen Frears, Sundance TV, 2019.

Steiner, Wendy, 'Pictorial Narrativity', in *Narrative across Media: The Languages of Storytelling*, ed. Marie-Laure Ryan (Lincoln and London: University of Nebraska, 2004), 145–77.

VanArendonk, Kathryn, 'Theorizing the Television Episode', *Narrative* 27, no. 1 (2019): 65–82.

The Good Wife, created by Robert King and Michelle King, CBS, 2009–16.

The OA, created by Brit Marling and Zal Batmanglij, Netflix, 2016–19.

The X-Files, created by Chris Carter, Fox, 1993–2002.

Transparent, created by Jill Soloway, Amazon, 2014–19.

Twin Peaks: The Return, created by David Lynch and Mark Frost, Showtime, 2017.

VanDerWerff, Emily, 'Netflix is Accidentally Inventing a New Art Form – Not Quite TV and Not Quite Film', *Vox*, 30 July 2015. Available online: https://www.vox.com/2015/7/29/9061833/netflix-binge-new-artform (Accessed February 2024).

CHAPTER 7

'Minute by Minute': Short Form Seriality and Social Viewing and Waiting in *SKAM*

Sara Tanderup Linkis

The third season of the popular Norwegian web-series *SKAM* (*SHAME*, 2015–17) focuses on the growing relationship between two young boys: the protagonist Isak, an insecure and closeted 16-year-old, and Even, who is a few years older and suffers from bipolar disorder. One morning, Even expresses his deep anxiety about the future, but Isak calms him down by asking him to play a game. 'It's called "Isak and Even: Minute by Minute." It, um, it's about that the only thing we need to worry about is the next minute' (Figure 7.1).[1]

Figure 7.1 'Even and Isak – minute by minute' (S03E10).

The concept of 'minute by minute', which is thus presented in the series as a therapeutic strategy, also relates to *SKAM*'s overall approach and mode of narration: the web-series was released online in short clips of 2–20 minutes on the series' webpage, skam.p3.no. The clips were presented in real time as each clip appears to take place at the same time as it is posted on the webpage – for instance, Isak and Even's conversation took place on a Saturday morning, October 12, 2016 and was also posted at this time (Figure 7.2). In this way, the viewers get the sense that they are following the story as it unfolds, minute by minute. 'Minute by minute' is, notably, also the label of the producer of the series, the Norwegian public service broadcaster NRK's famous slow television productions presenting, for instance, a train ride minute by minute. The reference in *SKAM* may indicate how the series represents a movement away from conventional 'fast' television, including a culture of on-demand streaming and binge-watching. Like slow television, it slows down serial narration and consumption, unfolding a story literally minute by minute, almost as a therapeutic strategy, in order to help teenagers like Isak and Even handle the big and small problems of life – together.

In this chapter, I want to investigate how *SKAM* makes use of short form seriality and real time narration to shape serial storytelling and frame the modes of social viewing and engagement that surround the series. According to Vilde Sundet, NRK's aim was 'to produce a drama series that portrayed young Norwegians in an authentic relevant and entertaining way, then present it in a novel form that fit naturally into these teens' media habits' (Sundet 2018, 2), and in this, *SKAM* greatly succeeded. Originally emerging as a 'secret' online

Figure 7.2 Clip from Saturday 10.15, (S03E10).

phenomenon in 2015, intended to bring a specific target group of 16-year-old Norwegian girls back into the audience of the public broadcaster, the series quickly developed into an international phenomenon, with fan groups all over Scandinavia, and, eventually, the world. The series is thus interesting as an example of a fiction created by a national public service broadcaster, using the short form to reach a specific target group while also leading to transnational success, as reflected in the production of, e.g., French, Belgian, American and Italian versions of the series.

The series' success may be partly explained by its innovative mode of storytelling, using digital distribution and social media such as Facebook, YouTube and Instagram to tell a story in real time, thus reaching the target group through the very media that structure their everyday lives. Accordingly, the existing research in *SKAM*, which has so far primarily been conducted within a Scandinavian context, has highlighted the series' innovative aspects – speaking of the series as a 'game changer' and distinguishing between television 'before and after *SKAM*' (Kann-Rasmussen, Quist and Veel 2017). In the first part of the chapter, I emphasise this aspect of the series, as I consider how its real-time presentation in short clips reflects the effects of social media logics and digital distribution methods on contemporary serial narration and consumption.

While I recognise *SKAM*'s innovative qualities, I also want to underline an aspect of continuity, as I investigate how its use of short clips and real-time narration affects the modes of consumption and the social environment surrounding the series. As stressed by Ruth Page, digitalisation not only leads to innovation, but may also pave the way for a return to previous forms and methods of telling, selling and consuming serial narratives. Thus following her claim, that '[a]nalysts of serial forms in social-media contexts would [. . .] do well to characterize those forms in terms of evolution rather than radical creation' (Page 2013, 36), I argue that *SKAM*'s use of the short format allows the series and its viewers to return to a mode of storytelling and social engagement that defined broadcast television and even Victorian 'feuilleton' novels. That is, in a post-network age, where whole seasons of series are often released and consumed at once, alone and on demand, *SKAM* re-introduces the aspect of social viewing and waiting in serial consumption.

After a brief introduction to the specific modes of distribution, narration and consumption that individuate *SKAM*, I investigate how the real-time presentation of the series in short clips serves to point out the gaps and breaks in serial storytelling, allowing its viewers to use *SKAM* as a social meeting place and as a space for handling life together, like Isak and Even, minute by minute. I conclude by considering how this social aspect of the series relates to its brevity at other levels, discussing the decision to end the series after only four seasons.

SHORT CLIPS IN REAL TIME: *SKAM* AS A MEDIA EVENT

SKAM focuses on a group of Norwegian high school students, mostly girls, attending the Hartvig Nissen School in Oslo. Each of the four seasons has a new protagonist, namely Eva, Noora, Isak and Sana respectively, and focuses on her or his private and social life and problems with friends, sexuality, love, religion, et cetera. The series was released in short video clips during the week, from Saturday to Friday, on the webpage skam.p3.no, following the everyday rhythm of typical school life.[2] The videos were continuously supplemented by other material on the webpage, such as SMS-chats between the characters, Facebook posts, Instagram updates, YouTube clips, et cetera, reflecting the protagonist's interaction with the others through smartphones and social media. Every Friday, the clips of the week were collected into one whole episode (20–50 minutes), which was broadcast on national television on Friday night. Because of this structure, all of the essential aspects of the story had to be told in the video clips, whereas the other material on the website served to 'substantiate storylines and characters and make them more relevant and in sync with current events', as the project leader of *SKAM*, Marianne Furevold-Boland, explains (quoted in Sundet 2018, 9).

Following the series 'live' as it unfolds across platforms in short clips and with the extra material on the website thus provides a significantly different experience than the one resulting from watching *SKAM* in the form of the weekly episodes, as a conventional television series.[3] This makes the series an interesting case for studying the effects of short forms and digital distribution on serial narration and consumption. First and foremost, the real-time presentation results in a sense of authentic 'presence'[4] and immediacy. I refer to Jay David Bolter and Richard Grusin's concept of immediacy, as presented in *Remediation: Understanding New Media* (1999). Bolter and Grusin describe how 'the logic of immediacy dictates that the medium itself should disappear and leave us in the presence of the thing represented' (5–6). Yet, they also underscore that '[i]mmediacy depends on hypermediacy' (6); that is, on the presence of media. In the case of *SKAM*, the relation between immediacy and hypermediacy is demonstrated, as the series' real-time aspect emphasises the presence of social media such as Facebook, YouTube and Instagram. The use of these platforms furthermore enables what the producer Mari Magnus describes as a 'fictional slide into reality' (Magnus 2016, 33–4), as it allows the fictional material from the series to merge in the viewers' feeds with other, authentic social media content, such as actual news and updates from real users.

A large part of the series' success may therefore be explained by the fact that it integrates the logics of social media into its storytelling method, producing an authentic image of young people's everyday lives as it is shaped by

Figure 7.3 SMS chats on screen (S04E07).

these media. The social significance of these media is enhanced in the series at a diegetic level, as the characters are often presented interacting on social media. Usually, their Facebook messages and SMS chats are presented directly onscreen in the video clips as well as on the webpage, further contributing to creating an effect of (hypermediated) immediacy and producing a sense of intimate familiarity and identification with the characters (Figure 7.3).

The use of short clips and real-time-narration in *SKAM* may be considered in this context as a direct consequence of its reference to, and use of, social media. Focusing on serial storytelling in social media, Ruth Page notes that 'social media genres are inherently episodic, consisting of posts, comments, and updates that are published over time: the environment par excellence where seriality might flourish' (Page 2013, 36). Whilst being 'inherently episodic', social media, according to Page, also alters the conditions of serial storytelling, for instance by reversing the chronology, telling the most recent events first, as is also the case at the *SKAM* webpage. Ruth Page further points out that social media usually are characterised by real-time-narration: 'real-time narration found most prominently in social-network sites like Facebook and Twitter favours present-tense or non-finite verb forms, creating an on-going sense of an ever-present "now" that bridges the asynchronous gap between the time of narrative production and narrative reception' (Page 2013, 41).

As a narrative that imitates and incorporates the logics of social media, *SKAM* too produces this 'on-going sense of an ever-present "now"' – or what might be described as a sense of 'liveness' (Jerslev 2017). Not only is the fictional story posted at the same time as it apparently takes place; the series also, much like most social media feeds, integrates the character's personal – fictional – stories with comments on actual political and cultural events. For instance, the then 2016 US presidential election is mentioned in the third season along with the recent release of the Netflix series *Stranger Things* (2016–present), and in Season 4, Sana posts an Instagram update, sympathising with the victims of a terror attack in Manchester the day after the attack took place (May 23, 2017). In this way, the series, in the words of Page, bridges 'the asynchronous gap between narrative production and narrative reception'. In fact, while the video clips were produced beforehand, most of the extra material, Facebook and Instagram posts on the skam.p3.no-website were produced continuously as the series was released in order to make the story more realistic and in sync with current events.

Through its digital distribution and real-time narration, *SKAM* itself also gains the status of a media event – like the US election or the *Stranger Things* release. In other words, each posting of each clip stands out as a one time-experience, since the series in its original real-time format can only be experienced once. According to media scholar Joos van Loos, the event is something that stands out from the rhythm of everyday life: 'The event is what is marked, what stands out, in time. Standing out in time becomes a time out' (Van Loos 2010, 111). As noted by Anne Jerslev, each posting of clips and other material in *SKAM* produces the experience of an outstanding media event, not only because of its real-time aspect, but first and foremost because of the series' irregular and unpredictable publication rhythm: '*Because* the *SKAM*-clip is staged as an intense time-out from the continuous rhythm of everyday time, and *because* the clips are uploaded irregularly, they stand out as (media) events; they become *outstanding* and function autonomously and independently, not referring to anything outside of themselves'[5] (Jerslev 2017, 77).

The status of *SKAM* as an event is enhanced by the reception of the series on social media. For instance, in the Danish Facebook group dedicated to the series, each clip emerging at the *SKAM* webpage was received as breaking news – the fans would alert each other, crying out 'Klip!' ('Clip!'), emphasising the status of each post as a social event. This practice reflects how the series' digital distribution and real-time aspect affects the modes of consumption and the social use of the series. The real-time aspect and the irregular publication rhythm encourage viewers to continuously update and check the website for new clips and material. Waiting for clips thus becomes a central aspect of watching the web-series, and, as I further explore below, the activity of waiting gains significance as a social activity in the community surrounding *SKAM*.

Thus, watching *SKAM* in the form of short clips in real time certainly resulted in a radically different experience than watching the broadcast version in the weekly episodes. Whereas the series in the latter form of a conventional television series quickly became popular with an older audience, following the series online, to some extent, allowed the young target group to keep the authentic one-time real-time *SKAM* experience for themselves. Below, I further investigate this experience as a result, on the one hand, of *SKAM*'s innovative strategies and use of digital media logics, and on the other hand, of its return to the traditional values of serial storytelling, encouraging the activities of social viewing and anticipating.

'WILLIAMMÅSVARE': SOCIAL ANTICIPATING AND THE SERIAL GAP

On May 20, 2016, at 2.15 p.m., *SKAM*'s Season 2 protagonist Noora's heart was broken as her boyfriend William ran away from her and out of the school yard, angry about her possible betrayal – she might or might not have slept with his brother during a party, which she did not herself remember. In the following five days, he did not answer any of her messages, resulting in a period of silence and anxious waiting on the *SKAM* webpage. That is, Noora's waiting for William to answer in the diegesis was shared by *SKAM*'s viewers in real time, as reflected by the discussion fora at the webpage and in the various fan-groups on social media, where the hashtag 'WilliamMåSvare' ['WilliamMustAnswer'] quickly emerged – until, on May 25, William's awaited reply finally ticked in.[6]

The 'WilliamMåSvare' incident reflects how the series uses the gaps or pauses between the clips to create suspense and identification with the protagonist. Although the collective waiting for William to answer unfolded across more than one weekly episode, the effect of his long silence was most significant when following the series in real time, as the viewers found themselves in the same situation as Noora, constantly checking the website for messages from William over the course of several days. Kristin Veel accordingly notes how the real-time consumption of the series adds significance to the gaps and pauses between clips: 'When watching *SKAM* in real time, the gaps between new posts (clips, SMS conversations, Instagram pictures, et cetera) get to take up relatively more time than the posts themselves, and they gain their own significance, as they are used with great dramaturgical effect in the construction of suspense' (Veel 2017, 70).

While creating suspense, the gaps also contributed to the social experience of the series. Through the fan groups and discussion fora, the real-time waiting for William to answer, or generally for the next clip or chat in the series to emerge on the website, *SKAM* becomes a collective experience, as also illustrated by the Facebook group's practice of announcing and sharing new clips (and even translating and texting the clips for viewers who do not understand Norwegian). Furthermore, the waiting time between the posts becomes significant, as it is filled out with social activities, as fans discuss the series online and in real life, re-watch and analyse the clips together, create and share fanfiction, and engage in other participatory and analytical activities.[7]

This social aspect of serial consumption is obviously not new. Indeed, the reception of Victorian 'feuilleton' novels was characterised by the collective consumption and shared waiting for new instalments. Most famously, this is exemplified by an anecdote about Charles Dickens' American readers, who stormed the wharf at the New York harbour when the ships from England arrived with the next and final instalment of Dickens' novel *The Old Curiosity Shop*, shouting anxiously to their British fellow readers at the ships and asking whether or not the beloved character Little Nell had died in the final instalment. In the twentieth century, the fan cultures surrounding broadcast television series were characterised by similar practices of social viewing and waiting. Notably, these television series, which were typically broadcast once a week and often included commercial breaks that made up gaps within the episodes, contributed to developing the function of the serial gap. Writing about the significance of gaps in broadcast television, Jason Mittell thus notes that,

> television series in their original broadcast form alternate between episodic instalments and mandatory temporary gaps between episodes – it is these gaps that define the serial experience. Serial temporality is thus lodged primarily within the realm of screen time through the material reception contexts of television broadcasting, which enables the regular and ritualistic consumption of a series that lies at the core of the serial experience. Additionally and importantly, these gaps allow viewers to continue their engagement with a series in between episodes, participating in fan communities, reading criticism, consuming paratexts, and theorizing about future instalments. (Mittell 2015, 27)

It is the gaps that define the serial experience, according to Mittell, since they frame the 'regular and ritualistic consumption' that is associated with television series. Furthermore, they provide the context for the social engagement with the series. *SKAM* may be characterised by a more irregular online distribution; however, the function of regular and ritualistic viewing practices is present in the series as the fictional characters gather to watch the weekly episodes of the Norwegian version of the reality show *Paradise Hotel* (TV3, 2009–present). Just like *SKAM*, the popular show functions as a social meeting space as the girls watch it together and discuss the show's development week by week – as reflected, for instance, by Eva's comment in SMS-chat during Season 4, 'weird week in Paradise'.[8]

The *Paradise* reference reflects how serial consumption structures the social lives of the target group. However, contrary to the broadcast reality show, most television series in the 'post-network-era' (Ames 2012) are watched on demand and alone, either on DVD, as pointed out by Mittell, or via streaming platforms such as Netflix or HBO. The new modes of distribution result in viewers gaining increasing control over the modes of viewing, and consequently transform the serial experience, as described by Todd M. Sodano, among others (Sodano 2012). Summarising Sodano's argument, Melissa Ames notes that '[t]oday's viewer can time-shift and/or binge on favourite series through DVD, DVR, on-demand and online viewing. Consequently, the standard gap (traditionally, the week between episodes) that used to predominate TV discourses now has shrunk, increased or been eliminated all-together' (Ames 2012, 24). When the gap disappears, the aspect of social waiting disappears as well; rather than waiting together for the next episode, catching up on the latest episode around the water-cooler, viewers may 'binge' any number of episodes on demand. The transformation of serial consumption is further stressed, as noted by Ames, as the number of series and platforms increases and thus, 'viewing audiences are sure to fragment into smaller pieces' (24). Similarly focusing on the impact of digitalisation on the social aspects of television, Jason Jacobs concludes '[I]t is true [...] that digital television threatens the universal experience of television's social function. Digital television's promises of control imply disconnection and separateness from the usually nationally socialized presence of television' (Jacobs 2011, 267).

SKAM, in this context, appears as the exception that proves the rule. Rather than promoting individual binge-watching, its digital distribution and use of short clips serve to re-introduce the social significance of the gap in serial storytelling, encouraging collective viewing and waiting, as exemplified by the 'WilliamMåSvare' episode. In this way, *SKAM* may be considered to return to the modes of consumption that characterised traditional serials, Dickens' novels as well as *Dallas* (CBS 1978–1991) – while also, significantly, transforming the serial experience according to the logics of digitalisation and social media, for instance, by replacing the 'regular and ritualistic' consumption of broadcast series with the irregular and real-time publication rhythm.[9] Indeed, it may be argued that precisely because *SKAM* is produced specifically for a 'post-network era' and adjusted to the modes of consumption that delineate the specific target group of 16-year-old girls, it becomes able to transcend the tendencies towards audience fragmentation and individual viewing practices described by Jacobs, Sodano and Ames. While the fan cultures that surround *SKAM* and are represented on Facebook and on the *SKAM* website certainly do exemplify the kind of specific online niche-culture that surrounds many contemporary television series, *SKAM* has also succeeded in moving beyond and has become something that is frequently discussed more broadly, in real life – indeed, around the water-cooler – bringing together not only the (Norwegian) nation but all of

Scandinavia, and even growing into an international phenomenon with the recent remakes.[10]

Thus, *SKAM* has succeeded in returning to the social roots of serial storytelling precisely through its use of short clips and real-time seriality, allowing an audience across the world to follow the series' development, minute by minute, together.

TOWARDS A CONCLUSION: BREVITY IN THE POST-NETWORK ERA

In spring 2017, the creator of *SKAM*, Julia Andem, announced in an Instagram update that the fourth season would be the end of the series. This decision was surprising, as the internal logic of the series would have it follow the protagonists all the way through their three years of high school. From the beginning, the protagonists' discussion and preparation for the celebration of their graduation according to Norwegian custom had been a central issue in the series, leading viewers to anticipate that this graduation would be the culmination of the series. However, with each season covering one semester, the four seasons only covered two years. Ending the series at this point thus meant that we would not get to see Eva, Sana, Noora, Isak and their friends graduate. Furthermore, the decision to end the series also went against general tendencies in an age where, as noted by Jason Mittell, the success of a series usually implies its continuation (Mittell 2015, 33–4). Thus, an international success such as *SKAM* would be expected to be continued. In this context, the fact that *SKAM* sticks to brevity, not only in the sense that it tells a story in short clips, but also in the sense of its short duration and its almost untimely end, stands out as a statement.

In her Instagram post, Andem – true to the social media context – motivates the decision personally. The series' success had gone over her head and its production had become too exhausting, a '24-hour job'. However, this personal explanation should be supplemented with the fact that *SKAM*, as a product of the public service broadcaster NRK, reflects a radically different mode of production than the usual Netflix series. Although NKR was of course interested in attracting viewers, the main purpose of the series was not commercial, but rather to provide a public service by presenting relevant content for the specific target group. In this context, rather than promoting its continuation, the series' unexpected success seems to have contributed to its end, as it became too big to keep serving its purpose as a 'secret' online phenomenon, speaking directly to the target group alone. When the 16-year-olds' mothers started watching as well, the game was over.

Like the presentation of the series in short clips, its overall short duration thus served to keep it relevant to the target group, maintaining its 'cult' status.

In other words, sticking to brevity is what makes *SKAM* stand out from the mainstream tendency of long-form television. Telling a story minute by minute, it provided a one-time-experience which was specifically adjusted to social media habits and consumption methods, and partly because of the sense of immediacy and authenticity that this mode of storytelling produced, the series became popular, also in the form of broadcast weekly episodes. Its short duration added to its authentic profile because it signalled that the series did not fall prey to the logics of commercial serialisation; on the contrary, just like the idealistic youths in the series, who repeatedly articulate scepticism towards modern consumerism and capitalist modes of thinking, it sought to resist this logic through the very decision to end it.

SKAM did not, however, end with Season 4. Rather than continuing the story, the series has been re-made and remediated: as mentioned above, there have been American, French, Belgian and Italian versions, and in Denmark, it has been turned into a popular theatrical play, while NKR has followed up with similar web-series such as *Semester*, which is targeted towards a slightly older audience, around 20 years of age. More generally, the transmedial form of storytelling, exemplified by *SKAM*, using social media and platforms such as YouTube to tell stories, is in rapid development, not least in Scandinavia, as exemplified by the Danish web-series *29* and *Centrum*. However, *SKAM* still stands out for its unique mode of integrating these transmedia aspects in the story, using the short form and real-time framing to produce a more immersive experience than what we find in most recent examples. The continuing status of the series is reflected by the fan communities: at the moment of writing, years after the release of the final clip in Season 4, fans are still active, discussing the series in various Facebook-groups. In this way, despite, or rather because of *SKAM*'s short duration and its presentation in short clips, as a one-time real-time experience, it has made a lasting impression.

NOTES

1. Clip posted on skam.p3.no on Saturday 10, 2016, 8.10 AM. My translation. Due to restrictions in copyright, the clips are no longer accessible outside of Norway (the series was geo-blocked in spring 2017).
2. That is, the series' weekly publication rhythm followed the rhythm of the school week, from dull Monday mornings to the culmination Friday night, just as the seasons follow the educational calendar and the seasonal holidays, with the season finales culminating, respectively, with Christmas vacation in December and graduation in June. In this way, the series invited the viewers to identify with the everyday lives of the characters. Its digital distribution allowed its integration into the target group's everyday lives, exemplifying what Hämmerling and Nast call 'quotidian integration' (Hämmerling and Nast 2017, 248).

3. For further analysis of the aspect of real-time, or concurrent, narration in *SKAM*, see Andersen and Linkis 2019.
4. I refer to the concept of presence here in accordance with Hans Ulrich Gumbrecht's conceptualisation of the notion in *The Production of Presence* (2004), that is, as 'a dimension in which cultural phenomena and cultural events become tangible and have an impact on our sense and our bodies' (n.p.); in the case of *SKAM*, the digital distribution and real-time narration (along with e.g. the many close-up images) produces a sense of the story and the characters as present.
5. All quotes from articles in Danish (by Jerslev and Veel) are translated by the author of this chapter.
6. For further analysis of this passage, see Veel 2017.
7. Especially the widespread activity of re-watching clips in-between clips and seasons bears witness to the fact that, while on the one hand, the real-time presentation promotes the experience of *SKAM* as a one-time event, the short clips also pave the way for a practice of repeatedly returning to the series and closely analysing every scene and clip. For further analysis of the viewers' activities and the participatory culture surrounding *SKAM*, see Andersen and Linkis 2019.
8. 'Weird uke på paradise, ass.' The comment functions as a meta-comment, referring to the fact that *Paradise Hotel*, in that same week, had a *SKAM* theme (*Paradise Hotel*, TV3, Season 9, 2017).
9. It should be noted in this context that the series' irregular publication rhythm means that viewers lose control of their consumption. Just like Noora, waiting for William to reply, we are powerless, waiting for the next post. At least, that is, if we choose to consume the story in real time. Although the online presence of the series to some extent makes it possible to watch 'on demand', we cannot choose to fast-forward and binge-watch when consuming it in real time.
10. For further discussion of *SKAM*'s development into an international success, see Sundet 2018.

WORKS CITED

29, created by Jesper Zushlag and Julie Rudbæk, Xee, 2018–20.

Ames, Melissa, 'Introduction. Television Studies in the Twenty-first Century', in *Time in Television Narrative: Exploring Temporality in Twenty-First Century Programming*, ed. Melissa Ames (Jackson: University Press of Mississippi, 2012).

Andersen, Tore Rye and Sara Tanderup Linkis, 'As We Speak. Concurrent Narration and Participation in the Serial Narratives *SKAM* and @I_Bombadi', *Narrative* 27, no. 1 (2019).

Blank, created by Knut Næsheim and Hege Gaarder Nordlie, NRK, 2018–19.

Bolter, Jay David and Richard Grusin, *Remediation: Understanding New Media* (Cambridge: The MIT Press, 1999).

Centrum, created by Jonas Risvig et al., YouTube, 2020.

Gumbrecht, Hans Ulrich, *The Production of Presence: What Meaning Cannot Convey* (Stanford: Stanford University Press, 2004).
Hämmerling, Christine and Mirjam Nast, 'Popular Seriality in Everyday Practice: *Perry Rhodan* and *Tatort*', in *Media of Serial Narrative*, ed. Frank Kelleter (Columbus: The Ohio State University Press, 2017), 248–60.
Jacobs, Jason, 'Television Interrupted: Pollution or Aesthetic', in *Television as Digital Media*, eds James Bennett and Niki Strange (Durham: Duke University Press, 2011), 255–80.
Jerslev, Anna, '*SKAM*s "lige her" og "lige nu". Om *SKAM* og nærvær', *Nordisk tidskrift for Informationsvidenskab og Kulturformidling* 6, no. 2/3 (2017), 75–81.
Kann-Rasmussen, Nanna, Pia Quist and Kristen Veel, 'Efter *SKAM*. Kollektive perspektiver på den individuelle oplevelse', *Nordisk tidskrift for Informationsvidenskab og Kulturformidling* 6, no. 2/3 (2017), 1–6.
Magnus, Mari, 'SKAM – når fiksjon og virkelighet møtes', *Nordicom Information* 38, no.2 (2016): 31–8.
Mittell, Jason, *Complex TV: The Poetics of Contemporary Television Storytelling* (New York and London: New York University Press, 2015).
Page, Ruth, 'Seriality and Storytelling in Social Media', *Storyworlds* 5 (2013): 31–54.
Semester, created by Alexander Johansson and Ulrik Imtiaz Rolfsen, null.video, 2020–present.
SKAM, created by *Julie Andem*, NRK, 2015–17. www.skam.p3.no
Stranger Things, created by Matt and Ross Duffer, Netflix, 2016–present.
Sodano, Todd M., 'Television's Paradigm (Time)shift. Production and Consumption Practices in the Post-Network Era', in *Time in Television Narrative: Exploring Temporality in Twenty-First Century Programming*, ed. Melissa Ames (Jackson: University Press of Mississippi, 2012).
Sundet, Vilde Schanke, 'From "Secret" Online Teen Drama to International Cult Phenomenon: The Global Expansion of *SKAM* and its Public Service Mission', in *The Scandinavian Invasion: The Nordic Noir Phenomenon and Beyond*, eds Richard McCulloch and William Proctor (Oxford: Peter Lang, 2018).
Van Loos, Joos, 'Modalities of Mediation', in *Media Events in a Global Age*, eds N. Couldry, A. Hepp and F. Krotz (London and New York: Routledge, 2010), 109–23.
Veel, Kristin, 'Fortællingens dynamiske arkiv. Fortælleformer og narrativt begær i *SKAM*', *Nordisk tidsskrift for Informationsvidenskab og Kulturformidling*, 6, no. 2/3 (2017): 67–74.

CHAPTER 8

Narrative Efficiency and the Constraints of the Short Form in *Les Engagés*

Stéphane Sawas

Les Engagés (Studio 4, 2017–21) was the first LGBT-themed television series produced by the French national public television broadcaster France Télévisions for its Studio 4 web platform.[1] The first season, which will be the focus of this chapter, was shown between 17 May and 16 June 2017 every Wednesday and Friday at 7 p.m. It was then immediately released on DVD in June 2017 in Optimale's Rainbow collection (dedicated to gay- and lesbian-themed fiction) and screened every Monday to Friday between 19 and 30 June 2017 on the television channel TV5 Monde.[2] The series was initially designed as 30-minute episodes on the model of the British television series *Queer as Folk* (Channel 4, 1999–2000), a format unusual for French television (Ziemniak 2017, 162), but ultimately took the form of a web-series made up of ten episodes of between 8 and 12 minutes each. It was thanks to this format that the project, which its creator Sullivan Le Postec had been working on since the late 2000s, finally saw the light of day (Antoine 2017). The short form that *Les Engagés* uses is distinct both aesthetically and thematically from popular French 'shortcoms' like *Un gars, une fille* (France 2, 1999–2003), *Kaamelott* (M6, 2005–9), or *Nos chers voisins* (TF1, 2012–17) (Delaporte 2019), a format that has become increasingly popular in the French television landscape since the end of the 1990s (Bihel 2012, Ziemniak 2017, 47–9). It also differs from the short form of other French LGBT-themed TV series produced in 2017 and 2018, like *Louis(e)* (TF1, 2017), *J'ai 2 amours* (Arte, 2018) or *Fiertés* (Arte, 2018), all of which are structurally short, being miniseries of two or three 50-minute episodes, but whose brevity was ultimately limited by their broadcasting conditions, given that they aired sequentially on primetime over the course of a single evening.

The first season of *Les Engagés* is built around the two protagonists Hicham (played by Mehdi Meskar) and Thibaut (played by Eric Pucheu) meeting again after many years. Hicham leaves the outskirts of Saint-Etienne to join Thibaut in Lyon, with the intention of changing his life. Thibaut takes him to an organisation called *Le Point G* [The G-Spot] where he is an activist, hence the title *Les Engagés* [The Activists].[3]

The series aims to reflect something of the diversity of French society, whilst addressing a broader audience beyond the LGBT community. With the exception of Hicham's sister Nadjet (Nanou Harry), all the main characters are homosexual. Three generations are represented, with activists in their twenties, forties and sixties. Of the four groups represented by the letters 'LGBT', gay characters predominate. A few lesbian characters struggle to carve out a proper role, in particular the charismatic Murielle (Claudine Charreyre), who is a member of the organisation's board. There are no transgender characters in the first season, but this changes in Season 2 (2019) when they occupy centre stage, particularly through the character of Elijah (Adrián de la Vega). Finally, the question of bisexuality is not addressed directly; only one brief shot at the very end of the second season shows Liao (François-Xavier Phan) kissing a young woman, to the great displeasure of his partner Mickaël (Pierre Cachia), from whom he seems to be becoming more distant. However, this theme, suggested here, is not developed in Season 3, based on a broader political storyline set between Lyon, Saint-Etienne and Brussels.

The series sets out to avoid giving a monolithic, smoothed-out image of the LGBT community by revealing its various internal conflicts and drawing on these explicitly in the plot. For example, the heated debates in the first season around coming out (Hicham, then Thibaut) and outing (Amaury, then Thibaut again) are structured around the conflict between the right to indifference, advocated by Amaury (Franck Fargier), and the right to difference, demanded by Thibaut. This dividing line overlaps with an equivalent, albeit porous, line between the left wing and the right wing. Amaury, who is chief of staff to one of the district Mayors in Lyon, is open about his moderate right-wing political views (at the end of E06 he states, about the Mayor, 'C'est pas ma droite' [that's not the right-wing I belong to]). Alongside this key conflict, around which the first season is built, two further tensions emerge within the community itself: first, the organisation's gender imbalance or even misogyny, denounced by Murielle, who points out that it is rooted in the very name 'G-Spot' (E05), and second, more discreetly, the right-wing drift of some parts of the community, represented by Mickaël.

The series also represents diversity through characters from different sociocultural backgrounds (Gay 2020). Thibaut's surname, Giaccherini, suggests Italian origins, although this angle is never explicitly developed in the plotlines of the show's three seasons. The question of Hicham's Muslim culture does appear from the outset, but without any particular emphasis: no links are made between religion and disapproval of sexuality, nor is there any of the over-eroticisation present in so many of the characters played for instance by the actor Selim Kechiouche, particularly in the 2000s (Rees-Robert 2008, 27–35). The issue of Islam is above all addressed through the character of Hicham's sister Nadjet, who wears the Islamic headscarf in public and is the focus of tensions in the organisation as soon as she walks through the door (Mickaël asks her to remove her veil if she wishes to stay on the premises, which Murielle immediately contests in the name of feminism, S01E05); later, during a meeting of the feminist fanzine committee in S02E06, a conflict breaks out between the activists on the question of a woman's right to wear the Islamic veil and Murielle invites Nadjet to talk about her choice.

Although the series does foreground characters from minorities, it is intended for a much broader viewership. While the creator Sullivan Le Postec is openly gay (the series draws on his own experience of LGBT organisations in Lyon), the same is not true of the two directors of the first season, Maxime Potherat and Jules Thénier, nor of the two main actors, Mehdi Meskar and Eric Pucheu. The main actors were deliberately chosen to avoid falling into the caricatural representations of gay characters that are so prevalent on screen, and so to be neither too effeminate nor hyper virile. Maxime Potherat says, for example: 'What I find really interesting and what I liked in Sullivan, and in his writing, is that actually he didn't want our two heroes to be effeminate. [. . .] someone like Thibaut could just as easily be straight as gay, and Hicham too' (Gay 2022). Beyond the cast, the theme of the series, which is linked to the question of individual and collective political commitment, and which lies at the heart of the title itself, speaks to both a targeted viewership (the audience of Editions Optimale, whose DVDs are often classified in the 'Gay and Lesbian Cinema' shelves at sales points) and a broader one (the audience of Studio 4, TV5 Monde and YouTube, where the entire series is freely available online). The series' many awards testify to the recognition it has received not only for its particular theme (Best LGBT Series at the UK Web Fest in 2017), but also more generally (Best Web-Series at the nineteenth La Rochelle TV Fiction Festival in 2017, as well as Best Actor for Mehdi Meskar, Best Screenplay and Best Web-Series at the Toulouse Francophone Web-Series Festival in 2017, Best Foreign Language Series at the Stareable Fest in NYC in 2018, Best Drama Series at the HollyWeb Festival in Los Angeles in 2018, Best Web Creation and Best Supporting Actor for Denis D'Arcangelo at the Rome Web Awards in 2018). These distinctions reward its particularly accomplished use of the short form, which I shall now turn to, looking at its three guiding principles: variation, alternation and ellipsis.

VARIATIONS

The titles of the first season's episodes are striking: E01 'S'enfuir' [Running away], E02 'Se retrouver' [Finding yourself], E03 'S'ouvrir' [Open], E04

'*S'embrasser*' [Kissing], E05 '*S'émanciper*' [Emancipate], E06 '*S'acharner*' [Hitting], E07 '*Se découvrir*' [Discovering yourself], E08 '*S'associer*' [Partnering], E09 '*Se compromettre*' [Compromising], E10 '*Se confronter*' [Confronting].[4] In French, each title is a pronominal verb in the infinitive form and each title crystallises a tipping point for one or several characters, considered individually but also as reflecting an archetype. In the audio commentary to the DVD (E02), the scriptwriter specifies that it was the title of the fourth episode ('*S'embrasser*') that served as a model for all the others. The infinitive lends a dynamic form to these titles, by emphasising an action and beginning the episodes with the idea that that action can be generalised beyond the characters most directly concerned. Moreover, the pronominal verbs are sometimes reflexive, sometimes reciprocal, sometimes both, which reflects the series' overall project: the eight main characters move from individual quests to collective commitment, and from turning inwards on themselves to opening up to others.

Carrying out such an ambitious project within the economy of a mini web-series meant there were considerable pitfalls to avoid. In order to achieve the 'languorous mix of sounds and colours' (Sialelli 2017) that characterises the series, it was necessary 'to be visually interesting, with limited means in terms of both time and budget', to quote the director Jules Thénier (Thénier & Potherat 2017).

The work that the series does with colour is immediately visible in its poster, where pink (often associated with the feminine) provides a counterpoint to the dominant blue (often associated with the masculine). When Hicham arrives in Lyon (E01), a brief shot shows a street name that has been replaced by a woman's name, with a pink sticker covering the official dark blue plaque. This is explained in Episode 5, when Murielle tells Nadjet that it was part of an initiative carried out by women activists in many of the city's streets to raise awareness about the fact that so few are named after women. At the end of this episode, entitled '*S'émanciper*', Nadjet, who has decided to take control of her life, replaces the blue plaque of the 'rue Pouteau' with a pink one that reads 'rue Olympe de Gouges', after Murielle has explained the pioneering role played by Olympe de Gouges in raising feminist demands during the French Revolution (Figure 8.1).

Further work on colour can be seen in the décor of the organisation's premises, which on the ground floor has four coloured roller banners, visible in the very first episode, prefiguring the seven colours of the rainbow in the 'happening' at the beginning of Episode 4.

The characters' psychological and social development is also revealed through their clothing, and particularly through the tops worn by one of the two protagonists. Hicham progressively replaces his old-fashioned baggy diamond-print jumper (from the first episodes) with elegant, single-colour tops, sometimes worn without anything underneath (in the last episodes).

Figure 8.1 Nadjet (Nanou Harry) lays a sticker 'rue Olympe de Gouges' at the end of E05.

The question of clothing is even the subject of a humorous exchange between the two characters at the beginning of Episode 3 when Thibaut protests: 'Quoi, mon p'tit pull? Il fait pas pédé, mon pull, là!' [What about my jumper? Damn, it's not faggy!].

From one episode to the next, variations on compositional patterns allow for a crescendo in plot progression, based on the gradual revelation of each character's flaws. This is the case, for example, with the appearance of two important characters: Bastien (Claudius Pan), a prostitute who has been the victim of a homophobic attack, and Vincent (Benjamin Mayet), Thibaut's ex-partner. Bastien is mentioned verbally in E02 and glimpsed in E06, before entering Hicham's life in E07 and becoming the centre of the inquiry carried out in E08. Similarly, Vincent appears furtively within a reverse angle shot in E04, then as a vision in E06, before entering the storyline in E07 (when Hicham comes to question him), and being fully given a place in the final two episodes, as Thibaut's flaws are revealed – the season ends with Thibaut turning up at Vincent's flat.

Finally, this play on patterns leads to several mirror structures within the macrostructure. The season begins with Hicham's angst and ends with Thibaut's, as figured by a chiasmic construction: at the beginning of the first episode, Hicham is filmed with a shoulder camera and appears as fairly immobile, in an unstable image, while at the end of the last episode he is filmed with a fixed camera, mobile within a stable image; the exact reverse is true for Thibaut. In another mirror effect, Claude (Denis D'Arcangelo), an activist in his sixties, warns Hicham about Thibaut in Episode 3 and then warns Thibaut about Hicham in Episode 6. Similarly, a cross-cutting sequence in the fourth episode enhances Thibaut's desultory attitude and Hicham's seriousness, while it is the opposite at the end of the final episode when we are shown Hicham's carelessness contrasting with Thibaut's disarray. The same mirror effect is also present in the macrostructure of the whole series: Season 3 ends with a young black gay man arriving in the organisation just as the first season began with Hicham's arrival at Le Point G.

ALTERNATIONS

Maxime Potherat has stated: 'Alternation is a key word for me' (Thénier & Potherat 2017). This alternation is apparent on several levels. The many changes in rhythm provide the necessary breathing space between action and introspection. Comic scenes (in which improvisation plays a decisive role) alternate with action scenes and lyrical sequences within the same episode (which mainly last under 10 minutes).

The thresholds of each episode contribute to creating the dynamic characterising this season. Certain prologues lasting around 1 minute alternate between a humorous sequence and a dramatic sequence, for example in the opening sequences of E08 (an amusing scene depicting a stock count in the organisation) and E09 (when the vandalism of the organisation's premises is revealed [Figure 8.2]).

Similarly, some of the final sequences are constructed around a cliffhanger (for example E04 and E06), while others solve an enigma by means of an image, for instance in Episode 9 when the viewer realises that it is Thibaut himself who vandalised the frontage of the organisation's premises. Moreover, the short form lends particular intensity to the beginnings and endings of episodes.

This alternation is also visible from one episode to another. Some episodes function almost autonomously, such as Episode 5 ('*S'émanciper*'), focused on Nadjet's quest for independence, or Episode 8 ('*S'associer*'), focused on the

Figure 8.2 Hicham (Mehdi Meskar) and Murielle (Claudine Charreyre) discover the homophobic tags at the start of E09.

characters resuming the inquiry into the homophobic attack upon Bastien, which means they can be watched as standalones. Others are presented as the continuation of the previous episode, beginning with the prologue before the opening credits, in which the last sequence from the previous episode is shown again (E03 and E05).

This work on alternation is extended by the careful use of alternating points of view: the scene with Hicham's first kiss is shown from Thibaut's point of view in E04; the attraction between Bastien and Hicham is shown from Nadjet's point of view in E05 after a series of angle/reverse angle shots; and the exchange of knowing looks between Vincent and Thibaut, testifying to their earlier romance, is shown from Hicham's point of view in E07. In all cases, the use of slow motion adds emphasis to this alternation.

The alternation in tone within the microstructure of each episode and within the macrostructure of the season leads to a considerable variety of sequences within this 10x10 minute format. The most striking example is perhaps the final sequence of Episode 9, marking Thibaut's downward spiral. Thibaut – a charismatic 'winner' figure who is very sure of himself, like the characters Stuart and Brian in the British (Channel 4, 1999–2000) and North American (Showtime, 2000–5) versions of *Queer as Folk* – has just won the election to be head of the organisation, but only by using more than dubious methods. He is filmed in slow motion dreaming of being back in Vincent's arms as he wanders the streets at night to the soundtrack of Pierre Lapointe's song 'Je déteste ma vie' [I hate my life], of which we hear the last two verses and the chorus. This is the second track on the Quebecois singer-songwriter's album *Paris Tristesse* (2014), and it is the only time vocal music is used in the season to accompany an emotional climax by putting it into words (in S02E03, a song is again used to important effect in the revelation of Elijah's trans identity). By unfolding in slow motion, that finale, which may be compared to a video clip, stands as a lyrical mise-en-abyme of the short form in a miniseries that is itself made up of brief episodes. Further, while there is no explicitly LGBT content in Pierre Lapointe's song, it comes from an album that ends with a cover of Charles Aznavour's 'Comme ils disent' [As they say] (1972), a pioneering song evoking homosexuality at a time when it was still taboo in France. The choice of this song hints at many offscreen implicit allusions that inscribe the series within a more extensive history of activism, as explicitly referred to in the second episode.

ELLIPSES AND OFF-CAMERA

By shifting to the 10x10 minute web-series format, the screenplay was necessarily condensed. As it gained in density, so certain narrative elements were left in a blind spot, at times barely comprehensible upon a first viewing of the series.

NARRATIVE EFFICIENCY & CONSTRAINTS OF THE SHORT FORM 141

Figure 8.3 Thibaut (Eric Pucheu) receives a message from Hicham before sleep at the end of E04.

For example, Nadjet's arrival in the series raises many questions. She appears at the end of Episode 4 when she rings the doorbell at Thibaut's flat, where Hicham is staying temporarily. Then at the beginning of the next episode, Thibaut greets her by name, as though he already knew her. Two points remain unexplained: how did she find her brother? How did Thibaut recognise her? In the initial screenplay available on Sullivan Le Postec's website (Le Postec 2017, 57), the fifth episode starts with a flashback in which Nadjet contacts Thibaut via social media, but this flashback has disappeared from the final cut. The only clue to this is when Hicham invites Thibaut to join his group of friends (Figure 8.3). But it seems difficult to piece together the missing link in the storyline. A blind spot seems to have been left deliberately in the final cut of the series.

These ellipses very often contribute both to the density and the acceleration of the storyline, which again can sometimes make it difficult to understand in all its dimensions when watching it for the first time. For example, the beginning of the fourth episode seems particularly complex. It shows the happening organised by Thibaut first thing in the morning in front of the district Mayor's offices, to denounce his homophobia. Three ideas are developed in this sequence: 1) the difficulty of setting up this rainbow happening; 2) the plan to out Amaury (which Thibaut hides from most of the participants); 3) Hicham's refusal to kiss the man he is paired with (he reveals in the next sequence that he has never kissed anyone on the mouth before). The end of the sequence is so intense that it is difficult to understand in all of its aspects: 1) the president of the organisation confiscates the tracts; 2) Amaury is humiliated, to Thibaut's great satisfaction; 3) Murielle leaves the happening, showing her disapproval. The viewer therefore wants to see the sequence, the episode, or even the whole season again – something that the web-series makes possible, since it is available on many online platforms, and that is also facilitated by the short format, which does not require watching hours of TV fiction (Season 1 lasts 98 minutes in total). The aesthetic pleasure of re-watching is combined here with a desire to make sense of the sometimes striking blind spots and ellipses that the creator and screenwriters retained in the montage.

Finally, the work done outside the narration proper is also developed in the bonuses to the DVD that anchor the series in reality, from a documentary perspective. In *Les Engagés*, the blogger Rose (Anaïs Fabre) produces reports and interviews in connection with Le Point G's latest activities. The character is a synthesis of several bloggers present in the original screenplay, on an idea of the directors Potherat and Thénier, as specified by Le Postec in the audio commentary (E01). She also appears in the bonuses on the DVD (taken up and expanded on the YouTube channel 'Le Monde de Rose' [Rose's world] for a series of reports entitled '*Paroles d'engagés*' [Talking with activists] in which she interviews real-life members of Lyon's LGBT activist community). The DVD thus offers a documentary miniseries made up of eight episodes (and enhanced to thirteen episodes on YouTube) that runs parallel to the main series: the miniseries is actually a miniature version of the original longer series as it is composed of episodes that are even shorter as they last between 2 and 5 minutes. A fictional character therefore goes out and meets the real-life actors of a community. As the homepage of the 'Le Monde de Rose' channel puts it: 'Rose has left the fictional world to go and meet men and women who are committed to activism in the day to day. A series of interviews recommended to lift your spirits!' This interplay between fiction and reality, which is so typical of the web-series form itself (Rio 2013, 58–9), blurs viewers' relationship to the plot and prompts them to watch the season again. It also begs the question of what links there might be between the fiction itself and its sources of inspiration (the creator's experiences in LGBT organisations). Some features of Lyon's real-life LGBT activist community also figure briefly, for example on a yellow poster for the queer cinema festival 'Ecrans mixtes' in most episodes. In Episodes 6 and 7, the meeting of the board is shot in a room located in the LGBT Centre in Lyon, which we easily recognise in the first reports in *Paroles d'engagés*. Similarly, in the audio commentary of Episodes 1 and 7, Le Postec points out that the sauna and the gay bar where the protagonists see each other really existed in Lyon when the script for the series was underway.

In this regard, various elements, which, on first viewing, take the form of almost imperceptible nods to those in the know, emerge to create a sense of complicity within a community of fans. For example, Le Postec himself appears in a shot at the beginning of the first episode (when Hicham arrives in Lyon, in the street that has been renamed with the pink sticker) and can later be seen among the dancers in the nightclub at the beginning of E07 and in the General

Assembly in E09. Similarly, the fact that Thibaut lives at number 65 of his street is a reference to the web-series *On habite au 65* (2015) [We live at number 65] by Maxime Potherat, one of the two directors of the first season of *Les Engagés*.

The writing in the series *Les Engagés* makes the intertwined fates of three generations of activists resonate with each other, both within the microstructure of each episode and the macrostructure of the first season; the second season, directed by Slimane-Baptiste Berhoun (interviewed in the fifth report of *Paroles d'engagés*), also develops echoes with Season 1 that take some of its main directorial choices further, while the third season, directed by Sullivan Le Postec himself, chooses a longer format (three episodes of 45 minutes each).

In the initial season, the linearity produced by its composition around a set of varied patterns was tempered by the principle of alternating tone, rhythm and point of view, as well as by the ellipses that encourage the viewer to return to the series for further aesthetic pleasure and deeper understanding. What is more, the presence of short forms which reflexively appear as 'mis en abyme' (in the liminal parts of some episodes) or as running parallel (through the mini documentary web-series that is available on the DVD or on YouTube) multiplies the various layers of reading thanks to a constant to-and-fro movement between the past and the present, and between fiction and documentary. Thanks to the tension produced by the constraints of the short form, the writing provides a nuanced and multifaceted perspective on the characters' individual awakening and collective commitment and offers viewers a few emotional climaxes that are genuine 'moments of grace' (P.M. 2017).[5]

NOTES

1. Studio 4, now Studio par France.tv slash, is a web platform dedicated to French and foreign fiction web-series, which belongs to France Télévisions. These web-series are also broadcast on free web platforms, such as YouTube and DailyMotion (Ziemniak 2017, 62–3).
2. TV5 Monde is a French public television network, broadcasting across the world French-speaking programmes, available on satellite, online and via TVPlayer.
3. The series is broadcast in the English-speaking countries under the title *Woke*.
4. In square brackets, the titles of the episodes when the series was broadcast in the English-speaking countries.
5. The author of this chapter and the editors would like to thank Lucy Garnier most warmly for her translation of this text.

WORKS CITED

Antoine, '*Les Engagés*: rencontre avec le créateur de la série et les deux acteurs qui la portent', blog *Séries Chéries*, 13 July 2017. Available online: https://seriescheries.

com/2017/07/13/les-engages-rencontre-avec-le-createur-de-la-serie-et-les-deux-acteurs-qui-la-portent (Accessed December 2022).

Bihel, Ingrid, 'L'explosion des programmes courts comiques (shortcoms) en France', *Web-revue des industries culturelles et numériques*, 2012. Available online: https://industrie-culturelle.fr/industrie-culturelle/lexplosion-des-programmes-courts-comiques-shortcoms-en-france-ingrid-bihel/ (Accessed July 2023).

'Comme ils disent', written, composed and sung by Charles Aznavour, *Idiote je t'aime*, Barclay, 1972.

Delaporte, Chloé, 'Aux marges de la fiction sérielle télévisuelle: sémio-pragmatique de la shortcom familiale', *TV/Series*, no. 15 (2019). Available online: URL: http://journals.openedition.org/tvseries/3661; DOI: https://doi.org/10.4000/tvseries.3661 (Accessed February 2024).

Gay, Déborah, 'La représentation de l'autre. Enquête sur les conditions de production de personnages racisés dans une websérie LGBT', *Réseaux* 223 (2020): 107–28.

Gay, Déborah, '"Est-ce qu'il fait gay?": Analyse des questions soulevées lors du casting de comédiens pour des personnages gays dans une websérie', *Genre, Sexualité & Société* 28 (2022). Available online: http://journals.openedition.org/gss/7581 (Accessed December 2022).

'Je déteste ma vie', written, composed and sung by Pierre Lapointe, *Paris Tristesse*, Belleville Music, 2014.

Le Postec, Sullivan, '*Les Engagés. L'intégrale des scénarios de la première saison*', blog *Les Engagés*, 2017. Available online: https://data.over-blog-kiwi.com/2/32/93/26/20170705/ob_5662e4_les-engages-scenarios-saison-1.pdf (Accessed December 2022).

On habite au 65, created by Maxime Potherat, YouTube, 2015.

P.M., 'Analyse critique: *Les Engagés*', blog *Papiers Journaux. Fragments de vie culturelle*, 27 July 2017. Available online: https://papiersjournaux.wordpress.com/2017/07/27/analyse-critique-les-engages (Accessed December 2022).

Queer as Folk, created by Russell T. Davies, Channel 4, 1999–2000.

Queer as Folk, developed by Ron Cowen and Daniel Lipman, Showtime, 2000–5.

Rees-Roberts, Nick, *French Queer Cinema* (Edinburgh: Edinburgh University Press, 2008).

Rio, Florence, 'Du programme court télévisuel à la mini-série web: l'essor d'un dispositif novateur?', in *Les Formes brèves audiovisuelles: des interludes aux productions web*, ed. Sylvie Périneau (Paris: CNRS Editions, 2013), 47–62.

Salielli, Marine, '*Les Engagés* (critique saison 1): une belle humanité', *Les Chroniques de Cliffhanger & Co*, 12 June 2017. Available online: https://leschroniquesdecliffhanger.com/2017/06/12/les-engages-critique-saison-1-une-belle-humanite (Accessed December 2022).

Thénier, Jules and Maxime Potherat, 'La réalisation: entretien avec Jules Thénier et Maxime Potherat', blog *Les Engagés*, 2017. Available online: http://lesengages.over-blog.com/2017/06/realiser-les-engages-entretien-avec-jules-thenier-et-maxime-potherat.html (Accessed December 2022).

Ziemniak, Pierre, *Exception française: de Vidocq au Bureau des légendes, 60 ans de séries* (Paris: Vendémiaire, 2017).

CHAPTER 9

Crisis on Earth-X or the Status of the Crossover Event

Claire Cornillon

The Arrowverse,[1] or the CW DCVerse, includes seven shows aired on The CW (*Arrow, The Flash, Supergirl, Legends of Tomorrow, Black Lightning, Batwoman* and *Superman & Lois*) that take place in the same fictional universe and are thought of as being part of one single large story, inspired by the DC Comics superheroes. The oldest of these is *Arrow* (developed by Andrew Kreisberg, Greg Berlanti and Marc Guggenheim, 2012–20), then *The Flash* (Andrew Kreisberg, Greg Berlanti and Geoff Johns, 2014–present), *Supergirl* (developed by Greg Berlanti and Ali Adler, CBS then The CW, 2015–21) and *Legends of Tomorrow* (developed by Andrew Kreisberg, Greg Berlanti and Marc Guggenheim, 2016–22). The different series are (or were) broadcast on different weeknights, and the schedule has varied from year to year. Therefore the CW's whole week is scheduled with DC shows, creating a sense of continuity and a vast space for the creation of fictions for the viewers. The possibilities in terms of narration and fiction are unique, especially because of the diversity of these shows in terms of tone, atmosphere and genre, leading to a broad range of characters and fictional situations. Thus whereas *Legends of Tomorrow* is a met a fictional and sometimes delirious comedy, *Arrow* is a very dark action series. Moreover, because of their science-fiction/fantastic nature, within all four series, the fictional universe incorporates time travel, different dimensions, other planets and magic.

In this context, I would like to analyse one very specific case, the crossover event called *Crisis on Earth-X*, which aired in November 2017 and which linked four series of the Arrowverse (*Arrow, The Flash, Supergirl* and *Legends of Tomorrow*) together into one story in four episodes. It had been done already the year before (and was done again in 2018 and 2019), but *Crisis on Earth-X* took the crossover game to another level. These four episodes have a very specific status within this group of series and could almost be considered as a spin-off miniseries of the four shows, creating a short format within the ever-expanding vastness of the narrative. They also lead us to think about network television today, and about the way it keeps on using its old techniques in terms of narrative constraints and format in a very clever way, to transform television into an event. In the case of *Crisis*, it is the scale of this event that is important. Crossovers have existed for a long time, especially within series already linked as spin-offs (for example, between *Frasier* [NBC, 1993–2004] and *Cheers* [NBC, 1982–93]), but also between series from the same network and linked by the programming schedule (such as *The Pretender* and *Profiler*, both simultaneously broadcast in NBC's Thrillogy, 1996–2000) or by their creator (such as David E. Kelley's *Ally McBeal* [FOX, 1997–2002] and *The Practice* [ABC, 1997–2004]) – some actually combining several of those criteria, such as *Angel* (created by Joss Whedon and David Greenwalt, The WB, 1999–2004) and *Buffy* (created by Joss Whedon, The WB/UPN, 1997–2001). But crossovers were generally limited to one or two episodes, with few characters moving from one show to the other, and with plots that did not have much incidence on the shows ('I will remember you', *Angel* S01E08, plays with this trope as Buffy forgets everything that happened at the end of the episode). On the contrary, *Crisis* was not the usual two-series crossover, but an entirely separate show with all the familiar characters – as well as some new ones – interacting just for the duration of this specific week of television. In this sense, this specific crossover constitutes a short form in itself inside the much larger form of the *Arrowverse*. But what *Crisis* kept from the tradition of the crossover, and amplified, is the pleasure of world-building by connecting shows (in diegetic and narratological terms) and the capacity to create an event, something that will please the fans (in a production/reception perspective). This tension between autonomy and continuity, a key element of seriality, will be the focus of this chapter. Because most of the characters of these shows already existed as comic-book characters, these series play with the idea of transfictionality, as analysed by Richard Saint-Gelais (Saint-Gelais 2011). But the specificity of the crossover is to question the status of the transfictional character by considering each of the series as a part of a super-series and therefore belonging to the same work. The group of characters in the crossover does not have the same status as, for instance, Nemo and Jekyll in the comic-book series *The League of Extraordinary Gentlemen* co-created by Alan Moore in 1999.

Crisis on Earth-X is an event, for the production and for the viewers. First, for a very simple reason: fun. The crossover context allows the production to play with its characters and with its fictional universe at a scale that is not usually possible during a basic episode. Crossovers have always been events on network television.[2] The idea is to create must-see television, something special that viewers cannot miss, but also a sort of gift to the fans, and to the production crew itself. The first sequence after the opening credits in the first episode sets the tone and announces what is at stake in terms of storytelling and of production/reception in these episodes (*Supergirl*, 'Crisis on Earth-X Part 1', S03E08). The sequence is a montage of the different characters shown consecutively over the course of a single song, which gives a sense of continuity, introducing every group of characters in the context of their own shows but responding to the same event: the invitation to Barry and Iris's wedding. It thereby blends all the Arrowverse characters together, while at the same time contextualising each group. It creates an impression of simultaneity because all the scenes reference the same event, creating a cross-cutting effect. Every show is therefore individually introduced, with the main characters and some elements characterising each series, in case some viewers had not yet seen them, which – it is important to highlight this point – is very possible. Because of its particularities, each show has a specific audience. Of course, many viewers watch all of them, but this is not universally true. Therefore, for many viewers, the crossover obliges them to watch an episode of an unfamiliar show. This explains why all the locations are indicated, in the same graphic style as the main characters' logo. Everything is in place to immediately identify each of the four groups, but also to link them together. The sequence equally makes it obvious that it is a special episode: the aesthetics are very sophisticated, with complex and expressive shots and many CGI effects. It is composed mostly of action scenes, so this opening specifies the style of every show, but also blurs them into one vast epic sequence (especially through the use of music), which is after all the whole point of the crossover pattern. What is interesting is that it is also a way to create a contrast between this non-superhero event, the wedding, and the everyday lives of these heroes, which are, of course, extraordinary. In the sequence, they are all risking their lives fighting (aliens, a mutant shark, ninjas) or travelling through time. Therefore the sequence creates a funny image of the everyday life of superheroes: not only do they have to save the world, but they also have to have a life. The dialogue between Felicity and Oliver sums up this aspect of the situation. When he protests that he is currently occupied, she responds that he is 'just' fighting ninjas, that it is not the end of the world and that they can therefore have this banal conversation, because it is not as if he were in any real danger of dying. And the fact is, of course, Oliver, the protagonist of the series, is going to win this momentary struggle. So, what is often treated as tragic in the four series is reinvested here in both an epic and a comic way. This example of a change of tone is a characteristic of what the crossover can bring: it displaces the ordinary dynamics of the series to show them from another point of view (tragic, comic, epic, et cetera).

This change of point of view can be created simply through the contrast between characters from different shows who bring with them the tone of their respective series. It is obvious that characters from *Legends of Tomorrow* shed a different light on the events than the ones from *Arrow*. This collusion effect is not new at all; it was already a primary characteristic of some crossovers of 1990s TV series, for instance between David E. Kelley's two law shows: *Ally McBeal*, a romantic bittersweet musical comedy, and *The Practice*, a realistic dark series, both taking place in Boston. Characters Bobby Donnell and his team, from the latter show, are shown to be stunned by the antics of *Ally McBeal*'s Cage and Fish, when they work together in a crossover (S01E20 in *Ally McBeal* and S02E26 in *The Practice*). But little by little, they come to understand each other's style and they learn to respect one another. Something similar happens in the DCverse crossovers. In the previous iteration of the Arrowverse crossover event, entitled 'Invasion!' (November 28–December 1, 2016), this interpersonal conflict is a primary aspect of the plot, especially in terms of the relationship between Arrow and Supergirl, which is initially difficult. Indeed, the Green Arrow is the least powerful of the group of superheroes, but is always considered as their leader, whereas Supergirl is the most powerful but is also younger. These tensions evolve, leading to a mutual respect at the end of the crossover. What is interesting in this element of the plot is that this hierarchy is not only linked to the fictional universe itself, but can be explained also by the real-life context and production of the shows. The DCverse is usually called the Arrowverse, simply because *Arrow* is the oldest show, and that is also the reason why the Green Arrow is at the centre of the group. As such, the logic derives not necessarily from the story but from the context of production, which is crucial in understanding the many levels of interpretation of the crossover's functions, a point that will be further developed later.

Indeed, very different characters – some more comic, some more dramatic – are suddenly in the same room and in the same story. This creates discrepancies which are often funny, but it also compels the crossover to make some choices to create a unified narrative. For example, the story begins in an episode from *Supergirl*, but the tone is not the one we are used to in this specific series, which is a lighter tone, underlined by a vision of the city mostly by day and with the use of colours. The sequence looks more like a scene from *Arrow*, as it is very dark and urban. Therefore, it is immediately clear that the crossover, in its autonomy, is here more important than the original show, which is subordinate to the needs of the television event. This dominance of *Crisis on Earth-X* is one of the reasons why we can understand it as a sort of short-lived spin-off of the shows featuring the different characters as a united group (as has been done in other franchises such as the MCU, with *The Avengers* or *The Defenders*).

Once the group unites, the interesting aspect of a crossover of this scale is the mass effect of the superhero group. Every one of these shows is built on a team of superheroes. Therefore, gathering all the teams offers a very large number of characters, enhancing the possibilities in terms of the scale of action scenes. The director frequently uses specific camera angles to obtain wide shots with all the teams together for the purpose of this epic dimension, especially in fight scenes. More than the visual aesthetics, this mass effect also influences the plot. Indeed, which enemy can be strong enough to threaten such a group? There are two possible answers to that question that are used in *Crisis*: an army and doppelgangers. In 2016, the crossover had already used the trick of creating an army, but in this case it was extraterrestrials, called 'dominators', coming to invade Earth. In *Crisis*, the superheroes fight against Nazis coming from another Earth where they won WWII and where Hitler died only in 1994. However, although the scale is the same in the two crossovers, the nature of the enemy is different. Nazis are a traditional enemy for superheroes who were born in comic books at the end of the 30s – but one can argue that in 2017, representing Nazis in this kind of fiction is not neutral, given the rise of the far-right and especially because of the neo-Nazi marches which occurred a few months before the airing of these episodes.[3] The political aspect of the crossover is quite obvious. For instance, there is a strong and explicit discourse against homophobia.

Dominators were the 'other', whereas the enemy in *Crisis* is simply what we can be as humans. It is something which has been often explored within the shows: the idea that, in another context, one can be a different person, and that good or evil is not our essence. But in the crossover, this concept is specifically underlined because of the presence of evil doppelgangers[4] of the main heroes. What is at stake in these episodes is consequently very different. Supergirl says about the dominators at the beginning of the first part: 'These guys are so last year.' The crossover will therefore be metafictional and fun, as was the first one, but the creators are stating that they have to do something better every year and that they will propose a story on another scale.

The crossover opens up many possibilities in terms of the form and the content of the story, but it also has an effect on the reception, because it transforms the episode into a special event. For instance, fans see the characters on their screen but at the same time, they also see the actor playing a new version of a familiar character. As such, this kind of episode creates an expectation, not only for the fictional world, but for the production of this fiction. Fans are interested in seeing what the actor is going to do as the doppelganger and this aspect contributes to the special status of the episode. *Crisis* plays on this element at several levels. Because his character has lived through very dark periods of time when he considered it was fine for him to kill or torture, Stephen Amell's performance as the doppelganger, for example, is not that different from what we already know of him. The Green Arrow in the show is sometimes his own evil doppelganger. On the contrary, Overgirl, the evil Supergirl, has to be played by Melissa Benoist in a very different way, as a cruel and dark character whereas Kara is usually nice and caring, and it is entertaining to see that change of tone. Leonard Snart (Wentworth Miller), a thief in his original version, is, in this new dimension, a very moral person and, as a consequence, an interesting variation on the character that we know. The idea of doppelgangers also allows the production to orchestrate a comeback for actors who had left the show, such as Colin Donnell, who plays Tommy Merlyn. His character died, but he appears in this episode as the Earth-X Nazi version of Tommy. The very structure of the crossover highlights the importance of this discovery, constituting one of the episodes' cliffhangers. All these elements are not necessarily new to the shows,[5] but they are combined here more densely in order to create something that is worth waiting for, a crystallisation of the characteristics of the different series designed to appeal to viewers.

To make this even more eventful, the writers briefly presented a new character during the final wedding scene, leading to much fan speculation as to the mystery character's identity. It was later revealed that it was Barry and Iris's daughter, come from the future. This is another example of the way that the episodes play with all the tricks that are expected in an event like this, especially with fan-friendly 'Easter eggs'. The crossover event is essentially geared towards fan interaction and fan service: fans can be active on forums and social media before the airing in their attempts to glean further information about it, and then comment on it during the show, before trying to decipher all the new information in each episode afterwards,[6] such as this new mystery character. These events not only increase fan engagement; they also strengthen links inside the fan community.

The most important aspect of *Crisis*, I think, is a certain play on the duality between continuity and autonomy – obviously a key element of seriality. *Crisis* presents itself as a unit that has a special status, and that is not simply four episodes of four different shows. In a way, it is a miniseries, or at least it is presented this way, which calls into question the dynamics of contemporary storytelling and the context of production and reception on network television.

The autonomy of this crossover is underlined by the fact that we explore a new Earth, with a new fictional universe and new versions of characters that we know as well as new characters. Thus the crossover is used to introduce The Ray, another superhero from Earth 1, who lives on Earth-X and is in love with the Earth-X Leonard Snart. When we see him for the first time, it is in a concentration camp where he bears the pink triangle on his clothes. Jax, the young ex-quarterback who became one half of the superhero Firestorm with the scientist Martin Stein, does not know what this symbol means, so he explains it to him. Again, this scene is linked to the political dimension of the crossover and has a didactic purpose, especially for the young audience.

This choice of plot, with new locations and characters, is a playground to try other things, but it is also a way to mingle. There are characters who did not know each other and who met in the crossover. This is often a technique to create funny scenes, but it is also used to develop characters, for instance, in this occasion, Sara (from *Legends of Tomorrow*) and Alex (from *Supergirl*). They have sex in the episode and this relationship is a rebound for Alex after her break-up with Maggie. This element of the plot is specific to the crossover as it implicates characters from different shows who meet at a special occasion, but at the same time it contributes to the narrative arc of both characters. It plays with the specificity of the crossover but feeds into the storyworld as a whole. The fact that these series are both highly formulaic and highly serialised[7] suggests that this hybridity is innate, but it is heightened with the idea of the crossover. Every episode of this type of show is both autonomous and interlinked. Therefore, the crossover is a means of foregrounding the question of the status of the episode. It is an opportunity to re-invest each show's respective narrative possibilities, but on the scale of the entire DCverse. A similar experiment was broadcast in the musical crossover between *Flash* and *Supergirl* the year before. It played with several layers of the shows, both narrative and extradiegetic, as in *Crisis*. Melissa Benoist, who plays Supergirl, and Grant Gustin, who portrays The Flash, both had a part in the musical TV Series *Glee* (Fox, 2009–15) and are accomplished singers. It was therefore expected that they were going to use these talents in a musical at some point in the shows. This musical crossover therefore does not necessarily follow a fictional logic. Instead, the storytelling is built on something exterior, taken from the context of production, but which adds a meaningful layer to the fictional world as well. The musical crossover follows the logic of integration of the musical as it has been analysed by Jane Feuer (Feuer 1993), and allows the characters to re-enchant their life, which leads to the proposal from Barry to Iris, the two main characters from *The Flash*. Fictional and metafictional aspects are so intertwined that it is not possible to really determine where one ends and the other begins. Moreover, in *Crisis*, during Barry and Iris' wedding, Kara sings again, because Barry now knows that she can, repeating the song used by Barry during the musical episode to propose ('I'm running home to you'). There is, consequently, a circulation of references within and outside the storyworld.

What makes this crossover a mini spin-off? Both marketing and aesthetics offer clues suggesting that the crossover was a separate entity, though interconnected to its four original shows. For instance, the opening credits of the shows have been replaced by credits specific to *Crisis*, featuring the characters from all four shows. This indicates that viewers are not watching *The Flash*, but rather a show called *Crisis on Earth-X*. Moreover, during the broadcast of the episodes, each commercial break would conclude with a written reminder on the screen: 'You are watching *Crisis on Earth-X*' (replacing the usual 'You are watching *The Flash*'). A special poster was made for the crossover, which looked like a movie poster and emphasised the unity of these four episodes as a whole. What is more, the episodes have no individual titles: they are called 'Part 1, 2, 3 and 4'. So when viewers watch the entire fifth season of *Arrow* for instance, they discover in the middle of the other episodes a part 2 of something for which they have neither the beginning nor the end. The airing schedule was also changed for this event, creating a two-night event instead of a series of episodes over the course of four different nights. The impact of this is both practical and symbolic: the usual schedule which allows viewers to identify each show was erased in order to look like they were launching something different. After all, the concept of a crossover created in this way makes sense only in the context of a weekly airing of the shows. It is rooted in a specific temporality which can be a special event, in one specific week. It is possible and it makes sense because the production controls the broadcasting. It would be more difficult in a streaming context where the whole season of the show is available on the same day. It could be possible, but it would not have the same effect. This is another example of contemporary strategies by producers who understand that the Netflix model is not necessarily the only way. Disney+ series and their weekly episodes have proved over the past years that what The CW was doing was not just a relic of another era of television. The recent success of *The Mandalorian* (Disney+, 2019–present), *WandaVision* (Disney+, 2021) or *Loki* (Disney+, 2021–present) has partly come from the possibility for the audience to follow the series in real time, to engage with it and to transform it into an event. *Crisis* is the epitome of this logic for The CW.

The fact is that you cannot watch any part of the crossover without the others. Without its counterparts, the individual episodes make no sense, because they are part of one vast, highly serialised story, with cliffhangers, in close continuity, and indeed the shows from which they are taken are not identifiable without outside information. There is no real dominant story arc which could indicate that you are watching *The Flash* for example. The episodes are not marked as belonging to one show or the other, which feeds the idea of a separate show, a spin-off. However, each part actually belongs to one specific show as it is part of the episode list of each show (Part 1 is listed as Episode 8 of *Supergirl* Season 3, Part 2 as Episode 8 of *Arrow* Season 6, Part 3 as Episode 8 of *The Flash* Season 4, and Part 4 as Episode 8 of *Legends of Tomorrow* Season 3). But almost nothing in the episode itself allows us to identify the different shows. There are a few clues, such as the fact that in *Legends of Tomorrow* the Legends appear more often than in the other episodes for instance, but those elements are not very obvious. Moreover, crucial events for characters from one show take place in another. The most obvious example of this aspect is the fact that Barry and Iris (the main characters from *The Flash*) and Oliver and Felicity (the main characters from *Arrow*) get married in the *Legends of Tomorrow* episode. This is a very surprising decision from a production standpoint because fans were waiting impatiently for these events to happen. But they had to watch *Legends of Tomorrow* to have the complete *Arrow* or *Flash* story. It is a sign of the confidence which the CW and the creative teams have in their fans, who are supposed to follow their lead and accept this special event. Of course, this is what happened and it was a success. Over time, the CW has developed a strategy in terms of broadcasting and of marketing based on interactions with a very supportive community of fans. Following the example of one of their lead shows, *Supernatural*, The CW pushed towards a very strong presence of the actors of the Arrowverse on social media, in order to feed the expectations around the shows. Lead actor Stephen Amell has an important following. This kind of fandom is not only in demand for events like crossovers but also possesses the literacy and the media habits to receive it and make the most of it. *Crisis* is therefore the result of the whole strategy of The CW in terms of production and marketing strategy.

Compared to traditional crossovers, such as the one between *Ally McBeal* and *The Practice* – which were playful and interesting but not very useful in terms of the story arcs, because they could be omitted from each series without much change – *Crisis* is, on the contrary, crucial to the long-term story. Important events, such as two weddings and the death of a central character occur during the crossover, making it impossible to remove it from the shows without breaking continuity. Of course, crossovers from the past, such as some between *Angel* and *Buffy*, were sometimes linked to main story arcs, but here, again, it is the scale of the complexity in *Crisis* that is so striking. The crossover chooses to insist on the characters' personal lives and relationships: two weddings, but also Alex and Sara's one-night stand, the father-and-son link between Jax and Martin, et cetera. All the specific story arcs of these episodes are pretexts for character development and that is why those episodes cannot be avoided in terms of the storyworld and storytelling dynamics.

These episodes are therefore presented as a spin-off, but at the same time the continuity with the original shows is crucial. This gives rise to a sort of super-series, in the sense of a supergroup in music, where members of successful bands gather to create a new band together. There is a similar logic to *Crisis*: all the characters bring with them the characteristics of their show, but they exist in a new context together. It is an interesting configuration because what bears the identity of the show is not the show itself but characters, places, plots – in a word, the fictional elements.

Therefore, I would like to argue that *Crisis* demonstrates that the network television pattern still exists besides other ways of creating TV series. This format is heavily linked to a specific temporality and relationship with fans. But what could be seen as old recipes take on new meaning and offer new possibilities because of the scale of the crossover event. With four episodes of four different shows on two nights, it is possible to create a miniseries. In fact, even though there are many references to storylines from each show, it is probably possible to just watch these four episodes, and to understand them. On the contrary, it is impossible not to watch these episodes to follow the narrative of the four shows, because of the key elements that they present. I would say that it is a way to describe how a semi-serialised formula show works. In this kind of series, you can watch one episode and understand it. But at the same time, if you are watching the whole show, you cannot avoid any episode to understand the story and the discourse on a more global level. The specificity of the crossover is an amplification of this phenomenon. *Crisis* is consequently a fine example of what is at stake in contemporary network television in an era of streaming platform services and an ever-increasing number of series broadcast in one way or another every year. The specificity of *Crisis* is, therefore, to question the short form inside the pattern of seriality, by creating a new space which exists only thanks to an editorial project. This short form is spectacular and exceptional but, at the same time, it plays with all the characteristics already present in the type of seriality represented by each of these shows. It therefore takes the experiment to another level.

NOTES

1. For an analysis of the Arrowverse as a franchise, see Joseph 2018.
2. On the use of crossovers, see for instance Benassi 2007, 111–29, or Feyersinger 2011, 127–57.
3. During the 2017 summer, there were white nationalist rallies in the United States. See for example this article: https://www.washingtonpost.com/news/local/wp/2017/08/13/heres-what-a-neo-nazi-rally-looks-like-in-2017-america/ (Accessed January 2023).
4. Evil doppelgangers can be easily found in comic books. We can think, for instance, of the Crime Society of America, an evil version of the Justice League.
5. We had already encountered doppelgangers before, but not the evil versions of the leaders of each team as a mirroring group of supervillains.
6. See, for example, this paper regarding the speculations about the new character introduced in the crossover, who was revealed later as Barry and Iris' daughter: https://www.digitalspy.com/tv/ustv/a844099/dc-fans-theory-crisis-on-earth-x-barry-iris-daughter/ (Accessed January 2023).
   Alternatively, see this other example of fan theories about the character of Tommy Merlyn: https://www.digitalspy.com/tv/ustv/a844092/arrow-crossover-episode-crisis-on-earth-x-tommy-merlyn-prometheus-fan-theory-colin-donnell/ (Accessed January 2023).
7. I classify all four shows as semi-serialised formula shows. For more details on this classification, see Cornillon 2018.

WORKS CITED

Ally McBeal, created by David E. Kelley, FOX, 1997–2002.
Angel, created by Joss Whedon and David Greenwalt, The WB, 1999–2004.

Arrow, created by Andrew Kreisberg, Greg Berlanti and Marc Guggenheim, 2012–20.
Batwoman, created by Caroline Dries, The CW, 2019–22.
Black Lightning, created by Salim Akil, The CW, 2018–21.
Buffy, created by Joss Whedon, The WB/UPN, 1997–2001.
Benassi, Stéphane, 'Spin-Off et Crossover. La transfictionnalité comme figure esthétique de la fiction télévisuelle', in *La Fiction, Suites et variations*, dir. René Audet and Richard Saint-Gelais (Rennes: Nota Bene and Presses Universitaires de Rennes, 2007), 111–29.
Cheers, created by James Burrows, Glen Charles, Les Charles, NBC, 1982–93.
Cornillon, Claire, 'Opening Credits', *Episodique*, 2018. Available online: https://episodique.hypotheses.org/158 (Accessed January 2023).
Feuer, Jane, *The Hollywood Musical*, 2nd ed. (Bloomington, Indiana University Press, 1993).
Feyersinger, Erwin, 'Metaleptic TV Crossovers', in *Metalepsis in Popular Culture*, eds Karin Kukkonnen and Sonja Klimek, Berlin: De Gruyter, 2011, pp. 127–57.
Frasier, created by David Angell, Peter Casey and David Lee, NBC, 1993–2004.
Glee, created by Ryan Murphy et al., Fox, 2009–15.
Joseph, Charles, 'The CW Arrowverse and Myth-making, or the Commodification of Transmedia Franchising', *SERIES*, 2018. Available online: https://series.unibo.it/article/view/8177 (Accessed January 2023).
Legends of Tomorrow, created by Andrew Kreisberg, Greg Berlanti and Marc Guggenheim, The CW, 2016–22.
Loki, created by Michael Waldron, Disney+, 2021–present.
Profiler, created by Cynthia Saunders, NBC, 1996–2000.
Supergirl, created by Greg Berlanti, Ali Adler, CBS then The CW, 2015–21.
Superman & Lois, created by Todd Helbing and Greg Berlanti, The CW, 2021–present.
The Avengers, created by Joss Whedon and Zack Penn, Marvel Studios, 2012.
The Defenders, created by Douglas Petrie and Marco Ramirez, Netflix, 2018.
The Flash, created by Andrew Kreisberg, Greg Berlanti, Geoff Johns, The CW, 2014–present.
The League of Extraordinary Gentlemen, written by Alan Moore and illustrated by Kevin O'Neill, Vol. 1, DC Comics, 1999.
The Mandalorian, created by John Favreau, Disney+, 2019–present.
The Practice, created by David E. Kelley, ABC, 1997–2004.
The Pretender, created by Steven Long Mitchell and Craig W. Van Sickle, NBC, 1996–2000.
WandaVision, created by Jac Schaeffer, Disney+, 2021.

Part 3

Blurring Boundaries: Production, Paratexts and Reception of the Short Form

CHAPTER 10

Loops, Bottles and Clips: Structuring Brevity in American Television

Shannon Wells-Lassagne

The fascinating nature of time as represented in fiction is particularly acute when studying television: more than any other medium, small-screen fictions are narratives defined by their temporality. Though this new golden age of TV seems to evoke associations with cinema and with length, offering series as '10-hour movies', television in its genesis was much more similar to radio, because as Caren Deming reminds us, television's very nature was based on immediacy and the ephemeral – and initially this was what made the new media intriguing:

> Television is inescapably about time. The sense of immediacy originating from simultaneous 'seeing at a distance' arose from genuine excitement about television as a new technology. Television's capacity (if not its dominant practice) to deliver events in real time remains its most salient claim to importance. (Deming 2005, 127–8)

While this aspect of television remains in our 'breaking news', sporting events or more recent experiments in live musical productions, it is worth noting that originally, television was all broadcast live, with no recording of its productions, and this immediacy (and its ephemerality) remains in television news of course, but also in television fictions' tendency to mimic the seasons the viewer is experiencing although they were filmed months before (an inevitable Christmas episode, et cetera),[1] perhaps explaining both the viewer's identification with the narrative and the seeming rapidity with which these narratives are forgotten.[2]

Moreover, as the very definition of what constitutes 'television' changes, and no longer signifies fiction broadcast on a television network, or even necessarily shown on a television set, time may in fact have become television's defining characteristic. Rosemary Huisman suggests that this was largely conditioned by American television's foremost characteristic as a commercial art form, where economic conditions were central in creating a good number of its traditions, notably in relation to time and its impact on the episode. Here are three characteristics of television narrative that economic constraints frequently would impose:

- the risk of investing leads to a conservative attitude to creative production, with great reliance on narrative conventions already established as successful (narrative repetition within the episode);
- the structure of the narrative of the individual program episode has to accommodate the interpolation of advertising texts within the episode as it goes to air (narrative segmentation);
- series and serials will preferably resist closure and be open-ended; for budgetary reasons the company prefers to find a successful formula for a program, then repeat that formula (narrative repetition between episodes).
- Given the circumscriptions described above, the production of narrative coherence in a television program is a conscious construction, and therefore explicit and established codes of television production are likely to be followed – and repeated (Huisman 2005, 164).

In this case, then, examining television's relation to time allows us to better understand the very nature of the medium and its content. The 'loops, bottles and clips' of my title refer to three time-honoured but high-concept television techniques that are all wilfully striking, while also being deeply related to the idea of time and more specifically, brevity in American television fiction. The bottle episode, the clip show and the time loop are all tried and true formulas in television fictions.[3] Examining these three techniques will allow us concrete examples of the repetition and segmentation that Huisman describes as typically televisual, while emphasising the importance of brevity and its relationship to length or duration in the traditions of American television. At the same time, the extreme nature of these techniques and the strain on realism that they create, the bravura implicit in their implementation, makes them all 'appointment television', thus fusing our interests in the intensity of this short form. What I hope to demonstrate is that these techniques are extreme examples accentuating underlying aspects of the televisual that are already present – these 'special episodes' are examples of evanescence in television's relationship to time.

To study these forms, I've chosen a series about series: *Community* (NBC, 2009–14; Yahoo 2014–15) was a sitcom that appeared in 2009 on one of the traditional broadcast networks, NBC. As a broadcast sitcom appearing on Thursday night primetime (a slot previously occupied by overwhelmingly successful sitcoms like *Seinfeld* [NBC, 1989–98], *Friends* [NBC, 1994–2004], *The Cosby Show* [NBC, 1984–92] or *Cheers* [NBC, 1982–93], and dubbed 'Must-see TV' by the network), the series seemed primed for success on a well-trodden path. The story of the series is also fairly classical: a successful lawyer, Jeff Winger, is found to have fraudulent credentials, and has to go back to the local community college to get a degree. While there, he meets a motley crew who make up his study group (and who correspond to the grand tradition of straight-man protagonist and wacky sidekicks long made standard in the genre). However, this apparently banal premise is in fact an opportunity to discuss the traditions of television in general and the sitcom more specifically, while the series ultimately subverts its forerunners and arguably could be seen as marking a turning point in the sitcom form itself.[4] It serves, therefore, as a shining example of metafiction, as is made clear in David Roche's work on the subject. In this chapter, the bottle episode, the clip show and the time loop will each be illustrated with an example from *Community* that deconstructs it, which will hopefully allow us to better understand the malleable nature of time in television.

The first of these combines the two defining characteristics of the television medium (time and money): the bottle episode is a standard form where creators make a 'budget episode' featuring only regular cast members in one of the pre-existing sets, which generally leads to significant character studies. In *Community*'s example, ambitious young student Annie has lost her pen, and while the other members of the study group want to leave and attend a 'puppy parade' on campus for pet adoption, she insists that they find it (or whoever stole it):

JEFF: (sarcastically) OK, whoever insidiously and with great malice aforethought abducted Annie's pen, confess, repent, and relinquish so we can all leave. [. . .]

ABED: Are we going to the Puppy Parade or not? 'Cause this is starting to feel like a bottle episode.

PIERCE: Again with the TV crap! Hey meatball! Did you take Annie's pen to make life more like *Benny Hill*, or whatever you do?

ANNIE: (suspiciously) Abed?

ABED: I wouldn't do that. I hate bottle episodes. They're wall-to-wall facial expression and emotional nuance. I might as well sit in a corner with a bucket on my head. [. . .]

JEFF: All right, everyone breathe. Do you know what this is?

ABED: Yup.

JEFF: Shut up. This is a normal day with a bunch of friends who are done studying and a pen that maybe rolled away.

ANNIE: (scoffing) Rolled away?

JEFF: Or maybe fell down someone's shoe.

ANNIE: Let's check shoes.
JEFF: Annie! Fine, fine. Someone in this room is hiding your pen. Wanna know why? They feel terrible. They made a mistake. They waited too long to come forward and now they feel bad. [. . .]
(PIERCE raises his hand. Everyone gasps.)
JEFF: Pierce, do you have something to tell us?
PIERCE: Yes. Is it me or has it become really obvious that Jeff took the pen? (Chorus of yeses.)
JEFF: You wanna bet, you jerks? Lockdown! Abed, seal the doors! Nobody leaves until this pen shows up.
ABED: I don't like this.
JEFF: Yeah, tell it to the pen you might have. [makes phone call] Gwennifer? Yeah, it's me – I can't make it. Well, tell your disappointment to suck it. We're doing a bottle episode.
('Cooperative calligraphy', S02E08, 2:31–8:55)

The low stakes (a missing ballpoint pen) are of course comic, though nothing new, whether you consider that it harkens back to *Seinfeld* being a series about nothing or to Hitchcock's beloved Macguffins. In fact one of the reasons this series is so interesting (and so useful for this specific study) is because of the character Abed, who by his own admission was 'raised by television' ('Home Economics', S01E08); his constant references to film and television are of course clearly metafictional, positioning *Community* firmly as postmodern, but it also points to the way that television traditions have become an integral part of a shared culture; as showrunner Dan Harmon noted, it would be completely unrealistic for some of these typical sitcom tropes to occur and not have someone refer back to its fictional counterparts (Dan Harmon 2010). This idea is confirmed by the irony of the remark that follows, when Pierce, a much older character who often finds himself befuddled by the group's contemporary references, mocks Abed's propensity towards TV fiction with what seems an outdated reference to *The Benny Hill Show* (BBC/ITV 1955–89), while actually using a television reference from a series that is approximately contemporary, and that has seemingly become a part of his lexicon: 'meathead' is an insult made popular by venerable sitcom curmudgeon Archie Bunker in landmark series *All in the Family* (CBS, 1971–9), a character that Pierce is obviously modelled after. The juxtaposition makes clear that while both character and technique might seem to be relegated to the past, they continue to have significance and relevance today. Here Abed's contributions underline that this is going to be a bottle episode, while also getting to the heart of what the bottle episode is generally about: while this episode with members of the main cast in a single setting was often an economic measure, ensuring cheap production costs with the means that were easily at hand, this tradition (especially – but not solely – of the sitcom genre) was in fact an opportunity to really examine the nature of the characters and their interactions: all 'facial gestures and emotional nuance'. All but the last minute of the 22-minute episode will take place in this single room, and the action is relegated to the characters reacting to one another, something that we can already see in the depiction of Annie (the highstrung pen loser) and Jeff (the smooth-talking leader). As Annie herself says, 'It's not a pen, it's a principle' – though the technique might be simple, and the reason basely materialistic (be it a budgetary measure or a pen), ultimately the artistry necessary to pull this situation off and make it funny and true to the characters is the ability to boil down the characteristics, the principles of screenwriting and performance to their very essence, and take the time to look inside everyone's bags/characters to see what they're hiding (the rest of the episode will include all of the characters actually stripping to reveal any hidden secrets – or pens). In so doing, the bottle episode also reveals the fundamental nature of television fiction's chronotopes. Bahktin's insistence on the inextricable nature of space and time is highlighted in this type of episode – while space has only recently expanded through increased television budgets allowing easier access to both location shoots and special effects in small-screen fiction, the bottle episode focuses on a location that is also the heart of the show, and on the relationship that space has to time (both for the characters, and as sole setting for an episode). Through this technique, then, by simplifying setting, chronology and storyline, the ephemeral nature of the 22-minute episode is ultimately thwarted – the bottle episode largely serves to show us just how subjective time in television is. Ironically, by focusing on both time and space and their limitations, the very banality of both time and space is part of what makes the episode exceptional, allowing us to delve into character and experience the time of the episode more intensely. When the group finally leaves 'lockdown', the dean passes by the study room now demolished by their feverish pen hunt:

DEAN PELTON: What the hell did you people do in there?
ABED: Something you and your puppies could only dream of, you non-miraculous son of a bitch. (19:50–19:53)

The transformational nature of this strip search for pens is of course played for humour, but the fact that the characters insist on the exclusive nature of their perception again points to the idea that the bottle episode is in fact foregrounding the intensity of real-time narrative, thus demonstrating the nature of the distinctions Ricoeur makes between the time of narrating, the narrated time and the fictive experience of time experienced in the relationship between the two.

The episode's conclusion also points to larger issues relating to television structure: unable to find the pen, the study group resorts to storytelling to resolve their quandary, deciding that a ghost must have stolen the pen rather than continuing to accuse one another of treachery. The viewer discovers a less supernatural, but equally unlikely resolution: a long-lost monkey belonging to one of the characters has been living in the air vents, and has been stealing various tokens (like Annie's pens): the camera pans over the different objects, which not-so-coincidentally link the episode back to previous events, like a mug made for the fictional morning show 'Troy and Abed in the Morning' that two of the characters repeatedly pretend to film (S01E20, S02E07, S02E12, S03E16, S03E19, S04E13), or the bracelets that one of the characters had made for the fellow members of the study group ('Comparative Religion', S01E12). In so doing, the conclusions (both for the characters, and for the viewer) privilege character over logic (the ghost over a pen thief), and the effect of the past in making this non-logic appealing to an audience – be it the study group deciding to believe that a long-deceased lover seeks pens to write a love letter, or the viewer acknowledging that our attachment to the characters and their previous adventures, as symbolised by the objects on display, ultimately outweigh both the unsatisfactory conclusion to this enigma, and indeed the illogical premise of the bottle episode altogether.

If the technique of the bottle episode focuses on the subjective nature of screen time, then, the time loop is even more explicit in its use of a tradition of artifice to explore character and structure. Normally, the time loop belongs to a certain genre (science-fiction or fantasy), where a character finds themselves trapped in a repeating sequence, and tries to free themselves; this also sometimes manifests in the possibility of alternate timelines, where it is the viewer's experience that is endlessly repeating, while the characters themselves remain unaware of their place in the time loop. This was most widely popularised by the film *Groundhog Day* (1993), but existed well before it; the concept appears to have originated in E.R. Eddison's novel *Worm Ouroboros*, published in 1922, a fantasy narrative where the heroes decide to repeat the recently ended war in the hopes of reliving the glorious battle endlessly. In its screen iterations, it seems to have first appeared in *The Twilight Zone* (CBS, 1959–64).[5] A first version appears in 1961's 'Shadow Play' (S02E26), though it ultimately uses the dream as its justification; a second episode from 1963 entitled 'Death Ship' (S04E06) is closer to the conventions of the trope. Set in the 'distant' future of 1997, spaceships are being sent from an overpopulated Earth to find planets suitable for colonisation; three astronauts are searching an unexplored planet when they discover a crashed ship – with their own corpses inside. The search for explanations occupies the rest of the episode (complete with seeming hallucinations of far-off Earth) before they find the solution . . . and start all over again. Both episodes are in fact adaptations of short stories (like many of *The*

Twilight Zone's episodes), but their application to television seems crucial: the association of a science-fiction and metafictional version of the Flying Dutchman is typical of the series, where the ship is endlessly roaming like its predecessor, but ironically is a portent of doom only to itself. This metafictional aspect of the narrative suggests that just as the spaceship mirrors itself, so the episode reflects on its medium: the inescapable nature of the loop the characters are stuck in suggests the indelibly repetitive nature of television.[6]

Community's version of the time loop tends to confirm this reading of the technique: in 'Remedial Chaos Theory' (S03E05), the group is celebrating Troy and Abed moving in together with a party, and when they order pizza, Jeff decides that they should roll the dice to see who goes downstairs to pick it up. Media-savvy Abed announces that this creates six different timelines – and the viewer experiences (almost) all of them. It is in the final 'timeline', where Abed refuses to allow Jeff to roll the die, therefore breaking the loop, that the series posits its views on the technique:

JEFF: OK. Starting on my left with one, your number comes up, you go.

ABED: Just so you know, Jeff, you are now creating six different timelines.

JEFF: (sarcastically) Sure I am, Abed.
(Graphics depict the die soaring through the air and falling to one of six designated spaces, before it cuts to Abed catching it in mid-air.)

ABED: I don't think you should. Chaos already dominates enough of our lives. The universe is an endless raging sea of randomness. Our job isn't to fight it, but to weather it, together, on the raft of life. A raft held together by those few rare, beautiful things that we know to be predictable.

BRITTA: Ropes? Vines? Let him finish!

ABED: Us. It won't matter what happens to us, as long as we remain accepting of one another's flaws and virtues. Annie will always be driven, Shirley will always be giving, Pierce will never apologize, Britta's sort of a wild card from my perspective, and Jeff will forever remain a conniving son-of-a-bitch.
(Cries of protest)

ABED: There are six sides of this die, and seven of us. He devised a system where he never has to get the pizza.
(Cries of outrage)

TROY: I think we just found our pizza-getter.

JEFF: Oh, like it matters who goes. (16:38–17:48)

The fact that this happiest and final timeline is created by Abed is typical of *Community*'s simultaneous depiction and deconstruction of television tropes, where it is the absence of the ostensible lead that actually leads the more beloved sidekicks to a more positive outcome (they begin raucously singing The Police's 'Roxanne', and begin dancing while Jeff stands on the sidelines, grumbling 'You see what happens when I leave you alone, huh?').[7] The episode (repeatedly) posits the limits of this time loop – only six sides to the die, so only six possible outcomes, and with the exception of Abed, the characters display reluctance to believe that alternate timelines exist at all,[8] refusing the science-fiction/fantasy nature of the premise. In so doing, the series positions itself outside these tropes – and thus better able to comment on them. In fact, the characters are not trapped in the time loop – only we have heard these lines and seen variations on the same acts again and again. As such, the episode clearly becomes a mise-en-abyme of television writing, the narrative repetition both within and between episodes that Huisman describes as characteristic of television: as Abed says, the characters exist as a point of predictability in a universe of chaos. Television fictions rely on this very predictability, this repetition, to retain their viewers – while also depending on the chaos that surrounds them to create enough difference to sustain the viewer's interest (like suddenly coming up with a seventh possible timeline despite the repeated insistence on limiting the time loop to six iterations). The fact that the new apartment features an Andy Warhol-like rendition of its two new occupants (reminiscent of the artist's depictions of Elizabeth Taylor or Campbell's soup) is no doubt symbolic here: no matter the colour scheme, Troy and Abed are always the same.

We can see this tension between the familiarity of repetition and the importance of evolution and novelty clearly, for example, in the explicit references

Figure 10.1 Troy and Abed's portrait (background centre): repetition with (limited) variation.

to narrative structure: the initial timelines are largely comic, but as the episode continues, the outcomes become increasingly dire, a clear manifestation of the classic three-act structure of the television episode; indeed, the initial timeline makes screenwriting clichés into actual plotlines, as Annie's bag holds the *Community* version of Chekov's gun, while in the darkest timeline it does, indeed, go off, resulting in Pierce's death.

The other aspect of the televisual made manifest through the use of the time loop, of course, is the importance of segmentation. By offering seven different timelines in a 22-minute episode (each loop lasts between 1:30–2:30), the episode highlights the strict framework of the American television series, a narrative divided not only by episodes or acts, but also by the commercial breaks typical of broadcast television: it's significant that the exchange that repeats through each timeline, Jeff explaining the rules, Abed remarking that this creates different timelines, and Jeff's sarcastic dismissal, immediately precedes each of the two commercial breaks for the episode, foregrounding how this extremely segmented text is in fact just an exaggerated version of the segmentation to which viewers of American television have become accustomed. One could also see a reference to the importance of segmentation in film studies since David Bordwell or Christian Metz and their attempts to discern a film grammar, but of course television is structurally segmented in a way that film never was – while films might have credits, they never had commercial breaks; with the exception of early film serials, they did not have episodes (though the increasing emphasis on franchise storytelling could call that into question somewhat). Segments have become increasingly fixed in TV culture, with the 'cold open', the credit sequence, the sequences between commercial breaks, the three-act structure, the closing credits, the 'previously on' and the reminders to 'tune in for scenes from next week'. Some of this has become less common with quality TV, but none of it has truly died out, and in some cases, the individual segments of the show are just as beloved as the episode as a whole, as with Bart Simpson's weekly blackboard punishment, or Chuck Lorre's numbered vanity cards at the end of his different TV sitcoms, from *Dharma and Greg* (ABC, 1997–2002) to *Two and a Half Men* (CBS, 2003–15) and *The Big Bang Theory* (CBS, 2007–19).[9] Time loops, therefore, are a way of highlighting the fundamentally divided nature of television, the way that brevity is part of the very structure of television storytelling, whether you're watching on a private channel with copious commercial breaks, or a streaming service where episodes follow one another, but are still separated into teasers, credits, three acts and end credits, and often associated with 'previously on' sequences or scenes from upcoming episodes afterwards. As Deming and Tudor remind us, this segmentation is fundamental to the medium:

> In stark contrast to the classical Hollywood narrative (often characterized as seamless), the televisual text is always about seams, or segment

markers, which don't interrupt the programs so much as help to constitute them. Television narratives use classical Hollywood rendering (such as shot-reverse shot patterns) within acts to inject television's highly elliptical narratives with natural illusion. More often than disguising divisions, then, the televisual flow manifests a preoccupation with division at the expense of continuity. (66)

Though television may generally use film techniques to hide their segmentation, here the time loop makes them manifest, where each repetition reminds us of the constitutive parts that make the episode and/or the series whole. The narrative repetition and narrative segmentation that Huisman spoke of as characteristic of television are one and the same, focusing our attention on both television's brevity (the many components that go into each and every episode) and its duration (through repetition of these elements, or of plot more generally).

My final example is one that is yet again motivated by economics, and perhaps more than any other has been thoroughly denigrated by contemporary viewers: the 'clip' show, where in yet another attempt to remain under budget, an episode is devoted to repeatedly reminiscing about past adventures – and showing clips from those previous adventures. By recycling sequences shot earlier, of course, studios can make considerable savings, but the tension between familiarity and novelty, repetition and innovation, becomes even more tenuous. The reason that these episodes are even an option, of course, is the power of memory (and indeed nostalgia) in the long-running series: the format appeals to the faithful viewer, who is now recalling long-past images placed in a new context. In so doing, the clip show foregrounds the idea of reaching out beyond the individual 'special episode' to consider the series as a whole, or at least to require the viewer to consider it in relation to its previous episodes.

In recent years, with the advent of VHS, DVD and streaming making episodes easily available for re-watching, versions of the clip show have become much rarer, and largely limited to satires; this is also the case for *Community*. 'The Paradigms of Human Memory' (S02E21) is an episode awash with clips and flashbacks to the narrative past only barely tied together with a frame story in the narrative present. The characters are making a diorama as a class project, when the long-lost monkey appears to steal a paintbrush. One of the characters follows him into the vents, where the objects from 'Cooperative Calligraphy' are rediscovered, and Jeff and Britta wax fondly over the memories they evoke (in the form of clips). This soon devolves into an argument about different members mistreating others in the group (again, complete with examples in the form of clips), or secretly harbouring romantic feelings for one another (showing yet more clips) before the episode concludes (and the members of the group forgive one another) after Jeff delivers an inspirational speech (itself splicing together different speeches from the different pasts that previous clips have introduced). As Jeff speaks, the series moves from one setting and situation to the next, suggesting that each speech supposedly tailored to the occasion is ultimately the same as the one before; his cadence and the music remain the same, while setting and mise en scene vary from shot to shot:

JEFF: You guys, wait. I wanna say something.
ANNIE: You don't have to save us with a speech. We're not breaking up. So we don't need to get back together.
JEFF: I know I don't have to, but I want to. (swelling inspirational music) Look, we've known each other for almost two years now. (cut to the group in a cobweb-infested hotel lobby at night) And, yeah, in that time, I've given a lot of speeches, but they all have one thing in common. (cut to the group outside a church with a man holding a gun to Pierce's head) They're all different. These drug runners aren't gonna execute Pierce because he's racist. (cut to the group at a train station with Jeff dressed as an engineer and standing on the cowcatcher of a locomotive) It's a locomotive that runs on *us*! (cut to the group standing beside a boathouse) And the only sharks in that water (cut back to the cobweb-infested hotel lobby) are the emotional ghosts that I like to call fear. (cut to the group in the Greendale cafeteria) Anchovies. (cut to the group toasting marshmallows in front of a campfire) Fear. (cut to the group in a padded cell wearing straitjackets, as Jeff struggles) And the dangers of ingesting mercury! (cut to the group in their underwear outside a building) Because the real bugs aren't the ones in those beds. (cut back to cafeteria) And there's no such thing as a free Caesar salad. And even if there were (cut to the group all wearing capes) *The Cape* still might find a second life on cable. And I'll tell you why. (cut to Jeff reading from a book in Spanish) El corazon del agua es verdad. (cut to boathouse) That water is a lie! (cut to padded cell) Harrison Ford is irradiating our testicles with microwave transmissions! (cut back to the original setting of the study room again) So maybe we are caught in an endless cycle of screw-ups and hurt feelings, but I choose to believe it's just the universe's way of moulding us into some kind of super group.
TROY: Like the Travelling Wilburys.
JEFF: Yes, Troy. Like the Travelling Wilburys of pain, prepared for any insane adventure life throws our way. I don't know about you, but I'm looking forward to every one of them. (16:22–17:49)

As is clear in this description of the episode, and particularly in the final monologue, the climax and dénouement of the episode corresponds to an ever-increasing proliferation of clips, becoming shorter and more incongruous as the episode goes on. The monologue essentially dramatises the echoes of past speeches implicit in each new iteration, making obvious that the title of the episode, 'The Paradigms of Human Memory' is central to the clip show premise. The *Community* version of the clip show ultimately focuses on the relationship between the viewer and their memory of a series, foregrounding two kinds of viewers, and their different relationships to the viewing of television fiction, through the lens of these brief clips of past events. Jason Mittell's remarks on television's unique relation to memory seem particularly pertinent in relation to this format:

> The television medium employs specific strategies distinct from other narrative media. For instance, cinematic narratives typically engage a viewer's short-term memory, cuing and obscuring moments from within the controlled unfolding of a two-hour feature film, while literature designs its stories to be consumed at the reader's own pace and control, allowing for an on-demand return to previous pages as needed. The typical model of television consumption, divided into weekly episodes and annual seasons, constrains producers interested in telling stories that transcend individual instalments, as any viewer's memory of previous episodes is quite variable, with a significant number of viewers having missed numerous episodes altogether. These constraints have helped lead to a specific set of story-telling conventions and poetic possibilities that distinguish television as a narrative medium. (Mittell 2010, 78–9)

Though the clip show is relying on nostalgia, a series cannot guarantee viewers will remember things from one episode to the next; indeed, the segmentation inherent to television (as highlighted by the time loop here) is partly created by the efforts to jog viewers' memories, through the 'previously on' or 'recap' segments preceding a new episode.[10] If the clip show is initially supposed to provide a moment of nostalgia for the viewer, *Community* ultimately turns that on its head, because it features *only* moments that were not previously featured on the show: these clips may be from the narrative or diegetic past, but they are all new to the viewer. They rely on the viewer's knowledge of past episodes, notably 'Cooperative Calligraphy' (with the re-discovery of the monkey and its treasure trove previously seen in that episode), as well as the running gag of the characters having to make dioramas (including this one, a diorama of them making their previous diorama); some of the clips feature 'unseen' moments in previous episodes, like a Claymation episode ('Abed's Uncontrollable Christmas', S02E11) where Abed celebrates the holiday season by seeing everything in stop-motion animation à la *Rudolph the Red-Nosed Reindeer* (NBC, 1964) – 'Paradigm''s version shows an excerpt from the episode without the animation, making it clear that Abed is experiencing a mental break; but inherently, the episode undercuts both the premise of the clip show and the notion of viewer memory. Watching the episode, particularly the first half, where the characters resort to the well-worn trope of using a signifying object as a premise to launch into a flashback, the viewer could find themselves questioning whether or not this is a traditional clip, whether they remember this moment from previous episodes or not. As such, through these clips, the show is actually pinpointing the limitations of viewer memories. Any uncertainty the viewer might initially have about whether or not these are previously-shown excerpts are allayed by the rest of the episode, which features increasingly outlandish adventures that are never fleshed out.

Meanwhile, a second use of clips in this episode highlights a more recent phenomenon in the viewer's relationship to memory: when Annie discovers that Jeff and Britta have been secretly intimate, she is offended because she insists that she and Jeff have been working up to a relationship, and offers up proof in the form of clips of innocuous moments, shown first at normal speed and then in slow-motion, to the strains of a love ballad. Jeff retorts that you could make this same argument for any two members of the group, and a similar series of clips shows the supposed budding romance of Abed and Pierce. The first of these is an adaptation of an actual fan video arguing for a future Jeff/Annie romance,[11] suggesting that in the contemporary landscape of YouTube and digital media, clips are no longer the sole property of the series itself, but are instead more likely to be found recycled and re-contextualised by the avid viewer. Though it insists on the dangers of over-analysis and de-/re-contextualisation, the episode as a whole offers a sort of panorama of the changing nature of the television series' relationship to time and memory through the use of these brief clips.

By choosing these 'high-concept' techniques that result in 'special episodes', and by choosing an example as metafictional as *Community*, I have inevitably chosen specificity over any exhaustivity in my study of brevity in American television fiction. However, despite these caveats, I would argue that this focus on the episode (with the bottle episode), the sequence (with the time loop) and the clip (with the clip show) nonetheless manage to represent larger truths about television fictions in general, and the importance of the tension between short sequences and long seasons, old and new television traditions, and writer, series and viewer.

NOTES

1. This of course heightens the irony of a series like *Game of Thrones*, which always aired in late spring/early summer even as the characters intoned that 'Winter

is Coming', thus implicitly insisting on the tendency of this series to break with television traditions (most notably in killing off the lead character in the first season . . .). See also Irvine 2012.
2. Though this is particularly true of current events shows (either late-night talk shows or satirical news shows), whose relatively rapid expiration of relevancy explains their open availability online, the relative dearth of studies on older series, as well as the literal absence of many of television's first shows, also point to this interpretation.
3. These techniques may occur occasionally in film as well, but never so frequently or with such impact, largely due to their being isolated within a given episode in a series in a way that is impossible for a feature film.
4. Perhaps in keeping with this subversiveness, *Community* did not do well on broadcast television, and was one of the first series to be 'saved' by streaming, having been picked up for a final sixth season on Yahoo's fledging platform, thus bridging the gap between broadcast and online television fiction. The series has since become fairly successful with a new generation on streaming services. See Venable 2020.
5. Some have argued that the first depiction of a time loop onscreen was *Turn Back the Clock* (1933), where a man finds himself several years in the past after having been hit by a car, and uses his knowledge of the future to improve his life; however, the return to the past turns out to be a dream, and the idea of repeatedly reliving the same time is absent from this version. See for example Jones and Ormrod 2015.
6. A more recent series, ABC's 2006 fiction *Day Break*, serialises the principle of 'Groundhog Day', as the character relives the same day in each episode. My thanks to Sylvaine Bataille for this suggestion.
7. See also Wells-Lassagne 2012 for a more in-depth discussion of the ostensible protagonist in the series.
8. Jeff repeatedly exclaims 'There are no other timelines!' throughout the episode.
9. Lorre's vanity cards are numbered and are currently archived both online (http://chucklorre.com) and in a coffee-table book entitled *What Doesn't Kill Us Makes Us Bitter* (Lorre 2012).
10. Indeed, to a certain extent both the clip show and the recaps serve similar functions.
11. See Bradford 2014.

WORKS CITED

All in the Family, created by Norman Lear, CBS, 1971–9.
Big Bang Theory, created by Chuck Lorre, CBS, 2007–19.
Bradford, Evan, '29 *Community* Jokes You Might Have Missed', *Vulture*, 15 May 2014. Available online: https://www.vulture.com/2014/05/29-community-jokes-you-may-have-missed.html/ (Accessed May 2022).
Cheers, created by Glen Charles, Les Charles and James Burrows, NBC, 1982–93.

Community, created by Dan Harmon, NBC, 2009–14; Yahoo, 2014–15.
'*Community* EP Dan Harmon explains Abed's evolution', 2010. Available online: http://blog.zap2it.com/frominsidethebox/2010/11/community-ep-dan-harmon-explains-abeds-evolution.html/ (Accessed January 2021).
The Cosby Show, created by William H. Cosby, Jr., Ed Weinberger and Michael J. Leeson, NBC, 1984–92.
Deming, Caren, 'Locating the Televisual in Golden Age Television', in *A Companion to Television*, eds Janet Wasko and Eileen R. Meehan (Hoboken: Wiley-Blackwell, 2005), 126–41.
Dharma and Greg, created by Chuck Lorre, ABC, 1997–2002.
Friends, created by Marta Kauffman and David Crane, NBC, 1994–2004.
Huisman, Rosemary, 'Aspects of Narrative in Series and Serials', in *Narrative and Media*, eds Helen Fulton, Rosemary Huisman, Julian Murphet and Ann Dunn (Melbourne: Cambridge University Press, 2005), 153–71.
Irvine, Colin, 'Why *30 Rock* Rocks and *The Office* Needs Some Work: The Role of Time/Space in Contemporary TV Sitcoms', in *Time in Television Narrative: Exploring Temporality in Twenty-First Century Programming*, ed. Melissa Ames, (Jackson: University Press of Mississippi, 2012), 218–31.
Jones, Matthew and Joan Ormrod (eds), *Time Travel in Popular Media: Essays on Film, Television, Literature and Video Games*, (Jefferson: McFarland, 2015).
Lorre, Chuck, *What Doesn't Kill Us Makes Us Bitter* (Los Angeles: Dharma Grace Foundation, 2012).
Mittell, Jason, 'Previously On: Prime Time Serials and the Mechanics of Memory', in *Intermediality and Storytelling*, eds Marina Grishakova and Marie-Laure Ryan, (Berlin and New York: De Gruyter, 2010), 78–98.
Ricoeur, Paul, *Temps et récit 2* (Paris: Seuil, 1984).
Roche, David, *Meta in Film and Television Series* (Edinburgh: Edinburgh University Press, 2022).
Rudolph the Red-Nosed Reindeer, created by Romeo Muller, NBC, 1964.
Seinfeld, created by Larry David and Jerry Seinfeld, NBC, 1989–98.
The Benny Hill Show, created by Benny Hill, BBC/ITV, 1955–89.
The Simpsons, created by Matt Groening, Fox, 1989–present.
The Twilight Zone, created by Rod Serling, CBS, 1959–64.
Turn Back the Clock, Edgar Selwyn, director, MGM, 1933.
Two and a Half Men, created by Chuck Lorre, CBS, 2003–15.
Venable, Nick, '*Community* is Everyone's Latest Netflix Obsession, and Fans Can't Get Enough', *CinemaBlend*, 12 April 2020. Available online: https://www.cinemablend.com/television/2494328/community-is-everyones-latest-netflix-obsession-and-fans-cant-get-enough/ (Accessed May 2022).
Wells-Lassagne, Shannon, 'Transforming the Traditional Sitcom: Abed in *Community*', *TV/Series*, no. 1 (2012). Available online: URL: http://journals.openedition.org/tvseries/1560; DOI: https://doi.org/10.4000/tvseries.1560 (Accessed February 2024).

CHAPTER II

Ovulate and Repeat: Temporal Uncertainties and the Serialising Effect of Narratives of 'Women's Time' in the Sitcom *Friends*

Jessica Thrasher Chenot

The ninth season of the iconic television sitcom *Friends* (NBC, 1994–2004) was originally broadcast from September 2002 to May 2003 and was, for most of those involved in the show's production process, considered to be the final instalment of the network television blockbuster. As such, the storytelling team began seeking ways to bring satisfying narrative closure to each of the six main characters by the season's end, an effort to respond to audience expectations. Creators Marta Kaufman and David Crane have explained on numerous occasions that their intentions were to reward the *Friends* fan base with the satisfying conclusions that fans were hoping for: 'we didn't see any advantage in frustrating them', Crane has stated (Snierson 2014).

For the newlywed characters of Chandler Bing and Monica Geller, and within the logic of the *Friends* universe – a universe explicitly concerned with the transition from early adulthood ('a time when your friends become your surrogate family' [Wilde 2004]) to an autonomous and independent existence at the head of one's own nuclear family – this meant moving from their New York apartment to a house in the suburbs and having children. To this end, in the final episodes of Season 8, a storyline about Monica and Chandler trying to conceive a child was explicitly introduced into the diegetic space of the series, establishing a potential period of suspenseful expectation for viewers, as well as the implicit anticipation of another childbirth episode over the course of Season 9. However, simultaneously and behind the scenes, an ultimately successful effort to produce a tenth and final season of the series was ongoing in the form of prolonged contractual negotiations with the series' stars. This final and somewhat last-minute decision to renew *Friends* for a tenth season meant that the writers ultimately had to 're-set' those narratives that had already been put in motion in order to accommodate the final instalment of episodes. As such, several episodes introducing narratives concerning Monica's tracking of her menstrual cycle, as well as questions concerning fertility and infertility, were integrated throughout the ninth season in an effort to prolong the inevitable moment of ultimate narrative closure, in this case represented by the arrival of a newborn baby.

In this chapter, I seek to articulate the ways in which narratives of women's bodily time, particularly as manifested by representations of the menstrual cycle, are deployed in *Friends* to manage a moment of temporal uncertainty for the series (the decision to add, or not, a tenth season). To do so, I will begin by discussing the twentieth-century American situation comedy as a short form of fictional, comic, televised storytelling composed mainly of standalone episodes and respecting a particular circular narrative logic. I will then point to the situation comedy genre's innate and historic capacity to adapt to telling stories that confound this conventional understanding, before examining the specific examples at work in *Friends*. Additionally, drawing on Diane Negra's concept of 'time panic' associated with representations of women's life cycles in popular postfeminist texts, I attempt to delineate some of the specific cultural discourses attached to these narratives concerning female reproduction.[1] I hope to demonstrate that these stories provide a particularly effective means to elongate and stretch out the short, episodic and circular televisual format that the sitcom has been conventionally understood to conform to, ultimately contributing to the genre's transformation into a longer-term, more serialised form with a heightened degree of narrative complexity.

SITCOM IN THE UNITED STATES: THE ORIGINAL SHORT FORM ON THE SMALL SCREEN

While it may seem counterintuitive to include discussion of a television program clocking in at over 200 episodes and more than 100 hours of fictional content in a volume predicated on the concept of brevity, the genre with which *Friends* is overwhelmingly associated can be understood as an unambiguously short form of televised narrative thanks to its formal and generic conventions. Scholars have noted how the situation comedy was transposed onto the medium of television from its immediate mass-media precursor, the radio.[2] Indeed, as televisions began to fill American living rooms in the post-WWII era, network executives began to feel with increasing urgency the need to fill potentially profitable airtime. In this context, popular radio programs, many of which were situation or domestic comedies, began new lives as televised productions.[3] In many cases these programs were simply filmed versions of their acoustic forms. Transposing radio fictions onto television screens meant not only that Americans could now watch the popular and familiar fictional worlds that they had grown accustomed to listening in on, but it also brought with it a set of television-ready corporate and conventional practices. One of those conventions was program length. While many sitcoms were 30 minutes in length, for a time, some were as short as 15 minutes. Those that were longer were divided into two shorter segments to allow for advertising from corporate sponsors. This shortened form of telling televised stories contrasted with the traditional hour-long programing reserved for 'serious' dramatic genres such as police procedurals, detective programs and westerns. While formal conventions remained experimental during the early years of television programming as the new medium was finding its footing, by the early 1950s program length had eventually sedimented, settling more or less into the accepted 23–26-minute period for comedy and hour-long segments for more dramatic fare.

Since that time and for the duration of the twentieth century, the American situation comedy has traditionally been understood as a televisual genre typified by short, autonomous episodes in which the plot is introduced, developed and resolved within the space of a single, finite instalment. According to this understanding of the sitcom, each episode launches its unique story from the same diegetic point of origin, only to return again and again to a reestablishment of the status quo. Such an episodic form, in which short narrative threads are concluded within less than 30 minutes, allows viewers to enjoy individual episodes of a sitcom without necessarily requiring a deep or long-standing commitment to watching a television show in a continuous and contiguous manner. Indeed, this narrative configuration may help explain the popularity of the sitcom genre during the network era at a time when episodes were broadcast in weekly instalments in several seasons over a number of months. Lawrence Mintz's 1985 definition of this televisual genre – published, it should be noted, at a moment when the genre was regularly attracting tens of millions of viewers weekly – underscores the cyclical, episodic nature of the network sitcom:

> episodes are finite; what happens in a given episode is generally closed off, explained, reconciled, solved at the end of the half hour (. . .) The most important feature of sitcom structure is the cyclical nature of the normalcy of the premise undergoing stress or threat of change and becoming restored. (Mintz 1985, 115)

Indeed, these brief but repetitive incursions into the fictional worlds sitcoms presented to their audiences appear to have been an ideal format from which to tell the types of intimate, familial and quotidian stories the genre, early on, made it its duty to transmit to audiences in the United States: Beaver and his brother Wally order a baby alligator by mail; Theo brings home a bad report card; Stephanie gets a part in a TV commercial her older sister tried out for.

That the genre was a perennial favourite, dominating television programming until the end of the twentieth century, suggests that these quick, humorous and (mostly) wholesome takes on American life proved extremely pleasurable for millions of viewers.

EARLY PREGNANCY NARRATIVES IN THE SITCOM

This conventional epistemology as described above, however, has been implicitly undermined from the earliest days of broadcast television by the presence of narratives pertaining to the fertility and pregnancies of female characters, narratives which inevitably stretch storylines over several episodes and even across several seasons. These storylines have been hiding in plain sight, part of the sitcom's trove of storytelling tropes since the genre's arrival on the small screen. Indeed, sitcom's first female character, Mary Kay (*Mary Kay and Johnny*, Du Mont, CBS and NBC, 1947–50), appeared as an expectant woman and then young mother during her pregnancy and after the birth of her real-life child. This story of pregnancy and early motherhood, which undeniably altered the early sitcom's status quo, was written into the diegetic sphere of the program in its quest for verisimilitude.[4] The extent to which episodes of *Mary Kay and Johnny* were explicitly anchored around the female character's pregnancy can, unfortunately, only be surmised, as only one episode of the program still exists. However, it is reasonable to conclude that Mary Kay's pregnancy was not 'reconciled' or 'solved at the end of the half hour' as per Mintz's definition. Indeed, the author's supposed restoration of 'normalcy' is, with notable exceptions, inherently impossible in the case of a pregnant sitcom character, the prolonged expectation and ultimate arrival of a child precluding any possible return to the initial narrative status quo.[5]

Similarly, an early narrative arc of pregnancy is introduced in one of the genre's most iconic examples, *I Love Lucy* (CBS, 1951–7). As in the case of *Mary Kay and Johnny*, character Lucy Ricardo's pregnancy and the birth of her son, Little Ricky, were written into the sitcom to accommodate the real-life pregnancy and childbirth of the sitcom's co-creator and star, Lucille Ball. As Stephanie Bor has convincingly argued, the inclusion of a pregnancy-related story arc within the narrative of this extraordinarily popular television sitcom was effectively deployed by the network to incite media attention and encourage viewer enthusiasm *over a period of several weeks* of broadcasting. These early examples demonstrate the ability of this supposedly routine, episodic genre to adapt to a more serialised form of narration for the purposes of telling a story that by definition could not fit within a single episode. They also demonstrate, significantly, a willingness on the part of audiences to return to and follow the sitcom over a number of weeks in order to reach the emotional culmination of the story arc: the birth of the baby (Bor 2013, 464–78). Indeed, in recounting pregnancy and childbirth on screen, in showing female characters (and their partners) in a state of anticipation, their bodies expanding and changing, as well as their early initiation into motherhood, these long term, life-changing stories associated with women's bodily time have, in fact, forced adaptations and accommodations onto the otherwise restrictive narrative structure of the television sitcom for decades.

FRIENDS: PEAK PREGNANCY STORYTELLING

While the two preceding examples of the genre telling elongated stories of pregnancy demonstrate an early capacity for the genre to stretch and adapt, and while many other sitcoms from television's network era have told stories of expectant and parturient women,[6] perhaps no network sitcom has exploited this capability of integrating stories of women's bodily time to such an extent and with such variety as *Friends*. One of this iconic sitcom's foundational storylines involves the surprise pregnancy of a secondary character, which in turn forces one of the main characters, Ross Geller, to consider his potential involvement with his biological child.[7] Far from wrapping up the story of this unconventional pregnancy within the space of a single episode, the expectant mother Susan, her evolving pregnancy and the confusion concerning Ross' future paternal role are revisited in multiple episodes throughout the first season of *Friends*.[8] While the penultimate episode of that season focuses on the birth of the child (bringing clear closure to the pregnancy narrative), the storyline involving this unconventional family is returned to repeatedly throughout the following episodes, maintaining the forever-altered status quo within the characters' and spectators' conscience over a period of several years.

Similar extended narrative threads relating to pregnancy and fertility include the surrogate pregnancy carried by the character of Phoebe Buffay through Season 4 and into Season 5 as well as the unintended pregnancy of the character Rachel Green spanning from the final cliffhanger episode of Season 7, through Season 8 and into Season 9. Through repeated and serialising examinations of non-normative pregnancies and family formation including lesbian motherhood (with its attendant interrogation of the paternal role), the complicated ethics and emotions linked to surrogate motherhood, as well as the continued controversies surrounding the politics of single motherhood in the United States, *Friends* demonstrated that it was 'clearly invested in making visible those kinships arrangements which challenge the dominant myth of the nuclear family' (Sandell 1998, 141–55).

While the extent to which these narrative arcs were truly politically progressive may be debated, what is clear is that such storylines were, until their explicit treatment by *Friends*, exceedingly rare in the sitcom genre. In *Friends*, they were not only possible but also incredibly successful thanks to the show's unusually deep commitment to character development. As Judy Kutulas explains, viewers 'returned to *Friends* as they might a drama, to see what happened next to people they cared about' (Kutulas 2018, 1172–89). Indeed while the care and commitment that viewers brought to *Friends*, as reflected by Nielsen ratings, fluctuated over the course of its broadcast, during the final seasons of the sitcom viewership increased significantly as fans continued caring about the characters they had grown to know so intimately: *Friends* was ranked first for the first and only time during its eighth season, second in its ninth, dropping to fourth during its tenth and last season (Brooks and Marsh 2007, 1696–7).

The continued popularity of the series, as well as NBC's and Warner Bros.'s continued desire to profit from that popularity, resulted in multiple and arduously extended contract negotiations between *Friends*' corporate partners and its stars. 'In its last seasons, *Friends* existed in a simultaneous state of unprecedented success and unsettling limbo', writes television critic Saul Austerlitz, as the 'costs of keeping all interested parties happy had risen so dramatically that no one could be sure that the current contract would not be the last one to be signed' (Austerlitz 2019, 282).

Between the end of Season 7 and the beginning of Season 10 of the sitcom then, the uncertain resolution of salary negotiations managed to unsettle the story writing process enough to create the impression of a number of false-start narratives of closure. Reporter Adam Chitwood explains in *Collider*:

> As *Friends* began production on its ninth season in 2002, all involved were under the impression that it'd be the last one. The actors' contracts were up and they were getting expensive ($1 million an episode expensive), so the first few episodes of this season set up the show's finale (e.g. Chandler moving to Tulsa). However, after much begging from NBC, the cast agreed mid-production to return for an abbreviated tenth season, and so showrunners Marta Kauffman and David Crane had to abandon their finale set-up and start moving things back to a place that could set up the next season. (Chitwood 2019)

It was within this context of narrative upheaval and temporal uncertainty that *Friends*' final and most extended collection of stories concerning female reproduction was conceived: Monica's attempt to become a mother. I will now turn to one particular aspect of this storytelling process, the mobilisation of narratives concerning the menstrual cycle to simultaneously bide narrative time while also elongating the overall story of Monica's journey to motherhood. In this final section, I also analyse some of the ideological implications of this type of narrative.

'PERIOD MATH': MONICA'S POSTFEMINIST JOURNEY TO MOTHERHOOD

To the extent that the character of Monica Geller was originally envisioned as the mother hen of the other five *Friends*, and, to the extent that the character was continuously portrayed as yearning to become a mother throughout the entirety of the series, it is possible to argue that Monica's narrative of coming-into-motherhood is, in fact, one of the overarching narrative arcs of the entire series. In any case, little doubt is ever left to the viewer that this character's narrative resolution will somehow involve motherhood.[9] Monica's inevitable arrival at that status becomes infinitely more concrete during the final, double episode of the eighth season,[10] not coincidentally during a visit to the hospital to attend the childbirth of fellow character and best friend, Rachel Green, as the latter makes her own transition to motherhood.

Into this narrative environment of parturition, already well-invested by *Friends* at this late point in the series (Rachel's giving birth is the third childbirth episode of the series), are planted the seeds of a different type of story concerning women's time: the management of Monica's menstrual cycle in an attempt to conceive a child with her husband. Positioned in a hospital corridor, opposite a glass-walled nursery full of swaddled newborns, Monica and Chandler make plain their intentions to start a family. As such, the *Friends* writing team simultaneously make plain their own intentions concerning the Monica and Chandler storyline to the viewer: the two will indeed start a family and become parents. To Monica's 'We . . . we're going to try? I mean, we're trying?' Chandler – after long panicking at the thought of having children – replies with the reassuringly affirmative 'We're trying to get pregnant.'

Implicitly acknowledging the fact that the following ninth season was to be the last (and with it, the possibility of there being little narrative time to waste), the character of Chandler immediately pursues the conversation, asking his wife 'So when do you want to start trying?' Monica's instruction to 'hold on a sec' may be understood as symbolic of the numerous questions of time, timeliness and temporality that this ultimate maternal narrative will introduce into the final seasons of the series.[11] In fact, Monica's request to Chandler to 'hold on' is accompanied by a most specific act: the young woman quite explicitly holds up her hands and begins counting on her fingers. Chandler, here the representative of a progressive, open-minded masculinity at ease with a woman's menstrual cycle, understands intuitively what his wife is doing: 'Period math?' he asks without a hint of embarrassment in acknowledging the reality of his wife's cycle. His intuition that Monica is in the middle of calculating her reproductive cycle in an effort to determine the precise moment of ovulation is indeed confirmed by Monica, and, as luck would have it, this 'period math' reveals that the young woman is currently at optimum fertility. 'Well, we could start trying *now*', she suggests.

The introduction of this particular narrative of conception, as that of a *process of trying to conceive* as opposed to a surprise announcement of pregnancy, and its configuration within the context of the menstrual cycle, is significant for two reasons. First, in openly discussing the menstrual cycle on a popular primetime television program, *Friends* begins to pry open what Iris Marion Young has termed the *menstrual closet* for a massive popular audience, 'outing' Monica as a menstruating woman.[12] While the allusion remains chaste – there is never any reference to menstrual blood, for example, and Chandler's 'period math' is as crude as things get – in openly discussing the 'mathematics of menses', *Friends* does not shy away from identifying its female characters as menstruating women nor does the sitcom, in this instance, ridicule them for it.[13] Secondly, and most importantly for our purposes, it introduces the possibility of 'reconciling the forward-moving hands of time with the circularity of women's cycles' (Nathanson 2013, 113). By introducing Monica's coming-into-motherhood story through the narrative of menses, *Friends* offers itself the ability to continually adapt to the uncertainty surrounding the sitcom's longevity, the possibility of repeatedly prolonging this narrative at least until certain decisions were made at the corporate level. The menstrual cycle, with its circular, episodic chronology, adapts perfectly to these circumstances in which a start-stop-restart approach is necessary, while simultaneously pushing this particular maternal narrative forward through time and towards its ultimate closure in the form of the arrival of a baby and the foundation of a new nuclear family for Chandler and Monica.

Indeed, during the following season, and in the context of continued contract negotiations playing out between the actors and the corporate entities behind *Friends*, the series returns to stories constructed around Monica's menstrual cycle in no less than four episodes. The narrative 'holding pattern' made possible by stories related to the female character's menstrual cycle effectively bought the series time and opened up new spaces in which *Friends* could continue its exploration of issues related to sexuality, gender, reproduction and family formation.

But if *Friends'* treatment of fertility/menstrual cycle narratives was efficiently employed to manage a specific moment of temporal crisis and uncertainty for the series' production, the repeated deployment of this type of story definitively positions this part of Monica's journey to motherhood within a postfeminist discourse in which pregnancy and motherhood are fetishised as paradigmatic moments in the feminine life cycle, to be achieved and celebrated at the appropriate moments of a woman's life.

In fact, Monica's marriage to Chandler and the absolute inevitability of her becoming a mother (combined with this sitcom's other narrative resolutions all taking the form of heteronormative coupledom with the promise of children on the way) suggest that *Friends*, with its emphasis on 'matrimonial and maternalist models of female subjectivity' (Negra 2009, 5), may be interpreted as a quintessential popular cultural text of the postfeminist era, presenting (consciously or not) 'conservative norms as the ultimate "best choices" in women's lives' (Negra 2009, 4).

This is particularly evident in the episodes dealing with Monica's menstrual cycle as these narratives insist on, to the point of fetishising, *ovulation* as the culmination or apex of the cycle. An example from the first episode of the ninth season (narratively speaking, a direct continuation of the storylines halted at the end of Season 8) illustrates this clearly.[14] When Monica's father, Jack Geller, inadvertently interrupts the couple in the middle of intercourse, the moment is profoundly embarrassing for all until the two clarify that they are trying to conceive a baby. The paternal figure's reaction changes swiftly from consternation and reproach to exaltation as he encourages the couple to 'get back in there' while he offers to 'guard the door'. The couples' discomfort is only exacerbated as Jack asks his daughter pointedly, 'Aren't you ovulating?' The father's intimate (incestuous?) knowledge of (and evident pride in) his adult daughter's menstrual cycle as well as his emphatic exhortation to take advantage of this singular moment positions the character's ovulation in such a way as to suggest that fertilisation and ensuing pregnancy are the 'goal' or 'point' of the menstrual cycle rather than simply one part of a physiological, cyclical phenomenon in which the possibility of pregnancy goes hand in hand with the possibility of not becoming pregnant. Monica's ovulation and menstrual cycle are thus firmly secured within an unambiguously heteronormative familial structure. Such a teleological perspective of the menstrual cycle tends to conflate, by extension, menstruation, womanhood and motherhood, thus configuring the menstruating body as an always and necessarily potential maternal body.

Furthermore, Jack Geller's own anecdote relating how he got his bad hip – in order to conceive Monica, he and his wife 'did it' ('bam!') 'whenever she was ovulating' – underscores the time-induced panic surrounding ovulation, that too-short window of opportunity which should be exploited even at the cost of self-injury. It simultaneously inscribes Monica within an intergenerational struggle to achieve fertilisation and reproduce at the right moment.

Thanks to the inherent episodic nature of the female reproductive cycle, the focus on Monica's ovulation, as well as its concomitant theme of correct time management in a quest for maternity, is redeployed within the linear narratological time of the series in further episodes from the ninth season.[15] In each, the pressure of conceiving at the right moment, the need to meticulously plan for intercourse at the point of sacred ovulation, the threat of missing the opportunity to conceive, result in upheaval for the couple and for those around them. Monica is ovulating, sex is planned, something goes awry and the cycles, physiological and televisual, are repeated. These narrative threads, with their emphasis on ovulation and the necessity to exploit its potential within a correct and appropriate temporality so as to achieve pregnancy, point to what Negra has identified as 'one of the signature attributes of postfeminist culture'; that is, 'its ability to define various female life stages within the parameters of "time panic"' (Negra 2009, 47).

Indeed, panic induced by the fleetingness of the female character's fetishised ovulatory status is a signature theme of the episodes featuring narratives of Monica's menstrual cycle. The character's obsession with having sex with her husband at the moment of ovulation results, on several occasions, in nearly disastrous consequences for the couple in the context of their friendships: Monica and Chandler put their friendship with Phoebe at risk by snubbing her birthday dinner in order to have sex; they are chastised by Joey as irresponsible when they leave the baby Emma asleep and unattended to have sex. Indeed, the panic to conceive is so pervasive in these episodes that their own relationship is strained as both participate in deceitful behaviour in order to manage the pressure of Monica's omnipresent and ever-ticking 'biological clock'. That these narratives are filtered through the comic framework of the genre, thus becoming sources of humour rather than pathos, mitigates the content to an extent, recuperating it as light-hearted and entertaining. Nonetheless, the menstrual cycle in *Friends* becomes a source of stress to be attended to, a disruption to negotiate, a female preoccupation to be successfully managed for as long as the series needs it to resolve its own 'time panic'. Monica's biological clock narratives parallel the clock ticking down on the series itself – in both cases, the final resolutions stretch the boundaries of the traditional sitcom.

CONCLUSION

In the penultimate season of *Friends*, Monica's long-standing desire to conceive, and the repetition of episodes concerned with her menstrual cycle, construct ovulation and female fertility as potential sites of 'success' in a postfeminist context in which women, having supposedly achieved political, social and economic equality, are implicitly and explicitly encouraged to 'have it all' by maintaining a fulfilling career, a nurturing relationship and a flourishing family. The woman who tracks her own physiological cycles closely and accurately enough to successfully lead to conception, these episodes appear to suggest, will be rewarded by the 'ennobling' status of incipient motherhood. For Monica, the constant surveillance of her menstrual cycle implied in these repeated episodes is materialised through the character's use of ovulation sticks and calendars. Conception is thus configured as the ultimate postfeminist domestic task, a mission of maternity requiring devoted attention, time and meticulousness. In these episodes, becoming pregnant is not a simple biological process; instead it presents as a rationally planned, well-scheduled endeavour, an objective to be achieved necessitating managerial precision and intelligence. Ovulation becomes a moment in which Monica may apply a near-professional level of expertise and strategising (the character's well-established penchant for manic-obsessive competitiveness chimes well with this undertaking) to her own reproductive system, the correct management of which will lead to the holy grail of pregnancy. This managerial approach to fertility establishes a seemingly harmonious merger of discourses of female empowerment and entrepreneurship with a more conservative domestic ideal of motherhood and childrearing. In effect, Monica's twin characteristics of perfectionism and motherliness position her as the ideal character for this narrative arc.

Following the episodes concerning Monica's ovulatory cycle, the ultimate narrative resolution for Monica and Chandler is finally established through a diagnosis of mutual infertility followed by the adoption of twins born to a young unmarried pregnant woman. Ironically, after all the careful tracking and organisation and despite the character's seasons-long desire to become a mother, Monica's body is ultimately written as being unable to reproduce. Elizabeth Nathanson argues that television 'captures' what she refers to as 'too-late' mothers in stories of 'infertility that do not represent infertility as a genetic and thus unavoidable problem, but rather one that is attributed to poor lifestyle time management' (Nathanson, 2013, 139). *Friends* may appear to disobey this logic – Chandler's coinciding diagnosis of reduced sperm motility, after all, seems to suggest that writers took pains to construct this narrative of infertility in a manner both sensitive to infertile couples and reflective of the reality in which men account for a significant proportion of problems with fertility in heterosexual couples. However, considering the repetition of episodes configuring ovulation and conception as *Monica*'s project, the ultimate diagnosis of infertility does appear to somehow be associated with poor management skills on the part of the female character, thus supporting Nathanson's claim that television's representations of infertility 'perpetuate anxieties that the ticking of women's biological clock *should* be cause for concern' (Nathanson, 2013, 139).

In mobilising the menstrual cycle's own 'narrative' form – with its complex hormonal and physiological changes and cyclical return to equilibrium, this sitcom comes full circle (so to speak), reappropriating the logic of circular, episodic time in its quest to sustain and prolong a satisfying serialised narrative in a context of temporal instability. The repetition of the ovulation/conception storyline may thus be clearly understood to have filled the empty narrative space available to the show's writers, and to have served, from a narratological perspective, its purpose in prolonging the series and building the suspense leading to its denouement. In so doing, the series dedicated significant narrative time and space to content highlighting some of the cultural anxieties surrounding female fertility and family formation at the turn of the millennium in the United States, fetishising those processes (ovulation, pregnancy, childbirth) that most closely align with the traditional norms of family foundation while simultaneously adhering to the sitcom's vision of narrative closure for its characters in a way that was deemed satisfying for its fans. The case of *Friends* confirms that such stories of 'women's time' can be a decidedly fruitful method for extending the life of a sitcom, offering a multiplicity of storytelling possibilities while acting as a cultural platform in which competing ideological pressures may coexist.

In this, we may witness both the limits and the potentialities of this genre, which appears paradoxically both rigid and elastic. Rigid, because as a shorter form of televised storytelling than traditional dramatic fiction, the sitcom may never run longer than its allotted 30-minute timeslot in spite of its desire or need to delve into more prolonged storylines; elastic, because in spite of this conventional restriction, it is in fact able to find creative ways to work around this constraint in order to introduce more narratologically and ideologically expansive content. Indeed, *Friends* demonstrates that the trend towards what Jason Mittell has identified as complex television, that is, 'rejecting the need for plot closure within every episode that typifies conventional episodic form' (Mittell 2015, 18), is within the purview of all fictional television genres, no matter their length.

NOTES

1. See Negra 2009, particularly Chapter 3, 'Time Crisis and the New Postfeminist Lifecycle', 47–85.
2. For detailed discussions of this process see, for example, Jones 1992 and Spigel 1992.
3. *Amos 'n' Andy* is perhaps the most famous example. Others include *The Rise of the Goldbergs* (shortened to *The Goldbergs* on television), *The Adventures of Ozzie and Harriet*, *Father Knows Best* (which lost its radio-version question mark to become an affirmative statement on television) and *My Favorite Husband* (which transitioned to television as *I Love Lucy*).
4. In a later interview, writer and co-star Johnny Stearns would explain the decision to include Mary Kay's pregnancy and the birth of their child within the sitcom's fictional universe: 'We wanted to be as close to ourselves as we could get so it would be effective.' Stearns' concern with including the details of their real lives within the fictional sphere of the program in an effort to 'be effective' suggests the extent to which these early television creators were attuned to the potential of the televisual form to become a conduit for viewer identification and adherence to specific programs. https://interviews.televisionacademy.com/shows/mary-kay-and-johnny/ (Accessed January 2023).

5. Exceptions to this may be found in two of Norman Lear's popular social relevancy sitcoms of the 1970s: *All in the Family* (CBS, 1971–9) and *Maude* (CBS, 1972–8). In the case of *All in the Family*, the character Gloria Stivic reveals she is pregnant and suffers a miscarriage within the space of a single episode (S01E06, 'Gloria's Pregnancy'). In the feminist sitcom *Maude*, 47-year-old Maude Findlay learns she is pregnant and decides to opt for an abortion in a special two-part episode (S01E09 and E10, 'Maude's Dilemma, Parts 1 and 2'). As such, only storylines of pregnancies ending *prematurely* can be contained and resolved within the space of a single finite episode (or, as in the case of *Maude*, two) allowing for the re-set and restoration of narrative normalcy that Mintz describes in his definition.
6. These include, but are by no means limited to, *My Three Sons* (ABC and CBS, 1960–72), *Bewitched* (ABC, 1964–72), *All in the Family* (CBS, 1971–9), *Family Ties* (NBC, 1982–9), *The Cosby Show* (NBC, 1984–92), *Growing Pains* (ABC, 1985–92), *Roseanne* (ABC, 1988–97), *Murphy Brown* (CBS, 1988–98), *Mad About You* (NBC, 1992–9) and *The Nanny* (CBS, 1993–9).
7. *Friends*, S01E02, 'The One with the Sonogram at the End,' originally aired on September 29, 1994. In this episode, Carol Willick, Ross's ex-wife, reveals that she is pregnant with Ross's baby and intends to raise the child with her lesbian partner, Susan Bunch. The very title of this episode, which explicitly positions the pregnancy-confirming medical exam in the final minutes of this sitcom's second episode, reveals the extent to which this narrative was conceived of to bring a suspenseful, cliffhanger element to the episode. Far from concluding the story of Carol's pregnancy, this episode's ending, in which the embryo is revealed through a close-up of a sonogram screen, is constructed to hook the viewer, to draw them into the story of the new life emerging, and, by extension, to Ross's newly uncertain world as well as to the uncertainty surrounding the familial configuration of this new life.
8. In addition to 'The One with the Sonogram at the End', this particular narrative thread is reprised in S01E09, 'The One Where Underdog Gets Away'; S01E12, 'The One with the Dozen Lasagnas'; S01E14, 'The One with the Candy Hearts'; S01E16, 'The One with Two Parts: Part 1'; and S01E23, 'The One with the Birth'.
9. Monica's desire to have children is made clear as early as the end of the first season when, awaiting the birth of Susan and Ross' baby, she openly pines over newborn babies in the hospital. Likewise, the reason given for her Season 3 breakup with the much older Richard is that he is too unenthusiastic about having children.
10. S08E23 and S08E24, 'The One Where Rachel Has a Baby, Parts 1 and 2', originally broadcast on 16 May 2002.
11. Indeed, the coda of this season-ending episode appeals specifically to the uncertainty of this moment in the series' production: as the couple emerges, manifestly post-coital from a janitorial closet, the probability of the series ending a year hence with another triumphant childbirth episode appears to be explicitly anticipated as Monica, satisfied, sighs to Chandler 'Do you realize that we may have just changed our lives forever? We may have just started our family. Nine

months from now, we could be here, having our own baby.' Chandler's humorous retort 'And if not, we got to do it on a bucket' anticipates, in turn, the possibility of pushing this desired outcome further along chronologically.
12. Drawing on Sedgwick's *Epistemology of the Closet*, Young suggests that, if the goal of feminists is to achieve equality with men, and if it is the heterosexual man in the male body that is upheld as the idealised norm and standard with which women are to achieve that equality, then it would seem 'apt [. . .] in this normatively masculine, supposedly gender-egalitarian society, to say that the menstruating woman is queer'. Young is careful to point out that in drawing this parallel, she is not attempting to say that the shame of the menstruating woman for 'deviating' from these normatively masculine body standards is on par with the shame and suffering caused by the oppression of homosexuality. See Young 2005, pp. 106–9.
13. It is perhaps possible to argue that a much earlier reference to menstruation in the series may, in fact, be a joke at the expense of menstruating women. In S04E12, 'The One with the Embryos', when Chandler and Joey allude to the fact that Rachel has bought some sort of menstrual sanitary care product, laughter ensues. However, the circumstances and overall allusiveness of the joke are, to my mind, enough to obfuscate any clear intent to specifically make fun of menstruation and menstruating women.
14. S09E01, 'The One Where No One Proposes', aired on 26 September 2002.
15. In addition to S09E01, other episodes that figure storylines specifically related to Monica's cycle include: S09E05, 'The One with Phoebe's Birthday Dinner' aired on 31 October 2002; S09E11, 'The One Where Rachel Goes Back to Work' aired on 9 January 2003; S09E14, 'The One with the Blind Dates' aired on February 6, 2003. Episodes which evoke Monica and Chandler's project of getting pregnant include S09E16, 'The One with the Boob Job' aired on 20 February 2003. Episodes that deal with the diagnosis of infertility and the couple's choice to adopt include S09E21, 'The One With the Fertility Test' aired on 1 May 2003 and S09E22, 'The One With the Donor' aired on 8 May 2003.

WORKS CITED

All in the Family, created by Norman Lear, CBS, 1971–9.
Amos 'n' Andy, created by Freeman Gosden and Charles Correll, WMAQ, NBC Radio, 1928–60; CBS, 1951–3.
Austerlitz, Saul, *Generation Friends: An Inside Look at the Show that Defined a Television Era* (New York: Dutton, 2019).
Bewitched, created by Harry Ackerman, ABC, 1964–72.
Bor, Stephanie, 'Lucy's Two Babies: Framing the First Televised Depiction of Pregnancy', *Media History* 19, no. 4 (2013).
Brooks, Tim and Earle Marsh, *The Complete Directory to Prime Time Network and Cable TV Shows, 1946–Present*, Ninth Edition (New York: Ballentine Books, 2007).
Chitwood, Adam, '"*Friends*' Seasons Ranked from Worst to Best', *Collider*, 26 December 2019. Available online: https://collider.com/friends-seasons-ranked-from-worst-to-best/#9/ (Accessed January 2023).

Family Ties, created by Gary David Goldberg and Lloyd Garver, NBC, 1982–9.
Friends, created by Marta Kauffman, David Crane and Kevin Bright, NBC, 1994–2004.
Growing Pains, created by Neal Marlens, ABC, 1985–92.
I Love Lucy, created by Lucille Ball and Jess Oppenheimer, CBS, 1951–7.
Jones, Gerard, *Honey, I'm Home! Sitcoms: Selling the American Dream* (New York: St Martin's Press, 1992).
Kutulas, Judy, 'Anatomy of a Hit: *Friends* and Its Sitcom Legacies', *The Journal of Popular Culture* 51, no. 5 (10 September 2018).
Mad About You, created by Danny Jacobson and Paul Reiser, NBC, 1992–9.
Mary Kay and Johnny, created by Johnny and Mary Kay Stearns, DuMont (1947–8); CBS (1949); NBC (1948–9, 1949–50).
Maude, created by Norman Lear and Bud Yorkin, CBS, 1972–8.
Mintz, Lawrence, 'Situation Comedy', in *TV Genres: A Handbook and Reference Guide*, ed. Brian G. Rose. Westport (Connecticut and London: Greenwood Press, 1985).
Mittell, Jason, *Complex TV: The Poetics of Contemporary Television Storytelling* (New York and London: New York University Press, 2015).
Murphy Brown, created by Diane English and Joel Shukovsky, CBS, 1988–98.
My Three Sons, created by Peter Tewksbury, George Tibbles and Edmund L. Hartmann, CBS, 1960–72.
Nathanson, Elizabeth, *Television and Postfeminist Housekeeping: No Time for Mother* (New York and London: Routledge, 2013).
Negra, Diane, *What a Girl Wants? Fantasizing the Reclamation of Self in Postfeminism* (London and New York: Routledge, 2009).
Roseanne, created by Roseanne Barr, Marcy Carsey and Tom Werner, ABC, 1988–97.
Sandell, Jillian, 'I'll Be There For You: *Friends* and the Fantasy of Alternative Families', *American Studies* 39, no. 2 (Summer 1998).
Snierson, Dan, '"*Friends* Finale: Marta Kauffman and David Crane Look Back', 16 April 2014, *Entertainment Weekly*. Available online: https://ew.com/article/2014/04/16/marta-kauffman-david-crane-friends-finale/ (Accessed January 2023).
Spigel, Lynn, *Make Room for TV: Television and Family Ideal in Postwar America* (Chicago and London: The University of Chicago, 1992).
The Adventures of Ozzie and Harriet, created by Ozzie Nelson, CBS, NBC, ABC Radio, 1944–54; ABC, 1952–66.
The Cosby Show, Marcy Carsey and Tom Werner, NBC, 1984–92.
The Nanny, created by Fran Drescher and Peter Marc Jacobson, CBS, 1993–9.
The Rise of the Goldbergs, then *The Goldbergs*, created by Gertrude Berg, NBC, CBS Radio, 1929–46; CBS, NBC, 1949–56.
Father Knows Best, created by Edward James, NBC Radio, 1949–54; CBS, NBC, 1954–60.
My Favorite Husband, CBS Radio, 1948–51.
Wild, David, *Friends . . . 'Til the End: The One With All Ten Years* (New York: Time Inc., Home Entertainment, 2004).
Young, Iris Marion, *'Throwing Like a Girl' and Other Essays* (New York: Oxford University Press, 2005).

CHAPTER 12

'Spoilers Ahead!': Short-circuiting Complex Series in Explainer Online Videos

Sébastien Lefait

INTRODUCTION

This chapter focuses on a paradox: the best way to expand a TV series may be to entice its fans to shorten it. Indeed, as Jason Mittell explains, the universe of TV series is now incomplete without its paratextual elements. In particular, transmedia storytelling encompasses 'orienting practices', which 'reside outside the diegetic storyworld, providing a perspective for viewers to help make sense of a narrative world by looking at it from a distance' (Mittell 2015, 261). In some cases, the work of orientation is explanatory. To quote Mittell again, 'We watch *Twin Peaks*, *The X-Files*, *Alias*, *Lost*, *Veronica Mars*, *Desperate Housewives*, *Dexter*, *Fringe*, or *The Killing* at least in part to try to crack each program's central enigmas – look at any online fan forum to see evidence of such sleuths at work' (Mittell 2015, 52). This epistemological reception mode sometimes encourages an even more specific rendition mode, the 'Easter Egg' fan video,[1] in which a viewer edits fixed shots or short clips from a TV series into a 5-to-10-minute compendium, highlighting details in the hope of clarifying the meaning of the show. These decrypting videos – which provide the equivalent in a different media format of the whodunit revelation speech popularised by Agatha Christie in her novels – thus seem to ruin the very premises of the shows whose goal is to hook their viewers by prolonging the mystery rather than solving it too soon. Their existence also stands in stark contradiction with our media environment's most widely shared implicit rule, against spoilers: spoiling the show is exactly what the videos undertake to do as many times per minute as possible. In other words, Easter egg videos short circuit the intended impact of the shows in that they cut their long stories short.

Ironically, this observation results from the development of serial storytelling across media platforms whose purpose is to extend the lifespan of a specific program. After decades of sprawling extension of fictional universes as governed by the new possibilities offered by transmedia narration, and despite the adequacy of one of Henry Jenkins' recent concepts, 'spreadable media' (Jenkins et al. 2013), there exists a contradiction between the extension of narratives, their continuation by fans as a way of appropriating their storyworlds, and a new mode of user appropriation, exemplified in the Easter egg video, which undertakes to shorten a show's narrative and condense its meaning. The point of what follows is to focus on these fan videos and make sense of their counterintuitive popularity. First, this will be achieved by identifying a few case studies which exemplify their own paradoxical nature. In the second phase of the chapter, an analysis of the trend will complement the analysis of the videos themselves, allowing us to draw conclusions about the current state of the relationship between fictional storyworlds and our world's stories.

EXPANDING THE STORYWORLD INTO THE REAL

My first case study is a video entitled '10 *Game of Thrones* Easter Eggs That You Might Have Missed!' (Screen Rant 2016). It features among numerous similar videos available on YouTube or other media platforms, and displays most of the attributes of Easter egg videos. In the video's introduction, the author says: '*Game of Thrones* is not a TV show that is known for its light-heartedness. Still the showrunners do like to toss in a few Easter eggs throughout the show for their viewers to enjoy.' This suggests that the series may not qualify as a mind game narrative,[2] and that it may not target forensic audiences primarily,[3] but that this should not deter its makers from pandering to the egg hunting trend, which is widespread among viewers of contemporary TV series. Accordingly, the video's opening speech is followed by the editing together of specific shots scattered along the series' seasons, drawing attention to visual details ('Gandalf's Blade', 'Jon Snow's Hobbit Friends', 'R+L=J', 'Tyrion's Nose'), to implicit metalepses identified in the lines spoken by the characters ('Littlefinger Predicts Death'), and to a micro analysis of the title sequence. Surprisingly, some of the details focused on are not obviously connected with the *Game of Thrones* (HBO, 2011–19) storyworld. One has to do with the identification of George W. Bush's head on a spike ('In season 1 when Joffrey Baratheon forces Sansa Stark to look at her father's head on a spike you can see the head of former American President George W. Bush. The showrunners insisted that it was not a political statement but just a way to reuse props. Still HBO released an apology and vowed to remove the head from future releases'). A second one includes a reference to Peter

Dinklage's (Tyrion Lannister) contribution to a different production, i.e. a video game ('Peter Dinklage's Ghost'). A third involves a disguised reference to *Monty Python and the Holy Grail* ('In the scene where the Meereenese rider challenges Daenerys's champion, he shouts at them. Nathalie Emmanuel's character Missandei translates the insults that the rider barks and he even pees in Daenerys's general direction. According to the show's linguist David J. Peterson, he is actually shouting insults from *Monty Python and the Holy Grail* including "Your mother was a hamster." If you caught that one you'd better be looking for a job as a linguist because only the producer and Peterson knew what they were doing since the language is made up for the show.'). In addition to exposing the private joke, the latter remark implicitly reveals that the purpose of the video is to allow fans to flaunt their superiority. The video maker must indeed, to be able to spot the reference, possess skills across different lines of work, and access information spread across several media platforms to be able to read so precisely into the show's hidden meaning.

This qualifies the original statement according to which *Game of Thrones*, as a serious entry in the fantasy genre, is not necessarily compatible with the detailed readings of forensic fans. Indeed, as a genre, fantasy seems prone to offer straightforward narratives, which seems to preclude the possibility of a forensic reading. Still, the fan here defends the idea that *Game of Thrones* is worthy of such a reading, which is in turn likely to be rewarding for the most perceptive viewers. Additionally, it is interesting to note that the fan video is featured on *Screen Rant*, an online news website mostly devoted to the coverage of popular TV shows, but whose landmark feature is the inclusion of fan theories. Consequently, it seems that the added value of *Screen Rant* as a type of pop culture journalism over more mature fan productions is the presence of an editorial line. The site has specialised in fan theories, yet since it covers major shows, it also includes fan interpretations of shows that apparently do not lend themselves to theory building. This is one of the possible explanations for the beginning of the fan's speech, where it is stated that serious shows are seemingly not compatible with the light-hearted game of Easter egg hunting. The statement is paradoxical, to say the least, as the very name 'Easter egg' derives its light-heartedness from being borrowed from the field of video games, but has turned into an analytical practice that makes the studied show worthy of the label 'quality TV'. The Easter-egg-hunting-activity, therefore, is only light-hearted in appearance. Here, when featured on a website that often features fan theories, it even becomes a practice that instantly seems to grant any TV show the label 'serious' or 'complex', in addition to the aforementioned 'quality' attribute.

Another possible explanation for what the fan describes as an apparent incompatibility between fantasy and egg hunting directly results from the showmakers' building complex fictional universes that must double as complex TV series. Creating as it does 'a world that users can explore', i.e. a storyworld,

Game of Thrones classifies as 'interactive fiction', according to Jeneen Naji et al. (Naji et al. 2019, 110). One of the consequences of this interactivity is that 'the more details that have gone into the development of a story and its world, the more likely readers/viewers are to believe in it and be able to immerse themselves more completely' (Naji et al. 2019, 110). *Game of Thrones* offers the perfect illustration of such a fan-friendly, immersive construction: 'it exists as books, television series, graphic novels, and games' (Naji et al. 2019, 110). This transmedia development of the show's storylines gives viewers access to a world that 'is extremely well developed and detailed', with full continents, each of which has 'specific characters, traits, themes, rules, and geography' (Naji et al. 2019, 110). As a consequence of this comprehensive world-building strategy, the TV show, while not a classical illustration of the mind-game series, nevertheless lends itself to decryption by fans who treat its storyworld as an enigma to be solved.

Paradoxically, then, the video offers shortcuts to a more comprehensive appropriation of the show that contributes to its expansion. Each detail makes sense, less in relation to another detail than to the global fictional universe it is part of, which creates the impression that the attention paid to detail makes this world realistic, as the creation of an all-controlling designer. In other words, the details are worth noticing even when they do not provide shortcuts to some hidden meaning. Paying attention to them is ultimately more valuable than obtaining access to an enhanced understanding of where the show is headed, since it improves the verisimilitude of the show's universe as a result of its authors' construction. Nothing, it seems, is there without a reason, which prompts viewers to further explore the ramifications of this storyworld online as much as the locations where the series was shot.

This invitation to TV series tourism is the crowning piece in a media strategy designed to bring the storyworld closer to reality by provoking detailed approximations of the latter through an implicit invitation to scan the former for meaningful, realistic details. Ironically, the compendium video, while shortening the show's narratives, does not short-circuit its goal as a media business operation. Quite the opposite, in fact, since this video summary acts as an incentive not to spend less time on the show, but to spend more time in its storyworld, possibly at the cost of taking trips to its shooting locations. Potentially, further exploration of the world is required for the show's storyworld to make full sense, as the frontier between the text and its paratexts is erased.

SERIALISING THE ANTHOLOGY

My second example is a *Black Mirror* (Channel 4 and Netflix, 2011–present) Easter egg video entitled 'Black Mirror_ Every Easter Egg in Seasons 1–4'

(ScreenCrush 2018), which pursues a slightly different agenda: to link together details found in episodes whose characters, timelines, locations and atmospheres are apparently totally unrelated to each other. Nonetheless, as the video demonstrates, the presence of references within certain episodes to other episodes is an indication that *Black Mirror*, like *Game of Thrones* and *Westworld* (HBO, 2016–22), introduces its own consistent storyworld. Once the fan video has connected the dots, the episodes' multiple plots seem to combine and form a single storyline. This is clearly stated in the video's introduction: 'We found over 60 Easter eggs across all four seasons of *Black Mirror*. Together, they confirm one big fan theory: all the episodes exist in the same universe.'

The illustration of how *Black Mirror* brings storylines together comes through the analysis of cross-episode references found in the *Black Mirror* Christmas Special, 'White Christmas'. To quote from the video hosts' speech:

> 'White Christmas' is Easter egg heaven for fans. The Jon Hamm episode featured the same futuristic pregnancy test from 'Be right back.' One of the single guys watching the video stream has the username Ian Waldo – a reference to the animated character from 'The Waldo moment.' The grain implant technology here called Z eyes also appeared in 'The entire history of you' and 'Men against fire.' The symbol from 'White Bear' appears on Joe's jail cell door in 'White Christmas.' When Joe turns on the TV he flips past 'hotshots', the reality show from '15 million merits', the late-night talk show from 'The Waldo moment,' and UKN news. Now look closer and you'll find even more goodies. Here, the news ticker has a headline about Michael Callow's divorce – He was 'The national anthem''s prime minister. There's one about Victoria Skillane, the killer from 'White bear' and one about Liam Monroe, the guy from 'The Waldo moment.'

Here, the point is to endow an anthology series, which by definition does not set out to construct such a self-consistent storyworld, with an independent, parallel fictional universe open for further exploration. Consequently, as the show is decrypted online, its entertainment value increases, since what was just an anthology series also becomes a story-oriented show.

More precisely, the added value offered by the *Black Mirror* video is the extra meaning that results from the deconstruction of a non-consistent universe made up of episodes taking place in different locations, at different periods in time, and involving numerous unrelated characters, followed by a reconstruction of that same universe as a now consistent whole. Such being the case, the explanatory video can be perceived less as a shortcut to the complex meaning of a several-season-long show than as the necessary premise to any form of meaning to be found in its universe. In other words, it guarantees that the show will make sense as a whole, even while its fictional universe remains sprawling in unpredictable ways. The explainer video thus endows *Black Mirror* with the features of a non-anthology, narrative driven, mind-game series, for the way it undertakes to help us make sense of a puzzling and puzzle-like storyworld that has to make more sense as a whole than as the sum of its parts. In this case, shortcuts across episodes create a potentially expandable storyworld for a show that originally lacked this attribute.

EXTENDING THE SHOW'S TIMELINE ACROSS MEDIA PLATFORMS

The third video short-circuits *Westworld* (HBO, 2016–22), a series which, according to Christina Wald, 'invites audiences' speculation on how the narrative might proceed and [which] led to intense conversation between dedicated viewers in online forums' (Wald 2020, 25). The video is entitled 'Biggest Easter Eggs in *Westworld*' (Looper 2016). It introduces itself by referring to the specific quality in the show that makes it susceptible for the kind of detailed analysis the video itself provides:

> Like most popular shows these days, HBO's *Westworld* is chock-full of extra goodies for eagle-eyed viewers. We've rounded up the biggest *Westworld* Easter eggs that you might not have noticed on the series so far. Oh, and just so you know, partner: there are spoilers ahead . . .

Nevertheless, the point of the details focused on here is to identify references to other works to be found in the show. This triggers an extension of its storyworld by encouraging forays into other, complementary fictional universes (among others: *Bioshock*, the series of video games [2016]; *Alice in Wonderland* [Tim Burton's 2010 film]; *Lost* [ABC, 2004–10]; a number of music videos shown to illustrate the presence of pop music songs in the *Westworld* mechanical piano soundtrack moments; *Jurassic Park* [1993]; *The Simpsons* [Fox, 1989–present], and, of course, the original 1973 Michael Crichton film).

All these cultural references are presented as necessary to access the complete meaning of the show. They therefore act as invitations to prolong the *Westworld* experience by exploring the show's paratexts, making it even more time-consuming to fully delve into than it is to watch, and suggesting that 'real' fans have an unlimited amount of spare time to spend on their favourite program. Indeed, according to Craig van Pelt, 'Free time is the time people have to spend in life not working, doing things they enjoy. But time is money. In the future forecast by *Westworld*, free time is very much a luxury. This reality is true today as well' (Van Pelt 2018, 223). This depiction of the series is not the one that first comes to mind (other labels – artificial intelligence anxiety, global surveillance-related fears, the distinction between reality and illusion – tend to spring to mind as possible descriptions of the serialised spin-off of the 1973 Michael Crichton film). Still, it resonates very consistently with the problems raised by shortened explainer videos of the show that thrive on the Internet. Indeed, while the first response watching *Westworld* is not likely to interpret the show's meaning to be that time has become more valuable than ever before, the Easter egg videos suggest that the value of how we spend our free time as viewers may have changed dramatically since the beginning of the new golden age of TV series, and perhaps because of them. Indeed, there are so many several-season-long shows available on so many different media platforms that choosing the right one to watch, and consequently subscribing to the right platform, has become an investment to be quantified in terms of money, but also in terms of the time spent consuming the show. The notion of investment, be it of time or money, seems to be one of the principal incentives to take shortcuts to a more comprehensive meaning of the shows.

The two videos studied before this one, related to *Game of Thrones* and *Black Mirror*, give value to the fictional universes of certain shows by looking at them in a different way. From their perspective, meaning is brought to the surface of complex storyworlds that would make little sense without the new angle offered by explanatory videos. Nevertheless, this is not necessarily a sign that audiences have adapted to the current media continuum. Although they stand as evidence that viewers crave meaning in relation to their favourite shows, the kind which is provided here through a series of shortcuts, this is qualified when one takes into account the type of meaning that is ultimately accessed and disseminated. Based on the first two videos studied above, this type of meaning can be defined as easily accessible, primarily visual, and essentially reconstructive. Complex storyworlds are made simpler through the editing of shots suggesting that the solution, like the purloined letter, had always been there, and becomes obvious on the second viewing. In other words, attention is rewarded, in the videos, saving the time that would be spent for a second viewing. It is not only time that is money, the videos suggest: directing one's attention judiciously is also a wise investment. In what follows, I focus on this quantitative factor in order to better understand why longer may no longer be better anymore, as the shows seem to indicate.

THE VIEWER'S WORK: PAYING ATTENTION

The starting point for this argument is self-evident: series want viewers on board for as long as possible. Indeed, as Jason Mittell explained, the long duration of complex TV series has become 'a significant issue for storytellers, who must design narrative worlds that are able to sustain themselves for years rather than closed narratives plans created for a specific run' (Mittell 2015, 34). Yet the most sustainable narratives also paradoxically call for explainer video shorts. Other symptoms of this are the proliferation of after-shows for extremely popular series such as *Game of Thrones* or *The Walking Dead* (AMC, 2010–22), and the popularity of podcasts for re-watching older shows. There seems, therefore, to be a contradiction between the (potentially limitless) proliferation of TV shows narratives and the (equally endless) dissolution of their meanings, which in turn give rise to orienting, riddle-solving videos. The long narrative patterns that characterise TV series, completed by numerous possibilities for transmedia appropriations or additions, seem to have reached a limit, as the continuation of narrative then demands further explanation. At the same time, plot developments incrementally impair logical closure, thereby constantly deferring an increasingly illusory wholeness of meaning. In other words, there seems to be no straightforward answer to the question, 'What does the show mean?'

It pays, however, to pay attention until the end – be it only pending the promise of an ending. Similar to the need for an ending described in many scholarly productions on TV series narratives (Lifschutz 2018; Wells-Lassagne 2017), the need for a synthesisable meaning seems to be increasingly present among viewers (Bost et al. 2016), intensifying the need for the ending to give its full significance to the narrative as a whole. In this sense, the Easter egg videos can be read as coping mechanisms. It seems that the narrative has become too long or the storyworld too complex, to the extent that it necessarily fails to make sense. To counter such a loss of meaning, someone needs to enhance viewers' understanding of mostly long-winded narratives told as they take place in mysterious storyworlds by retelling the shows, and by shortening them in the process. The viewers' work, therefore, becomes the equivalent of homework, as rereading the events of previous seasons amounts to reading for the implicit examination that understanding the next season is going to require. At least, this is what the name of a series of such videos, 'cram it', seems to indicate (Screen Junkies). The work 'pays' by providing forensic viewers with the ending they are missing, and which they sometimes create themselves, or at least prompt scriptwriters to include in their narratives.

If, then, the very existence of explainer videos must be interpreted as a symptom of narrative failure, or at least as a sign that the showrunners, or indeed the viewers, need to find their limits, it seems that the heart of the matter has to do with the notion of a show's accessibility with regard to viewers' specific skills. The limitation, it seems, is quantitative rather than qualitative – in the explainer videos, both the authors of the explanation and their addressees display top-of-the-range investigative and interpretative skills, great attention to detail, and a good command of serial narratology. The problem is the time effect: as the meaning of the show is the result of a several hour-long aggregate, it needs to be summarised to become accessible in one go – or pasted on shows that disturbingly seem to lack a decent ending.

Indeed, because they are explanatory, the very existence of these videos seems to point to another form of limitations in the viewers – their inability to understand what is happening in the specific storyworld, which may in turn be the consequence of showrunners' failure to make it consistent. In particular, in the case of 'Easter egg hunting games', eagle-eyed amateur video makers draw viewers' attention to specific details constituting clues that are necessary for a comprehensive, *global* understanding of what a specific fictional universe means. In their case, enhanced attention to visual details ironically stands in contradiction to the necessary attention loss that may occur after several hours of viewing, and to the very principle according to which the clues may be hidden in plain sight, given that they are still invisible without slow motion, the blow-up function of onscreen video players, and sleuth-like attention to tiny details.

Yet the most striking aspect of the fan videos under study, and especially of the one about *Westworld*, is that they convey the notion that paying attention to details is a way of spending one's viewing time sensibly. The existence of such videos can therefore be interpreted as a consequence of increasing awareness among viewers that the new form taken by capitalism is that of the attention economy. Claudio Celis Bueno reminds us in *The Attention Economy: Labour, Time and Power in Cognitive Capitalism*, indeed, that 'attention is becoming a scarce and hence valuable commodity, [so that] the question of time has been a central concern for both the apologists and critics of the attention economy. [In order to efficiently allocate attention, an option is to gauge] the attention-time necessary for the consumption of a given message' (Celis Bueno 2017, 11). The synoptic videos can therefore be read as a way of reducing the consumption time for a message that is scattered with detail after detail, clue after clue to be interpreted, over the course of several hours of audio-visual narrative, the watching of which is not compatible, it seems, with the full attention span of viewers. As a natural result of this phenomenon, which testifies to the existence of forensic viewers but also points to the limitations of effective forensic viewing where quantity is concerned, eagle-eyed viewers take the necessary shortcuts for their attention to be placed where it belongs – on the significant details that give the show its meaning.

To return to *Westworld*: this short-circuiting of TV series' extended narratives thus makes sense less as a destruction of the series' ambitious narrative project than as a consequence of the media context of the show. According to Berardi, one of the paradoxes viewers have to face in the context of the attention economy is the discrepancy or conundrum between 'the amount of semiotic goods being produced and the amount of attentive time being disposed of'

(Berardi 2021). Or to put it differently, in the words of Celis Bueno, 'attention economy appears as the result of an asymmetrical relation between the limited temporality of the subject (or human time) and the relatively unlimited temporality of the flows of information (or cyber-time)' (Celis Bueno 2017, 112).

With shows such as *Westworld*, this effect literally takes on epic proportions. Since the show extends over multiple narrative platforms and its storyworld sprawls across various types of screens, it offers an endless and therefore non-processable 'amount of semiotic goods' to be browsed through rather than consumed comprehensively. With the Easter egg videos, this is treated less as a negative turn taken by TV series narrative than as an adequate reaction on behalf of viewers who pride themselves on managing, despite the impossible immensity of the narrative universe offered for consumption, to spend their attention, *and therefore their time*, as wisely as possible.

In its third season, *Westworld* treats this dimension reflexively by introducing a global surveillance computer and disproportionate data centre registering human existences, which may suggest that the proliferation of data forces humanity to acknowledge quantitative limitations that account for the creation of artificial intelligence. Conversely, the revelation that the park's guests willingly placed themselves under 24/7 surveillance for their beings to be cloned and subsequently allowed to 'live on' as hosts in the park after their deaths similarly positions data as the source of potential extensions of storylines to be lived, in the future, across sprawling narrative universes, and therefore as a solution to the limitations of the human mind. To put it bluntly: no one but a machine can be eagle-eyed 24/7. Rather than the need for an ending, the video therefore illustrates the need for a conclusive interpretation of the show's meaning. Here, drawing the right conclusion leads to exposing the data collection capacity of machines as the biggest competitor to human attention, as their very mechanisms are illustrated by the reconstructive form of the explainer video itself.

VIEWER RESPONSE IN PROGRESS: A SHORTCUT TO TV SERIES' PREFERRED RECEPTION MODE

In his book, Jonathan Beller posits that the demand for synoptic meaning originates in the current status of the real world. For him, 'beyond all reckoning, the objective world is newly regnant with an excess of sign value, or rather, with values exceeding the capacities of the sign' (Beller 2006, 16). The Easter egg videos analysed in this chapter suggest that the same type of relationship exists between TV show viewers and their favourite storyworlds, also characterised by their excess of sign value. They also elicit a change in the nature of the connection between fictional universes and reality. According to Beller, indeed,

> The imaginary, both as the faculty of imagination and in Althusser's sense of it as ideology – the constitutive mediation between the subject and the real as 'the imaginary relation to the real' – must be grasped not as a transhistorical category but as a work in progress, provided, of course, that one sees the development of capitalism as progress. (Beller 2006, 10)

Similarly, the Easter egg videos illustrate the latest development in modes of capitalisation on visual labour[4] in the form of incentives to pay attention to details that effectively prompt viewers to spend more time watching more episodes.[5] Referencing the Frankfurt school of critical theory to support his reading, Beller also claims that entertainment is no longer the promulgation of exploitation after work: it has become work itself, due to its value-producing dimension.[6]

While I agree with Beller's views, which my own analysis of Easter egg videos tends to confirm, I have an alternative interpretation of his conclusions concerning the state of sign systems, especially after their deconstruction in the twenty-first century. For Beller,

> Deconstruction's crisis management of the sign, which could be grasped as a coming to terms with the withering away of the state of being under the analysis of the econometrics of the signifier, finds its historical conditions of possibility for its linguistic neurosis in the intensifying delimitation of the province of language by the image. Language just can't process all that visuality – it's like trying to eat your way out of a whale, which, of course, is somewhere you don't belong in the first place. (Beller 2006, 10)

But with the explainer video, which edits shots together into a reconstruction of a show's global meaning, visual language seems able to process that visuality. Based on this observation, I argue that the type of deconstruction offered here is not the symptom of a semiotic crisis. It is, rather, the sign of a narrative crisis which, unlike postmodernism, is born from the endless mediation of the real itself.

According to Jean-Pierre Esquenazi, TV series are not bona fide narratives, in particular since serial narratives never end (Esquenazi 2015, 95). They should rather be considered as an entanglement of multiple narrative threads, the global meaning of which is bound to elude the viewers' grasp. The examples studied above, all of which exemplify the narrative strategy that consists of regularly opening the screen as a window on a constantly expanding narrative universe that seems to live a life of its own, confirm this analysis. Series episodes are moments from the existence of this fictional, parallel universe. Seasons are, literally, years in the lives of the characters we have come to befriend over time. Under such circumstances, narratives may be interrupted but never fully end, as continuation through backward, forward or sideways extension always remains a possibility.

As the videos studied in this chapter suggest, this condition of serial narratives may have other consequences on audiences than the now well-known practices of textual poaching, fanfiction or vidding. Travesties abound on YouTube, imitative narratives or more or less official sequels heap up on Wattpad, and there seems to be no end to the imagination and editing skills of series vidding fans, but they all contribute to the further elaboration or at least to the maintenance of TV show storyworlds by endowing them with new building blocks. These kinds of practices confirm the persistence of the gap-filling habits of 'reader-response theory' (Iser 1997). They even seem to hyperbolise the concept: where, for Wolfgang Iser among others, readers were constantly compensating for a novelist's inability, by definition, to provide them with a whole self-consistent universe, TV show viewers now tend to open new gaps between their moments of access to an expanding, increasingly self-sufficient universe, in order to go about filling them not only during, but also after the consumption of storylines.

The logic of expansion through contraction may therefore only be paradoxical in appearance. Arguably, it may in fact be a strategy devised by showrunners to induce a specific reception pattern in viewers, by teasing their ability to be eagle-eyed or 'forensic'. In the case of the Easter egg videos described above, the narrative extension paradoxically takes the form of a compendium. Rather than adding building blocks to the storyworld as a *Minecraft* player would, some blocks from the original show are singled out for their ability to act as architectural linchpins. The proverbially forensic or sleuth-like viewers of complex TV thereby seem to restrict the expansion of the storyworlds by adding some sense of closure to the narratives. Rather than just filling a gap, the videos seem to act as stopgaps to an endless proliferation of meaning – similar to conspiracy theorists trying to exert control over an increasingly illegible reality by connecting some dots to form an intelligible framework of analysis, explanatory videos point to the overarching presence of an authorial force pulling the strings, checking on the logic of the story, providing users with the possibility of an interpretation. The more educated among viewers form an eagle-eyed elite, whose prerogative becomes the ability to summarise the hour-long shows, pulling out the hidden threads that give them meaning.

The videos under study thus fit very well, although paradoxically, within the expansion project of the media industry, which is to use 'these series as the basis for robust online fan cultures and active feedback to the television industry (especially when their programs are in jeopardy of cancellation)' (Mittell 2006, 32). The kind of feedback provided here is qualitative rather than quantitative: it helps the industry make sense of how contemporary audiences watch TV series, and of how they entice new types of audiences to endorse the same perceptive pattern as they do. The feedback, therefore, concerns viewing practices, and allows the channels to tailor their narratives and visuals to fit the newly popular forms of watching TV shows. In a way, they can be considered to be the equivalent of a worldwide scale study of how the shows are watched that dispenses from resorting to expensive eye-tracking devices equipping panels of viewers. Additionally, those acts of narrative condensation, contraction and reconstruction contribute to the imaginary expansion of the storyworlds. First, because they call for revisions of the shows to be operated by the consumers of the YouTube videos themselves. Second, because they contribute to the popularity of the shows, the meaning of which (whether reflexive or not) is guaranteed by the videos. Indeed, they tend to suggest that with the high-quality shows that have been selected, a disappointment of the kind that appeared when *Lost* fans realised the scriptwriters had no idea how the show would end seems to be impossible – perhaps because the showrunners now use the viewers' reconstructions to write their shows. Third, because this gap-filling in reverse – rather than adding to the implicit, 'between the lines' material that is necessary for a storyworld to make sense, the reader/viewer now contributes to the experience of fiction by providing the logical structure that the proliferating storyworld seems to lack – remains a form of expanding the imaginary life of the characters and the world they inhabit. With cinema, Beller reminds us, 'we sutured one image to the next (and, like workers who disappeared in the commodities they produced, we sutured ourselves into the image)' (Beller 2006, 9). The Easter egg videos suggest that the next stage in the same process has emerged, where we provide images with sutures in external and artificial ways in order to convince ourselves or others of their meaning, value and entertainment power.

CONCLUSION: HOW TV SERIES MIRROR OUR EVER EXPANDING REAL

In *The Ear of the Other*, Jacques Derrida famously claimed that deconstruction 'interrupts a construction' (Derrida 1985, 102). The deconstructive role of the videos described in this chapter similarly acts as an ironic type of interruption: re-centring on the meaning of expanding storyworlds starts with the identification of a central structure. The very notion of the stability of meaning is therefore at stake, and repeated attempts to apply logical closure speak volumes about our ways of relating (to) a Real that also seems to systematically lack logic and structure. But meaning, as Derrida also claims, is always constantly deferred, and the endless contradiction of previous assumptions is always on the verge of being replaced by the realisation that they, and we, were wrong. The shorter form, in this case cramming the meaning of several seasons into a 10-minute video synopsis or compendium, fits within this school of thought inasmuch as it illustrates a certain need for meaning to be re-stabilised.

Based on this deconstructionist reading, one may perceive the result, rather than the limitations, of the expansion of TV series on the state of fiction and our relationship to such a phenomenon. The very existence of eagle-eyed and forensic viewers testifies to a state of narratives as reflections of a reality that is in constant need of decryption. The Easter egg videos condense the result of their search for clues in a format that can be apprehended to form meaning, even pending contradiction. The synthetic mind, in which the shortened form of TV series' endless timelines originates, like the forensic eye whose access to meaning is always a form of decoding, speaks to the state of our construction of the reality we inhabit. It is, in a way, the next logical step in the same sequence. The increasing presence of eagle-eyed viewers suggests that we perceive all things mediated as fake – or at least as a front, as cryptic or coded. The explainer videos show that we increasingly perceive our reality as being meaningless – or at least as being less and less consistent – not because of a lack of information or knowledge, but because the ungraspable profusion of the same leads to the conclusion that by limitlessly expanding, our world, just like TV-show universes, will always necessarily supplant an established truth with its contradiction. The shortened form, then, is a shortcut which paradoxically confirms that TV shows, by becoming as inaccessible in their meaning as the reality around, are also, and are still, just becoming increasingly similar to the reality they represent.

NOTES

1. An import from the terminology of video games, where it describes an unobtrusive item that, when found, opens up a secret passage to a game's hidden level, the Easter egg has been redefined as a narrative clue (Hatchuel 2018, 9) for the purposes of its application to TV series. It most often is a detail in one of a TV show's shots that, if interpreted correctly, leads to an improved understanding of where the narrative is headed, and sometimes of its overall meaning. The term is very similar to the related concept of Chekhov's gun, defined as follows by Mittell: 'One of the pleasures of consuming a serialized narrative is trying to figure out whether a given event might be a kernel or a satellite in the larger arc of a plotline or series as a whole. Critics, fans, and television writers frequently reference Chekhov's Gun as a storytelling axiom: playwright Anton Chekhov's oft-repeated advice that if you hang a gun over the mantle in the first act, it must be fired by the end of the play. In Chatman's terms, Chekhov's Gun might be called a kernel initially presented as a satellite; thus serial viewers can attune themselves to look

for Chekhov's guns, searching for apparent satellites that might eventually turn into kernels in later episodes' (Mittell 2015, 24).
2. In her book on the use of Shakespearean references in TV series, Christina Wald undertakes a study of shows that seek to puzzle their viewers, presenting them as descendants from a cinematic tradition. One of her examples is *Westworld*: 'Westerns, science fiction, and the mind-game films (. . .) have gained prominence since the 1990s. A number of these puzzle films were written by Jonathan Nolan and directed by his brother Christopher Nolan, such as *Memento* (2000) (which can be seen as a rewriting of *Hamlet*) and *The Prestige* (2006). The series [*Westworld*] reflects on its appropriation of earlier films and genres' (Wald 2020, 22).
3. For an analysis of forensic viewing, see Mittell 2015, 52.
4. 'Imaginal functions are today imbricated in perception itself. Not only do the denizens of capital labor to maintain ourselves [*sic*] as image, we labor in the image' (Beller 2006, 1).
5. 'Such a new order of production not only extends the working day and therefore combats the falling rate of profit, it instantiates new orders of commodities such as air-time and vision itself, whose values are measured, for example, by a statistical estimate of the size and now the 'quality' of an audience' (Beller 2006, 28).
6. Beller comments, for this reading, on Antonio Negri's 'Twenty Theses on Marx' (Negri 1996): 'Statements like, "the inflection on the telephone or in the most intimate situation, the choice of words in conversation, and the whole inner life . . . bear witness to man's attempt to make himself a proficient apparatus, similar (even in emotions) to the model served up by the culture industry," seem to negate the creative aspects of fandom and performativity, but Negri himself almost inadvertently proposes a grim addendum to the Frankfurt school architectonic that "Amusement under late capitalism is the prolongation of work." In his words, with respect to the development of capital, "every innovation is the secularization of revolution."' (Beller 2006, 27).

WORKS CITED

Alice in Wonderland, directed by Tim Burton, Walt Disney Studios, 2010.
Beller, Jonathan, *The Cinematic Mode of Production: Attention Economy and the Society of the Spectacle* (Lebanon: Dartmouth College Press, 2006).
Berardi, Franco, *Time, Acceleration, and Violence*, September 2011. Available online: https://www.e-flux.com/journal/27/67999/time-acceleration-and-violence/ (Accessed May 2021).
Bioshock, created by Ken Levine, 2K, 2016.
Black Mirror, created by Charlie Brooker, Channel 4 and Netflix, 2011–present.
Bost, Xavier, et al., 'Narrative Smoothing: Dynamic Conversational Network for the Analysis of TV Series Plots', *2016 IEEE/ACM International Conference on Advances in Social Networks Analysis and Mining (ASONAM)*, 2016, pp. 1111–18. *IEEE Xplore*, DOI: 10.1109/ASONAM.2016.7752379.

Celis Bueno, Claudio, *The Attention Economy: Labour, Time and Power in Cognitive Capitalism* (London: Rowman & Littlefield International, 2017).

Derrida, Jacques, *The Ear of the Other: Otobiography, Transference, Translation*, translated from the French (1982) (New York: Schocken, 1985).

Esquenazi, Jean-Pierre, 'Histoires sans Fin des Séries Télévisées', *Sociétés et Représentations* 39, no. 1, Éditions de la Sorbonne (Juin 2015): 93–102.

Game of Thrones, created by David Benioff and D.B. Weiss, HBO, 2011–19.

Hatchuel, Sarah, '"What a Piece of Work is Your Machine, Harold": Shakespeare et la réinvention de l'humanité dans les séries américaines d'anticipation', *TV/Series*, no. 14 (2018). Available online: URL: http://journals.openedition.org/tvseries/3068; DOI: https://doi.org/10.4000/tvseries.3068 (Accessed February 2024).

Iser, Wolfgang, *The Act of Reading: A Theory of Aesthetic Response* (Baltimore: Johns Hopkins University Press, 1997).

Jenkins, Henry, et al., *Spreadable Media: Creating Value and Meaning in a Networked Culture* (New York: New York University Press, 2013).

Jurassic Park, directed by Steven Spielberg, Universal Pictures, 1993.

Lifschutz, Vladimir, *This is the End: finir une série TV* (Tours: Presses Universitaires François Rabelais, 2018).

Looper, *Biggest Easter Eggs in Westworld*, 2016, YouTube. Available online: https://www.youtube.com/watch?v=HLzq5xm896k (Accessed February 2024).

Lost, created by Jeffrey Lieber, J.J. Abrams and Damon Lindelof, ABC, 2004–10.

Memento, directed by Christopher Nolan, Summit Entertainment, 2000.

Mittell, Jason, *Complex TV: The Poetics of Contemporary Television Storytelling* (New York: New York University Press, 2015).

Mittell, Jason, 'Narrative Complexity in Contemporary American Television', *The Velvet Light Trap* 58, no. 1 (Austin: University of Texas Press, 2006): 29–40. Project MUSE, DOI: 10.1353/vlt.2006.0032.

Monty Python and the Holy Grail, directed by Terry Gilliam and Terry Jones, National Film Trustee Company and Python Pictures, 1975.

Naji, Jeneen, et al., *New Approaches to Literature for Language Learning* (Cham: Springer, 2019).

Negri, Antonio, 'Twenty Theses on Marx: Interpretation of the Class Situation Today', *Marxism beyond Marxism* (New York: Routledge, 1996), 149–80.

Screen Junkies, *CRAM IT*.

Screen Rant, *10 Game of Thrones Easter Eggs That You Might Have Missed!* 2016. YouTube. Available online: https://www.youtube.com/watch?v=iuWUykyueaw (Accessed February 2024).

ScreenCrush, 'Every *Black Mirror* Easter Egg You Missed in Seasons 1–4', *ScreenCrush*, 2018. Available online: https://screencrush.com/black-mirror-easter-eggs-season-4/ (Accessed February 2024).

The Prestige, directed by Christopher Nolan, Touchstone Pictures, 2006.

The Simpsons, created by Matt Groening, Fox, 1989–present.

The Walking Dead, developed by Frank Darabont, AMC, 2010–22.

Van Pelt, Craig, 'Exploring *Westworld* with Karl and Jean', in *Westworld and Philosophy: Mind Equals Blown*, eds Richard Greene and Joshua Heter (Chicago: Open Court Publishing, 2018), 218–24.

Wald, Christina, *Shakespeare's Serial Returns in Complex TV* (Cham: Springer International Publishing, 2020). *DOI.org (Crossref)*, DOI: 10.1007/978-3-030-46851-4.

Wells-Lassagne, Shannon, *Television and Serial Adaptation* (New York: Routledge, Taylor & Francis Group, 2017).

Westworld, created by Jonathan Nolan and Lisa Joy, HBO, 2016–22.

Westworld, Michael Crichton, Metro-Goldwyn-Mayer, 1973.

CHAPTER 13

Writing *En thérapie*: A Conversation with Vincent Poymiro

Sylvaine Bataille, Florence Cabaret and Shannon Wells-Lassagne with Vincent Poymiro

Vincent Poymiro is a celebrated French screenwriter for television and film, most known for television drama Ainsi soient-ils *(Churchmen, Arte, 2012–15), about a group of young men in contemporary Paris attending a Catholic seminary, which has won multiple awards and been broadcast in Canada, Belgium, Italy and Finland, as well as his work on* En thérapie *(Arte, 2021–2), the French adaptation of* BeTipul *(Hot3, 2005–8), an Israeli series still best known for its American adaptation,* In Treatment *(HBO, 2008–10, 2019–21). He has written about twelve scripts for fiction films and in 2022 he won the César [the French equivalent of the Academy Awards] for best original screenplay for* Onoda, *a film featured at the Cannes Film Festival's 'Un certain regard' and nominated for Césars for best original screenplay, best film, best director and best cinematography. He also teaches scriptwriting in France and abroad, and with fellow scriptwriter David Elkaïm they have launched their own production company, PERPETUAL SOUP, as well as a TV series department at the cinema school La Femis in Paris. Their goal is to promote and lead new projects involving innovative ways of writing and working in the French cinema and television industries, as well as welcoming young artists with whom to share old and new experiences and skills.*

The editors of this collection were fortunate enough to sit down for an interview with Vincent Poymiro to discuss En thérapie*'s genesis and first season, and to explore the very nature of the series, with its short episodes but recurrent format: each 20-to-30-minute episode focuses on a different character in therapy with the same therapist, Philippe Dayan, which then repeats week after week. Poymiro suggests that this format is* 'the minimum [. . .] that it takes to be able to make a real seriality,' *and pinpoints how this impacted not only the writing and production of the series, but ultimately may have influenced the broadcaster that produced it, public-service channel Arte, suggesting the central importance of format in television. Indeed, his discussion* *of the screenwriting process, highlighting both the cultural specificity of the French audiovisual landscape and of television writing (when compared to theatre or film) and the way that that process is made possible through a mixture of in-depth collective discussion and brainstorming in the writers' room, before then breaking down the whole into individual episodes, with characters attributed to individual writers, ultimately stresses the inextricable nature of length and brevity in the making of the television series. The interview has been translated from the original French and edited for concision and content.*

Could you first tell us about the genesis of *En thérapie*?

There was the genesis in temporal terms, and the genesis in conceptual terms, which is not quite the same process. In purely industrial terms, there was a series of convergent events, involving each of the actors of the project, i.e. [Franco-German public service television channel] Arte,[1] the producers, Eric Toledano and Olivier Nakache,[2] who were also the directors and to an extent the 'showrunners' (in a slightly polemic way, we have contested the fact that they were retrospectively designated as sole showrunners, but they were the initiators and industrial accompaniers of the project), and us, David Elkaïm and I, who were the co-designers of the project in the artistic and narrative sense.

In fact, this project of adapting *BeTipul* had been circulating in the French audio-visual landscape for more than ten years, very soon after the American adaptation [*In Treatment*, HBO, 2008–21] made it more widely known to the general public, internationally, and to a small but passionate audience in France. *BeTipul* series creator Hagaï Levi had also begun to accompany, sign and authorise adaptations in many countries. So the franchise quickly gave French producers ideas, especially as Hagaï had always wanted there to be a French and German adaptation, because for him, they were the two major European countries associated with psychoanalysis. Oddly enough, David Elkaïm and I were offered this project ten years ago, but there was no follow-up at the time. We started to talk about it again with Eric Toledano and Olivier Nakache when we worked together on another series project, and we discussed our appreciation for *BeTipul* and *In Treatment*. It so happened that at the time, they were in discussions to adapt other formats of Israeli television. Then it turned out that [*En thérapie* producers] Yaël Fogiel and Laetitia Gonzales from the Films du Poisson, who knew Hagaï, had also discussed how much they liked the show with Eric and Olivier, and finally they contacted Hagaï, whom Yaël knows personally, and discovered that the rights were available – so, logically enough, Eric and Olivier came back to us to suggest that we do the project. So it was a sort of series of coincidences.

Finally, it must be said that the other reason why the series had not been made in ten years was that there was a broadcasting problem; there was no channel open to a format like *BeTipul*'s, with daily episodes of 20–30 minutes. No broadcaster, be it [pay-cable channel] Canal,[3] or the Arte of the time, had either the possibility or the idea of developing a series of thirty-five daily episodes, especially one that was set in a psychoanalyst's office.

That's more the industrial dimension. But, obviously, David and I loved the American series, which led us to discover the original Israeli show. I also knew Hagaï for his subsequent work, including what he did on *The Affair* [Showtime, 2014–19]. David and I had no interest in sacrificing the original to this rather French sport of remaking a very good series and turning it into a disaster. From the outset, the original series was very important to us, as well as its American and even Italian adaptations (I also met Nicola Lusuardi, who directed the writing of the Italian adaptation). It is very clear that this is not a series about psychoanalysis; it is a series centred on society, the society of whichever nation hosts its adaptation. That is the incredibly efficient plasticity of Hagaï's concept; once you transpose it to another country, you wonder, 'What needs to be changed to make it consistent with that country?', and you open up an echo chamber of what is happening in that society. Anyway, we understood that. But we didn't really see what we could add to the original. So, at the beginning, when we started talking about it with Olivier and Eric, we weren't really sure that we should do it.

And then, as we were discussing the very sociological dimension of the original series and of the American series, suddenly, we got the idea of the Bataclan attacks that took place in Paris on November 13, 2015.[4] It was 2016 at the time, we were all very affected by this event, and we had all asked ourselves at one point or another about our duty as storytellers. Wasn't it our responsibility to find a way to quickly narrate something about it? Once again, we did not want to conform to the French traditional way of dealing with collective trauma and wait fifty years before talking about November 13.

Very quickly David and I, and then Eric and Olivier got on board. A few weeks later, we were in London, telling Hagaï about it – and he was immediately very supportive. That's how it started.

Then Yaël, Laetitia, Eric, Olivier and David and I pitched it to Arte. Yaël and Laetitia had connections with Arte. They are quite well known in the industry, but more for auteur cinema, which is of particular interest to Arte. Eric and Olivier had status and credit. It was their first series, but they brought Arte a guarantee of a wider audience. It was a gamble indeed and, yet, at the same time, they brought along their ability to promote and involve actors who came from the cinema and could attract viewers. So the project was seen as a kind of forerunner, since in the French industry, which is still very elitist, cinema actors have had a hard time switching formats in the recent past, because they were told so often that television is vulgar and that what matters is to make movies, though things have changed a lot over the past ten years.

Arte was immediately on board, at all levels. But there were obstacles because 35 episodes of 25 minutes each – which was what was planned at the beginning – would have used up half of Arte's fiction budget over a season. They didn't know how to broadcast it either. At the time there was no slot for this kind of episode length and everything seemed very complicated. That is why at first we had to write for several months in a row to complete and hone five episodes, which is not something usually done. We wrote the whole first week of the series, we made character cards, we had to work, rework, do a lot of versions of the show's bible and arrange a lot of appointments with Arte and deal with a lot of construction problems, give a lot of guarantees to each level of the Artesian decision-making system – and eventually, after two and a half years, they decided to take the plunge. I think that in the meantime, the idea of giving the platform a real identity probably played its part. I mean, this is how I tend to interpret it retrospectively given how they broadcast it.[5] That was also consistent with Arte's gradual development in terms of identity – that is, is Arte a Hertzian channel, or is Arte an online platform? And could Arte also possibly become – and time will tell – the bridgehead of an alternative European fiction proposal?

When Arte greenlit the project, we had to move very, very fast since the [35-episode-long] series had to be shot before the end of the following year, because of the rights. The writing period had to fit in with the rights transferred by Hagaï, but also with deadlines and other proposals he had, especially with regard to Germany. Eric and Olivier also had a very busy schedule, since in the interval, they had started to work on another film. All the episodes had to be written ten months later. But we had been fighting for two years to make the show, so we accepted the challenge.

Can you expand on this issue of time, starting with the very flexible time of your profession and then the time of the television production?

The need to produce quickly is one of the staples that remain highly counterintuitive from the point of view of the French industry, where even on TV, everything usually takes a long time. David and I saw that for ourselves at the beginning of our careers when we were writing *Ainsi soient-ils* [Arte, 2012–15], our first series as co-writers, and even before that, with series we didn't manage to make: we realised that development takes forever in France, both in the cinema and on television. Quite frankly, in those days, it was partly because of the writers saying they needed time, but also, very largely, because of the industry itself, the chain of command in TV. In cinema, it's never easy to finance a film, so a producer has several films on the go at the same time, they're often waiting for commissions, or some decision or other. In many instances the screenwriter and the director are sitting there waiting to know whether they'll get to the next stage. And on TV it's quite the same. We wait for the head of programming to read, they are overwhelmed with work of their own, then we have to wait until the channel has validated that step, and in the end, they don't really want to reject the project, but they would like us to rewrite it, and then suddenly there's a change in the head of programming and the project is put to one side, and so on and so forth.

As a result, and this is largely due to the cumbersome nature of the system, David and I, as writers, said to ourselves that we had to learn the Anglo-Saxon way, and the way series are done in other European countries. By exploring these models, we saw that it was possible, that there were techniques that would probably enable us to write rapidly in order to be competitive with other forms, or to encourage French decision-makers to say that we could be competitive with Anglo-Saxon and other forms.

In a process of trial-and-error, we and people like Fanny Herrero[6] learned to tinker with the work in the writers' room, which saved us a lot of time. And yet we still took the time necessary for conceptualisation at the beginning – that was incompressible, because it means that when you start writing, things can move very swiftly if the project is clearly delineated. It can be communicated to the co-writers and to the whole team in the workshop early enough so that everyone knows exactly what's going on. This is the method we devised with David, and so we learned to produce very quickly. We learned to play on this factor of time that is so essential in series: if you know how to work fast, you can manage it, including by mesmerising the management of the channel by delivering the texts in nothing flat, writing them at such a rhythm that they do not have enough time to find ways to 'torture' us by actually reading the script.

On the other hand, the industry itself is still a very intricate maze, so the fact that we learned to produce faster didn't after all make a huge difference in terms of manufacturing times. However, in a case like *En thérapie*, where, in the end, the amount of proper writing time was reduced to this minimal portion (which also shows how, aesthetically, the industry has trouble understanding the essential place of writing in serial work), the difference was that when they asked us to write all the remaining episodes in such a short time, it seemed impossible, but we knew how to do it. So we said yes, and I believe that we handed in Version 2 of the last episode three days later than the date we had originally planned when we had signed a year before. That was our great pride.

How long did the shooting take afterwards?

The filming was much faster. I think it was eighty days. Basically, each episode was shot in two days.

Were you involved in the filming, or was there a separation between the writing time and the shooting time?

David and I accompanied the shooting only by means of a delegated voice, which means that we respected the chain of authority of the French industry, where the screenwriter must on no account be on the set because no one can imagine for a single moment that if they are there, it's to make everybody's life easier. People immediately assume that we're going to take up more space in the competition of egos present on the set – since we're in France, and everyone is more interested in power than in the collective result.

From an industrial point of view, I think a good example of the many misunderstandings we had to cope with during the process is the conflict we had about the final episode lengths.[7] Three weeks before the shooting started, the episodes were timed by someone in the team – someone who was very competent but came from the cinema industry – to 45–50 minutes, which was a major concern that was directly addressed to us (though we had been previously asked to stay out of the shooting process). We told the production that, as professional scriptwriters, we knew that this timing was not correct. Besides, structurally, we had generally used the Israeli and American episodes as a model and, from our experience, we could see that our text for each episode corresponded to the same average duration [of around 30 minutes].[8] We made this point very clear, explaining that when the actors are here, and if they are directed at the correct tempo, it will take the time that we had implicitly anticipated. So we asked one of our juniors, Alexandre Manneville, to follow the filming from the point of view of the text. He constantly fought to ensure that the texts were not cut excessively. And of course, we were right about the duration of the episodes.

The final length of the episodes was just the result of an intestine struggle within the production teams – between the representative of the writers' room, i.e. Alexandre, Mathieu Vadepied (the shooting coordinator) and Eric and Olivier – against a backdrop of professional differences between TV series and cinema films. As it turned out, in terms of platform broadcasting, it didn't pose so much of a problem. It would have been more of a sales problem, but then the series being an adaptation, this issue of sales was less important. In retrospect, regardless of all the conflicts that we may have had, I do think that everyone succeeded in making the right concessions and settled for the better end result.

Could you talk about adaptation in terms of project design and explain to what extent previous versions influenced the texts you have written, but also in industrial terms, and tell us if it was easy to pitch the series to the network? You mentioned that it was easier to sell abroad, since the show is an adaptation of other shows that were already popular elsewhere.

It's obvious that we were adapting a format, which is a double-edged sword, because from the outset, we couldn't hide the fact that the series was going to take place over the course of a certain number of episodes in a psychoanalyst's office and that characters were hardly ever going to get out of the room. But it's clear that in terms of editorial policy, for a TV channel like Arte, the prestige of Hagaï's series and its multiple adaptations, including the American one in which Hagaï actively took part, was a definite asset. So that made it possible to pitch it much more clearly.

Then, I would say, an adaptation is essentially a series of constraints. And from our perspective, constraints are what helps us invent. So even when we do an original series, there is a long work of what I call conceptualisation, which consists of determining precisely the best way to tell this particular story, to approach this subject according to the way we thematised it, and therefore what is the best narrative, and also aesthetically, which pre-existing format, which genre we should work in. So, we impose constraints, ultimately, that we will accept, that will allow us to work faster, but also to create complicity with the viewer. And of course, these are constraints which we will be forced to transgress when we absolutely need to. This is what generally confers the project its singularity – giving ourselves the maximum number of constraints to force us to be creative and therefore to have a good reason not to respect them when the need arises.

In terms of temperament, David and I are pretty much in tune with each other: we tend to think that a constraint is an opportunity; so in the case of *En thérapie*, from the moment we found an angle to tell a story of our own, we were presented with the ideal configuration because we were dealing with an extremely well-constructed series, saturated with incredibly consistent rules. It was very interesting to experience: by taking certain elements and changing them and putting them back into the original structure, the series started to tell other stories, without us having much more to do. So by being thoroughly precise about what we wanted to keep from the original series and what it was necessary to change, we obtained this inventing machine. And we found that some elements which were almost identically transposed from the original series in a slightly renewed context initiated different meanings. We may have had the feeling that we were telling them ourselves, except that the stories already existed, so it was quite easy. It was a real pleasure.

Moreover, to go back to the time limits, I don't think we could ever have met those deadlines had it not been for the pre-existing constraints. The series was 'only' an adaptation. And the genius is Hagaï. What's brilliant is the serialised structure, and the underlying concept. Writing a series implies a special form of creativity that is not exactly the same as the creativity at work in the feature film, which rests on the paradigm of the closed ending. This is another kind of creativity: it's the conceptual creativity of inventing a narrative model that does not end and can develop, not indefinitely, but that can proliferate logically.

You are probably familiar with this plot/theme distinction that everybody knows in Anglo-Saxon criticism, and that Lumet explains very well in his book on how to write a feature film,[9] but that is still too little-known in France. For David and I, there is a very clear distinction between plot and theme. This distinction is not the same in feature films and in series. We consider *En thérapie* to be a miniseries, because it is still closed.[10] As our plot focuses on a psychoanalyst's office just after the attacks on November 13, our theme would be something like, 'Is it possible to leave the world at the door?' We recreated the theme, and of course it is more intensely shared by all the characters than in the original series, because the external trigger is the Bataclan attacks and therefore, in a way, you might say that the crisis is really external – even though very quickly, after the initial shock, any external crisis gets transformed into an intimate crisis. It was really about addressing the viewer questions that were centred on the issue of how we had reacted, collectively, to the attacks of November 13, and offering a kind of echo chamber for all these issues which we all had to face and which we debated amongst ourselves – because ultimately, that's what this series is about: people talking.

That was probably the specific, conceptual contribution that we brought to the original format, which we respected to the extreme in all other aspects, up to the portrayal of most of the characters. But the initial concept was a little different, and this had implications for what the series offers thematically. That's basically what I can say about the adaptation process viewed from an external, industrial, as well as aesthetic point of view.

Since we are talking about the link between a collective crisis and a more intimate, individual crisis, how did you choose the characters who were going to deal with the Bataclan shooting in particular – Adel and Ariane, a policeman and a surgeon? Why these two professions, and why a man and a woman?

I may think of several motivations behind our choice of protagonists. They still inherit quite a lot from the characters from the original series. I would actually say that three characters specifically carry the question of the impact of the Bataclan events – Adel, the policeman, Ariane, the surgeon, the third one being Dayan, the psychoanalyst himself. In terms of identification and empathy in relation to the viewer, he is gradually supposed to be the one in whom viewers most recognise their own affects, their own doubts; and in any case, he is the one who incarnates the entire experience as a character. But Hagaï's format is brilliant because he conjures up a double episodic temporality: it is both an episodic episodicity and a weekly episodicity. There are several bundles of episodes per character, so that the story in each episode, each singular cell, is informed both by this weekly recurrence that is the therapy of each single patient and the overarching journey of the psychoanalyst which, for its part, is truly episodic, inasmuch as Dayan remembers the previous episode and is the only witness of the different characters' arcs (plus his own narrative arc), while each patient remembers only their own storyline.

That dual temporality is absolutely incredible and is really a conceptual masterpiece, because it also puts viewers in a kind of dual attention. They are simultaneously empathising with the character who is in therapy, for many understandable reasons, and empathising with the therapist, who has a double position. Indeed, Dayan is either the protagonist or the antagonist of the session as well as of the therapy that is underway – and at the same time he is also the deeply internally-conflicted protagonist of what he is experiencing over the long term, which the viewer is aware of, because of the clinical supervision at the end of each week (Figure 13.1).

All this is a prodigious construction aimed at putting the audience in a state of maximum attention and psychological contemplation. That's what's so spectacular about the series. This is not just a purely abstract, theoretical construction, since everything is done to put the viewers 'in a state'. They are the ones who know everything, who understand everything and who therefore project themselves in a divided, complex way, which makes each episode extremely intense from the perspective of their experience. That's one of the reasons why the series worked so well.

The psychoanalyst is really the one who undergoes a crisis, who says to himself 'Since the Bataclan attacks, nothing can ever be the same, I can no

Figure 13.1 Philippe Dayan (Frédéric Pierrot) meeting his supervisor Esther (Carole Bouquet) at the end of each week (S01E05).

longer lead my life in the same way.' To show that, we had to specify who he was, historically speaking. He's a psychoanalyst, he's Jewish, he has roots in North Africa, which is very important. Also, he's a dissident Lacanian, that is to say a guy who left his Lacanian circle after human conflicts, someone who has done a lot of soul-searching and harbours a certain bitterness about his own tools, and who calls the usefulness of his practice into question. This character really had to be reimagined, for lots of reasons, because psychotherapy and the history of analytic psychotherapy are not the same in France as in Israel or in the United States.

As for Ariane, I would say that she didn't change much compared to the Israeli and American model. As a surgeon, she's on the front line of the terrorist attacks: obviously there's something crucial about this trigger, and it also contributes to narrative consistency. If it hadn't been for the Bataclan events, she would not have had this revelation that forces her to rush to confess to her shrink that she loves him. She embodies the idea that the external crisis is something that impacts everyone, but ultimately, very quickly, she does something very human, which is that in the midst of chaos, she brings it all back to her own issues and she makes it into an impetus that spurs her to move forward in her life, provoking a crisis with her therapist that will allow her character to develop. And probably, as it is implied at the end, to free herself from the grip of her analyst because she needed to detach herself from him as well as experience this attempt at a seduction with him, to then live her life fully as a woman.

In contrast, Adel Chibane is probably the character who changed the most. He couldn't be a military man who bears the repressed guilt of the use of force by Israel or the United States, because France's relationship with its own power is not the same. Clearly, in France, for example, a fighter pilot, or any high-ranking soldier has a completely different social aura. Maybe we're an older country, which is more disillusioned, I don't know. In any case, there is a very clear social mistrust of the issue of force and military power in France, which means that we couldn't use that Israeli or US aura at all, it would not have been consistent with the French social perception of this kind of man.

By turning him into a policeman we could make his affective trigger not the repressed guilt of violence, but on the contrary a guilt – which he is enormously conflicted about, but which ultimately is not so repressed – about having arrived too late at the Bataclan and not having been able to protect people. Obviously, this guilt conceals great depths which are connected with French history. It was very important for us to refer to the history of terror in Algeria in the 1990s, and the history of Algeria in general, at least since its colonisation by France in 1830 and beyond its war of liberation and independence in 1962. We wanted to use French history to tell that story, too. When we were investigating post-November 13, we met a lot of police officers who were sociologically of African descent, and they all had the same reaction after the Bataclan attacks – that in fact, they were not the ones who changed after November 13, but it was the way people looked at them that changed. Suddenly, French people of North African origins had become 'Arabs', and for many of them, it was a trauma, rekindling another former trauma: why did their family have to forget who they were to become French? All this seemed essential to us.

Moreover, Chibane made it possible to bring a popular voice into the analyst's office, i.e. the voice of the majority of people we know around us, in our families, who are anti-psychotherapy, because they've assimilated this idea that you shouldn't talk, you mustn't think about what hurts, you mustn't look back, you have to move forward – this very touching, and at the same time very self-destructive attitude. It was important for us not to elicit a kind of contrived, fake complicity with the viewer, as if, between ourselves, it was not worth talking about psychoanalysis since we are all extremely savvy about it and know all the tricks of the trade. On the contrary, we wanted the viewers to feel welcomed, to discover an unfamiliar field, to learn things, and at the same time we wanted their own reservations to be explicitly expressed on the screen, in the clearest and even most brutal way possible, so that they felt included in the fiction and not compelled to identify with so-called experts.

Chibane represents all this, but also provides a final essential opening about the questions raised after November 13, which we do not have the answer to, but which we were all confronted with. Chibane is probably the only one who ends up looking the shrink in the eye and saying, 'OK, I get it. You have understood all my neuroses, but in fact, I'm not a psychological subject, I'm a tragic subject. So I don't give a shit about my psychology. I'm in a tragedy, and that's it' (Figure 13.2). We wanted that to unnerve the psychoanalyst, who at that point has a moment of vertigo which he will probably feel bad about for a long

Figure 13.2 Dayan listening to an initially reluctant Adel Chibane (Reda Kateb) (S01E02).

time, because he thinks 'That's when I didn't know what to say to him, because maybe for a moment I thought, "What if he's right?"' So, Chibane represents all that disruption, in addition to other aspects of his character which were rooted in the police documentation that our co-writer Pauline Guéna brought in, as she worked on that character specifically.

Are you then telling us that there was one writer per character?

Yes, we did the same as Hagaï, and the same as Nicola Lusuardi in Italy. Once David and I had conceptualised the story, written the first five episodes, and started to build the story arcs, we decided to recruit three co-writers who would each take a character, so they would pay more attention to their character during the writing process – whereas we, who co-wrote with them, would focus on keeping the tension and ensure the consistency of the overall story.

David and I had decided to take the character of the controller in order to work on the episodes where Dayan is himself the patient, because that's what makes it possible to tie up the other episodes together, both in terms of dramatic irony and dramatic progress. Then everyone chose their character.

Could you tell us about the benefits and constraints of the short format, of short episodes, and the interaction between short formats and dramatic content that is quite original and too rarely seen on television?

The 26-to-30-minute format is developing more and more, but also less than before in the form of what was called the dramedy or the sitcom. Instead, there are now more and more miniseries of six, eight or ten episodes of 26 minutes that, for me, tend to fit into the paradigm of the feature film. It is rare to be able to serialize a story correctly in six parts of 26 minutes. In general, such a pattern is typical of feature films, or of '*unitaires*' [standalones], as we also say in the French TV industry, that are plot-driven – in other words, there's the promise of the trigger quite early on in the story, which calls for a closed response. And so, the viewer is ready to go all the way because they want to know whether the final answer will be 'yes' or 'no'.

These are questions about the destiny of aesthetic forms. The short format, which has long been the typical format of the ultra-serial program, that is to say the sitcom that can last for ten seasons of closed or semi-closed episodes, has now migrated, or is in the process of migrating to a format that I find a little 'cut-rate', because in fact, it's not a series, it's just a cut-up narrative unit, a standalone which is divided into parts but which is not especially serialised. Even though it can be very good, if you think for example of *Normal People* [BBC3, 2020]. And then there is the British format. You can see that the six-episode season is properly serialised, like *Ghosts* [BBC1, 2019–23] or *This Way Up* [Channel 4, 2019–21]. But then, to have a real dramedy season, you need two or three British seasons of six episodes. It's still a series for me, because there's this question of episodic unity.

So we chose the short format – also because Hagaï has never hidden the fact that when he got the idea for the format, he was actually writing soaps, working pretty much as a penny-a-liner, and so at some point a brilliant short circuit occurred in his head, connecting the duration of the soap and the duration of a therapy session, and he said to himself, 'I'm going to make a soap about shrinks.'

And it is true that when we made the show, we thought that we would have loved it if Arte had broadcast it one episode a night at the same time as *Un si grand soleil* [a popular daily French serial, France 2, 2018–present].[11] We would have really loved to make Arte's soap, Arte's daily show. But it was too complicated, there was no slot for it, even though we talked about it, even seriously at one point, with the head of programming. We couldn't do more than 35 episodes, so we were far behind our daily friends.[12]

Incidentally, I would also point out that it's not actually such a short format. You can see that when you look at the dramedies, even *Nurse Jackie* [Showtime, 2009–15]: in 26 minutes they manage to fit in a narrative in three or four acts with Plot A, Plot B, Plot C, Plot D. *Nurse Jackie* is a model in this respect: there's a theme and a serialised plot, two closed plots, and even sometimes a multi-perspective narrative in terms of characters, a real choral unity, an 'arena' series. So for me, 26 to 30 minutes is not a short format. It's the minimum, if you're concise and efficient in narrative terms, to be able to make a real seriality, often supported in the case of dramedies by comic stylisation, which allows you to go faster on many occasions, and in terms of tone, to go more directly to emotional places.

In terms of pure seriality, again, we were enormously inspired by Hagaï's work. The classic Freudian therapy sessions last 45–50 minutes. Anyone who has frequented the Lacanians knows that sessions can last as little as 10 minutes, but we didn't want that at all. Obviously, the series stages a stylisation of a psychotherapy session, of a psychoanalysis that does not exist. It is the movement that we found interesting, to narrate the effects and consequences over several sessions. An analysis in seven sessions doesn't exist either. But we still wanted to give the viewer an idea of what a session might look like. And then it's entertainment, it's a show, so that each episode is dramatised with the basic staples of a trigger, a protagonist and an antagonist.

In *En thérapie*, viewers figure out the psychoanalyst's goal quite rapidly and we see him struggling because we are aware of his internal problems. Sometimes we know, and sometimes we don't know, whether he will succeed in mastering the conflict or the attempt to escape, or catch the unconscious truth that is coming out. The patient's conflict is pretty clear. It is summed up in four acts, with quite obvious act breaks, and at the same time we, viewers, in a kind of dramatic irony, can clearly see that the psychoanalyst is dealing with another problem than the one raised by the patient, which has to do with his own story. These two entities within him, the therapist and the psychological subject, are in frequent conflict, and depending on the episode, one or the other of them wins over. So in the end, the dramaturgic consequence for the viewer of the episode is either a victory – which fuels serialisation since the victory also takes place in the therapist's inner journey, even in the context of the patient's therapy – or a defeat, which obviously calls for a follow-up since we suspect that Dayan will have to deal with the fallout next time.

And of course, we were quite aware, with the help of Hagaï, too, that this dramaturgy of speech, which relies heavily on what we would like to say, what we can say, what we don't say, has everything to do with psychoanalysis, but also with the classic Racinian dramaturgy. You can clearly see in Racine's great tragedies that what is at stake in all the conflict, and all the exposition of the conflict, is knowing what the protagonist would like to say, must say, does not want to say, as they go on stage. And the whole conflict for the spectator relies on the fate of this speech in the scene, which logically leads to the rest of the story and the final twist. Take any tragedy by Racine, it's designed that way, and that's why it's so dramatically intense.

You talked about establishing rules before breaking them. It is true that, as we reach the ending of the first season, we can feel a progression towards more scenes taking place outside Dayan's office (outdoors, or even in Ariane's flat) and more intrusions of new characters in his office (his own daughter and Chibane's father). So it is true that the viewer can experience what you said about rules that are internal to the series and that can be infringed on account of a logic that is also intrinsic to the unfolding of the series. Could you comment upon the crucial unravelling of rules in the writing process?

Naturally, once the rules have been established, the goal is to find a way around them. That's what a rule is for, it's to make you want to transgress it, and I guess psychoanalysts would say that too. But if the rule makes sense enough, if it is necessary enough, finding the means to transgress it in a coherent way obviously compels you to do something more with it, narratively speaking. And of course, the transgression always has a huge effect on the viewer who has become accustomed to the rules and comes back to check on them. That's how the show hits the spot, too: you watch because it's the same thing and you watch because it's something else. And this conjunction of the two opposites – it has to be the same thing, except that it also has to be something else – is what

Figure 13.3 Dayan trespassing the rules with Ariane (Mélanie Thierry), visiting her at her place (S01E35).

produces such a pleasurable tension. The viewers come back to check that the promise has been kept, that the show fulfils its program and sticks to its contract, but they also want to go through the gratifying experience that we found a way to trick them by telling them something they didn't expect.

Obviously, in something as coded as the series as we made it, in addition to the context of the therapy session where the shrink himself keeps insisting on rules ('There are rules here'), all the while struggling not to infringe them himself, even though he really wants to (he keeps asking his controller for permission to do so in the hope that she will tell him not to . . . so that he can), there is a constant play at all levels of the narrative about rules, and the pros and cons of setting rules for oneself (Figure 13.3).

To conclude, we were wondering if you have specifics to share about the broadcasting strategy. You've already touched on the idea of using the Arte streaming platform, with all the episodes that were put online in one go, while on the channel, the series was aired week by week – narrative week by narrative week.

I agree with you that the centrality of this kind of reflection for the series and for the writer's work needs to be underlined because in a way, the broadcaster is essential for the serial format and its editorial policy. So if the content is essential, broadcasting strategies are no less crucial. All the more so as we know that formats also evolve according to industrial constraints. Incidentally, let's never forget this essential idea that it is possible to turn constraints to our advantage. The idea that at some point we have to cut the episode to insert ads meant to sell soap or laundry detergent because that is going to finance the program. . . . Either you take it as a declaration of war and go off and write for a more selective audience who is more respectful of the beauty of art, or you remember a very old rule invented in the classical theatre, which is the acts. And you can turn this dreadfully industrial constraint, but that still allows the program to take place, to your advantage. And so, you come up with the idea of dividing your episode into acts, which allows the cut to be made in a place that does not compromise the story. And on top of that, you guarantee the soap makers that there's a chance the viewers will come back because you cut in the right place. So, we do our job well in industrial terms, but we're also likely to strengthen our narrative tool.

Broadcasting practices involve just other types of constraints. I think that there was a moment when Arte realised – because they were also in advance with Arte Creative[13] – that they had a chance to try something on their platform. In October [2020], they started airing exclusive content, in particular remarkable English series, on the platform, and three months later, they had an original series to release that would allow them to hook audiences in, becoming the first Hertzian channel to migrate to a platform.

Hertzian Arte is still for the over-60s. But they managed to open up their platform to a much younger audience. So this was an example of industrial inventiveness. Again, with this idea that they would succeed, not by competing in terms of content with what the big international platforms do with their specific knowledge, their address to an audience, but by proposing an alternative offer, which in my opinion, requires them, industrially, to be Europeanised. There's only Arte that already has the scope to do that, and I think that the future of a platform like Arte is really to become a European platform for alternative audio-visual content. As in, to attract viewers who might want something else. And on a European scale, that's a lot of people. They're working to produce ambitious programs aimed at a broad audience, but by positioning themselves as an alternative to the big American platforms.

Thank you really, dear Vincent Poymiro, for this captivating interview.

Thank you as well. I think it's important that people like you take an interest in these topics because I know we also need viewers who are specialists and who can reflect on all the narrative, sociological and technical dimensions of these forms that we are trying to invent. It was a great pleasure to take some time to share my professional experience with you.

NOTES

1. Arte (Association relative à la télévision européenne) is a channel that began broadcasting in 1992 based in Strasbourg, France, and which was resolutely

Franco-German, broadcasting alternately in each language and subtitling for each country. It was the result of a political initiative to strengthen ties between the two countries, and in turn, within Europe, largely financed by the European Union and each country's public broadcasters. Arte was the first French channel to make its programs available on a streaming platform (Arte +7, 2007), and in 2015 branched out into other languages on that platform (English, Spanish, Polish, Italian); it specialises in arthouse films/series and documentaries, and was the broadcaster for *En thérapie*. [*All notes are from the editors.*]

2. Eric Toledano and Olivier Nakache are a French directing duo, best known internationally for *The Intouchables* (*Intouchables*, 2011, starring Omar Sy and François Cluzet), one of the highest-grossing films in France and also among the most successful French films outside of France.
3. Canal Plus is best known outside of France as Studio Canal, a major producer of films, but originally the studio was France's first pay-cable channel, which soon branched out from broadcasting sporting events and recent film releases on the small screen to original content. The number of channels under the 'Canal' umbrella has since multiplied to nine channels at the time of publication, and Canal+ is a significant financier of French fictions on the small and silver screen.
4. A series of domestic terrorist attacks were carried out in Paris on November 13, 2015 at the national football stadium (Stade de France) during a France-Germany game, in several neighbourhood cafés in the 10th and 11th arrondissements, and at the performance hall Bataclan, where the band 'Eagles of Death Metal' was performing, and where the death toll was the highest (ninety deaths). The first season of *En thérapie* takes place in the immediate aftermath of the attacks.
5. From February to March 2021, the series was broadcast on Arte weekly, five episodes at a time, but the whole season was released on Arte's web platform, Arte. tv, in January 2021 and remained available (for free) until July of the same year.
6. Screenwriter of several successful French series; arguably best known as screenwriter and showrunner for *Dix pour cent* (*Call my Agent!*, France 2, 2015–20).
7. Although the original project was to produce 25-minute long episodes, the final duration of the episodes is irregular, varying from 20 to 29 minutes in the first season (see IMDb's episode list: https://www.imdb.com/title/tt11080216/episodes?season=1).
8. *BeTipul*'s episodes are 29 to 31 minutes long; HBO's *In Treatment*'s episodes are 21 to 30 minutes long in the first season.
9. '[T]he most important decision I have to make [is this]: What is this movie about? I'm not talking about plot, although in certain very good melodramas the plot is all they're about. A good, rousing, scary story can be a hell of a lot of fun. But what is it about emotionally? What is the theme of the movie, the spine, the arc? What does the movie mean to me? Personalizing the movie is very important. I'm going to be working flat out for the best six, nine, twelve months. The picture had better have some meaning to me.' Sidney Lumet, *Making Movies* (New York: Vintage Books, 1996), 10.

10. Since this interview, the series broadcast a second season, focusing on characters dealing with the Coronavirus pandemic (April–May 2022), but David Elkaïm and Vincent Poymiro were no longer the writers of this subsequent season as they had decided 'to throw in the towel' after the lack of financial and authorial recognition Poymiro alludes to in this interview (see for instance Thibault Lucia, '"En thérapie": les scénaristes de la saison 1 n'écriront pas la prochaine', *Les Inrockuptibles*, February 26 2021, https://www.lesinrocks.com/series/en-therapie-pourquoi-les-scenaristes-renoncent-a-la-saison-2-158039-26-02-2021/). That is why the writing team of Season 2 was supervised by Clémence Madeleine-Perdrillat.
11. The 26-minute-long episodes of this soap opera are broadcast every weekday immediately following the national news, in primetime.
12. The series was ultimately broadcast on Arte in weekly blocks: thus episodes S01E01–S01E05 were broadcast on February 4, 2021, episodes S01E06–S01E10 broadcast on February 11, 2021, and so forth, allowing the viewer to watch all the therapist's weekly sessions in a single sitting.
13. Originally developed in 2011, this participatory web platform focused on a younger audience and digital series and subject matter; it has since become Arte.tv.

WORKS CITED

Ainsi soient-ils, created by David Elkaïm, Bruno Nahon, Vincent Poymiro et Rodolphe Tissot, Arte, 2012–15.
BeTipul, created by Hagaï Levi, Hot3, 2005–8.
Dix pour cent (*Call my Agent!*), created by Fanny Herrero, France 2, 2015–20.
Ghosts, created by Mathew Baynton, BBC1, 2019–23.
En thérapie, developed by Eric Toledano and Olivier Nakache, Arte, 2021–2.
In Treatment, developed by Rodrigo Garcia, HBO, 2008–10, 2019–21.
Intouchables, directed by Eric Toledano and Olivier Nakache, Gaumont, 2011.
Lucia, Thibault, '"En thérapie": les scénaristes de la saison 1 n'écriront pas la prochaine', *Les Inrockuptibles*, 26 February 2021. Available online: https://www.lesinrocks.com/series/en-therapie-pourquoi-les-scenaristes-renoncent-a-la-saison-2-158039-26-02-2021/ (Accessed April 2023).
Lumet, Sidney, *Making Movies* (New York: Vintage Books, 1996).
Normal People, adapted by Sally Rooney et al., BBC3, 2020.
Nurse Jackie, created by Linda Wallem, Showtime, 2009–15.
Onoda, 10 000 nuits dans la jungle, directed by Arthur Harari, 2021.
The Affair, created by Sarah Treem and Hagaï Levi, Showtime, 2014–19.
This Way Up, directed by Alex Winckler, Channel 4, 2019–21.
Un si grand soleil, created by Olivier Szulzynger, Eline Le Fur, Cristina Arellano and Stéphanie Tchou-Cotta, France 2, 2018–present.

Index

act, 2, 6, 8–9, 10, 26, 29, 66–9, 110, 112–18, 167–8, 218–19, 221
Affair, The, 87, 208
Alfred Hitchcock Presents, 6, 7, 17–31
Ally McBeal, 146, 148, 153
Amazon Prime Video, 74, 75, 76, 79, 114, 116, 118
Angel, 146, 153
anthology (television), 6, 17–31, 192–4
arcs, 8, 38, 47, 62, 92, 109–12, 116–18, 151–4
Arrow, 145–55
Arrowverse, 145–55
Arte, 134, 206, 207–8, 209, 212, 218, 219, 221, 221–2n, 223n
Astier, Alexandre, 59–61, 62, 65, 67, 68, 69, 71n
auteur, 2, 7, 8, 60, 78, 93, 97, 98, 102–3n, 113, 208

Batwoman, 145
beats, 8, 80, 108, 109–10, 112–18
BeTipul, 11, 79, 89n, 206, 207–8, 222n
Bignell, Jonathan, 35
binge-watching, 2–3, 7, 9, 10, 11, 53, 76, 79, 80, 89n, 115–17, 122, 129, 132n
Black Lightning, 145
Black Mirror, 102n, 192–4, 195
bottle episodes, 10, 94, 159, 160, 161–4, 171
Breaking Bad, 93, 115
broadcast TV, 1, 4, 5, 7, 9, 10, 12, 21, 34, 35, 40, 54, 59, 60, 66, 70n, 71n, 75, 97, 115, 122, 123, 124, 126, 128–31, 134, 145, 146, 151–2, 159, 160, 167, 172n, 174, 176, 177, 206, 222n, 223n; *see also* network TV

Buffy the Vampire Slayer, 70n, 146, 153

cable, 4, 5, 8, 12n, 56n, 70, 76, 77, 92, 102, 110–17, 163, 169, 208, 222n
Cahiers du cinéma, 102–3n
Caméra Café, 62
Canal+, 70, 208, 222n
Chosen, 82
cliffhanger, 6, 8, 41, 42, 66, 80, 82, 102, 110, 112, 117, 139, 150, 152, 178, 186n
clip, 10, 35, 45–6, 50–1, 52, 122–31, 132n, 140, 159, 160, 161, 168–71, 172n, 189; *see also* newsreels/news clip
Columbo, 94
comedy, 7, 19, 23, 60, 61, 63–71, 71n, 75–7, 100, 145, 148, 175–6
commercials, 9, 19, 20–2, 75, 76, 110, 112–13, 114, 115, 128, 151, 167, 176
Community, 10, 159–73
Crisis on Earth-X, 145–55
crossover, 10, 145–55
CW, the, 10, 145, 152, 153

DC comics, 10, 145–55
Death of a Salesman, 21–2
Delorme, Stéphane, 92, 98
De Palma, Brian, 7, 78
Disney+, 114, 152, 155
documentary, 44, 142, 143
Dragnet, 23, 27, 81
drama, 4, 5, 6, 8, 9, 11, 17, 18, 22, 26, 27, 29, 32, 34, 40, 44, 56, 61, 66, 67, 68, 69, 74–81, 87–8, 89n, 92, 102, 109, 113,

114, 122, 136, 139, 148, 176, 179, 185, 206, 222
DVD, 11, 40, 108, 110, 114, 129, 134, 136, 137, 142, 143, 168
Dyer, Richard, 39, 41, 42, 50

Easter egg video, 150, 189–202
Elkaïm, David, 206, 207, 223
Engagés, Les, 9, 10, 134–44
En Thérapie, 12, 13, 206–23
episode, 1–11, 17–30, 32–6, 41–7, 50–5, 56n, 60–70, 71n, 72n, 74–91, 92–104, 108–20, 124, 126–9, 131, 134, 136–43, 145–54, 159–72, 174–87, 193, 194, 199, 203n, 206, 207, 208–11, 212, 214, 217–21, 222n
episode endings/excipits, 6, 7, 21, 22, 27, 28, 30n, 40, 41–4, 47, 49, 52, 53, 54, 65, 66, 67, 69, 79–82, 87, 88n, 89n, 112, 116–17, 138, 141, 152, 160, 167, 176, 196, 197, 213,
episode length, 42, 60, 65, 67, 74, 75, 76–81, 83, 87, 88n, 89n, 97–101, 102, 110–11, 113, 116, 160, 176, 185, 209, 211; *see also* runtime
episode openings/incipits, 6, 7, 20, 37, 42, 43, 44, 45, 49, 66, 68, 69, 79, 96, 100, 116, 139, 140, 147, 151, 167
Esmail, Sam, 7, 74, 77, 78, 80, 82, 83, 85, 89

fandom, 5, 10, 11, 70, 96, 107, 111, 123, 126–30, 131, 136, 142, 146, 149, 150, 152, 153, 154, 171, 174, 179, 185, 189, 190, 191–2, 193–4, 197, 200, 201, 202n, 203n
final cut, 93, 141
Flash, The, 145, 151, 152
flashback, 6, 35, 42, 44, 47, 49, 80, 89n, 94, 141, 168, 171
flow, televisual, 1, 3, 10, 75, 168
forensic viewing/audience, 11, 96, 107, 190, 191, 196, 197, 200, 202, 203n
France Télévisions, 9, 134, 143n
Friends, 11, 111, 161, 174–86

Game of Thrones, 2, 70, 79, 88n, 171n, 190–3, 195, 196
Gandhi (film), 37
genre, 4, 6, 11, 19, 22–4, 56–6, 28, 29, 32–3, 38–40, 55, 59–61, 70, 71n, 74–7, 79, 114, 125, 145, 161, 163, 164, 175–9, 183, 185, 191, 203n, 212; *see also* comedy, drama

Good Wife, The, 113
Granada ITV, 33, 34, 35, 56n

HBO, 2, 5, 12, 33, 74, 76, 79, 94, 95, 97, 102, 113, 114, 129, 190, 193, 194, 206, 207, 222n
heritage film, 33
Hitchcock, Alfred, 6, 7, 17–31, 78, 162
Homecoming, 7, 11, 74–91
Hulu, 89n, 114

I Love Lucy, 23, 177, 185n
In Treatment, 11, 79, 87, 89n, 206, 207, 222n

Jenkins, Henry, 190
Jewel in the Crown, The, 6–7, 11, 32–58

Kaamelott, 7, 11, 59–73, 134
Kubrick, Stanley, 78

Legends of Tomorrow, 145, 147, 151–2, 155
Le Postec, Sullivan, 134, 136, 141–3
Levi, Hagaï, 207–9, 212, 213, 217–19
Lost, 5, 111, 189, 194, 201
Lotz, Amanda, 57n, 93, 108, 111, 112, 113, 114, 115
Lynch, David, 8, 92–120

M6, 7, 13, 59, 60, 70, 71n, 134
Mad Men, 94
Mellier, Denis, 25
metafiction/metafictional, 149, 151, 162, 165, 171
miniseries (mini-series), 4, 6, 10, 36–58, 134, 140, 142, 146, 150, 153, 213, 217
mise-en-abyme, 7, 34, 108, 140, 143, 166
Mittell, Jason, 1, 2, 7, 8, 18, 19, 20, 23, 75, 79, 88, 88n, 96, 107, 109, 110, 111, 114, 117, 128, 129, 130, 170, 185, 189, 195, 196, 202n, 203n
Monty Python and the Holy Grail, 60, 64, 191
Mr. Robot, 78, 89n, 94

Nakache, Olivier, 207, 222n
NBC, 5, 6, 10, 11, 17, 23, 94, 111, 113, 146, 155, 160, 161, 171, 174, 177, 179, 186
Netflix, 5, 9, 32, 55, 75, 76, 77, 87, 89n, 97, 108, 114–18, 126, 129, 130, 152, 192
network TV, 1, 2, 9, 10, 17, 19, 75, 76, 108, 109, 110–14, 115, 116, 118, 143, 146, 150, 153, 154, 159, 160, 161, 174–8, 211; *see also* broadcast TV

Newman, Michael Z., 2, 4, 8, 76, 77, 78, 80, 89n, 93, 109, 110, 112, 115, 117
newsreels/news clip, 6, 7, 35–6, 44–6, 50, 52, 59, 60, 70, 193, 223n
NRK, 9, 14, 122, 130

opening credits, 20, 42, 43, 44, 79, 116, 140, 147, 151, 167
O'Sullivan, Sean, 2, 4, 12n, 111

paratext, 9–11, 20, 24, 29, 128, 189, 192, 194
Passage to India, A, 38, 56
Potherat, Maxime, 136, 137, 139, 142, 143
Poymiro, Vincent, 11, 89n, 206–23
Practice, The, 146, 148, 153
prestige TV, 4, 7, 34, 40, 74, 76–9, 87–8, 203n, 212; *see also* quality TV
prime time, 4, 7, 17, 59, 60, 61, 66, 71, 76, 109, 134, 160, 181, 223n

quality TV, 4, 7, 34, 36, 38, 56n, 74–8, 88, 107, 167, 191, 201, 203n; *see also* prestige TV
Queer as Folk, 134, 140

Raj Quartet, 35, 37, 56
Raj revival, 33, 37, 56
Rashomon, 87
real-time, 9, 10, 87, 123–33, 163
Rear Window, 18
reflexivity, 18, 19, 22, 28, 29, 66, 80, 81, 85, 111, 137, 143, 198, 201
runtime, 74–7; *see also* episode length

Saint-Gelais, Richard, 118, 146
Scott, Paul, 35, 55
season, 2–5, 7–12, 20, 23–4, 32, 54, 60–74, 77, 78, 79, 80, 82, 84, 85, 87, 88, 89, 92, 94, 95, 96–8, 102, 110, 111, 112, 114–18, 121, 123, 124, 126, 127, 130–1, 132n, 134–43, 151, 152, 159, 170, 171, 172n, 174–84, 186n, 190, 192, 193, 195, 196, 198–200, 202, 206, 209, 217, 218, 219, 222n, 223n
Sepinwall, Alan, 87, 92, 93, 116, 117
serial format, 2–6, 8, 18, 29, 32, 35, 41, 46, 48, 51–3, 56, 77, 79, 79, 81, 92–6, 99, 101, 102, 109–11, 114, 121–5, 127–31, 146, 150–2, 154, 160, 172n, 175, 177, 178, 184, 190, 192, 195, 196, 199–200, 202, 203n, 206, 210, 217–20
seriality, 2–4, 92–5, 102, 111, 121, 122, 125, 130, 146, 150, 154, 206, 218
shortcom, 7, 59–61, 67, 70, 71n, 134
showrunner, 2, 6, 23, 77, 78, 111–13, 162, 179, 190, 196, 197, 201, 207, 222n
Showtime, 8, 92, 102n, 110, 113, 140, 208
sitcom, 7, 11, 24, 61, 62, 71, 75, 76, 80, 81, 114, 160–3, 167, 174–88, 217
SKAM, 9, 10, 121–33
soap-opera, 4, 8, 11, 35, 38, 39–41, 44, 56, 75, 102, 218, 223n
social media, 9, 10, 123, 125, 126, 127, 129, 130, 131, 141, 150, 153
song, 86, 140, 147, 151, 194
Sopranos, The, 2, 4, 95
spin-off, 6, 48, 55, 146, 148, 151–3, 195
Stam, Robert, 18, 19
Staying On, 35
Stranger Things, 97, 126
streaming, 3, 5, 7, 8, 9, 11, 74–7, 79, 82, 110, 129, 152, 154, 167, 168, 172n, 220, 222n
studio, 4 9, 134, 136, 143
Supergirl, 145, 147, 148, 149, 151, 152
Superman & Lois, 145

theatre/theatrical influences, 7, 8, 18, 26, 36, 46, 60, 61, 64, 66, 68, 70, 71, 100, 108, 131, 207, 221
Thénier, Jules, 136, 137, 142
Toledano, Eric, 207, 222n
transmedia, 9, 118, 131, 189, 190, 192, 196
Twilight Zone, The, 18, 164, 165
Twin Peaks, 189; *see also Twin Peaks: The Return, Twin Peaks: Fire Walk with Me*
Twin Peaks: Fire Walk with Me, 8, 98
Twin Peaks: The Return, 8, 14, 92–120

Vertigo, 26

Westworld, 74, 193–8, 203n

X-Files, The, 70n, 111, 189

YouTube, 76, 123, 124, 131, 136, 142, 143, 143n, 171, 190, 201